Peaceful Transitions

Stories of Success and Compassion

Plan Now, Die Later—Ironclad Strategy

Excerpts from the Forewords and Essay

Millions who will be suffering from Alzheimer's and related dementias may receive treatment inconsistent with their preferences and values, treatment that may inflict longer and greater suffering. If you do not want this to happen to you, read this book! It offers a unique Advance Care Planning tool that offers substantial advantages over all alternatives.

—Thaddeus Mason Pope, JD, PhD, Widener University School of Law

Dr. Terman has had the courage to formalize a protocol for patients with Advanced Dementia whose quality of life is extremely low. [One form] explicitly lists *Palliative Sedation* as a method of Comfort Care for informed consent [that can be used] if all other modalities of treatment have not been successful to reduce pain and suffering.

—William C. Fowkes, MD, Professor Emeritus, Stanford University School of Medicine

Dr. Terman's book is full of illustrative and very moving vignettes, wisdom, compassion, and a whole lot of nuts-and-bolts recommendations that will seem controversial to some, but compelling to others... He offers a comprehensive series of sequential, complementary actions (forms, medallions, cards, suggestions for recording interviews, etc.), which combine to provide a guarantee that is closer to 100% than any other, [for] Advance Care Planning.

—Karl E. Steinberg, MD, Past President, California Association of Long Term Care Medicine

Sorting **My Way Cards** is an interactive exercise that could be very valuable in helping people consider what is important to them... I encourage you to read, consider, and discuss this most thorough, most-important, and perhaps life-altering book. Kudos to Dr. Terman for his monumental efforts in bringing us this work.

—Guy Micco, MD, Clinical Professor UC Berkeley—UC San Francisco Joint Medical Program

To ensure that patient preferences are honored and that physician orders are durable, Dr. Terman has thought of innumerable potential barriers for which he has devised strategic solutions... Ingeniously, he couples a specially designed Advance Directive with a set of **Natural Dying Physician's Orders**.... Some advantages of the **NDPO** include a recommendation for the implementing physician to consider important safeguards [since] Dr. Terman advocates strongly against ending life prematurely... Doctor Terman writes with compassion, passion, clarity, and expertise. His patient stories are compelling and illustrative... Ironically, a book about how to end life is really one that empowers readers to prolong meaningful and enjoyable life.

—Ronald B. Miller, MD, FACP, Founding Director of the Program in Medical Ethics, U C Irvine

The ***Natural Dying Living Will Cards*** [for religious observers] enable patients or their health care proxies to discern if even hand/spoon feeding becomes for them in some circumstances an extraordinary or disproportionate means of preserving life. Without conflicting with Catholic teaching, they will permit you or your loved one to identify the sorts of circumstances in which hand feeding or other treatments could and legitimately should be refused, withheld or withdrawn.

—Reverend Kevin McGovern, Director, Caroline Chisholm Centre for Health Ethics

Peaceful Transitions

Stories of Success and Compassion
Plan Now, Die Later—Ironclad Strategy

Second Edition

by

Stanley A. Terman, PhD, MD

With critical editing by
**Michael S. Evans, MSW, JD; Ronald Baker Miller, MD;
Guy Micco, MD; Thaddeus Mason Pope, PhD, JD;
and Karl E. Steinberg, MD, CMD.**

Includes an essay by **Reverend Kevin McGovern.**

For 14 million U S baby boomers and 1 of 3 of those over 65: Plan *now* to avoid lingering for years in late-stage Alzheimer's dementia.

For all: Plan *now* to prevent prolonged end-of-life pain and suffering.

Introduces: an optional, new, easy interactive tool that helps create *effective* Living Wills.

Publisher's Cataloging-in-Publication
(Provided by Quality Books, Inc.)

Terman, Stanley A.
    Peaceful transitions : stories of success and compassion;
    plan now, die later—ironclad strategy /
    by Stanley A. Terman. – 2nd ed.
    p. cm.
    Includes bibliographical references.
    LCCN 2008941522

    ISBN: 978-1-933418-27-8 (softbound)
    ISBN: 978-1-933418-26-1 (casebound)
    ISBN: 978-1-933418-28-5 (e-book)

    1. Advance directives (Medical care) 2. Life and
    death, Power over. 3. Terminal care.   I. Title.

    R726.2.T47 2011   362.17'5
                   QBI08-600336

© 2011 Stanley A. Terman, PhD, MD
Life Transitions Publications Carlsbad CA 92009

Other books by Stanley A. Terman, PhD, MD

The *BEST WAY* to Say Goodbye: A Legal Peaceful Choice at the End of Life (2007)

Lethal Choice, a medical-legal-psychological thriller (2008)

Peaceful Transitions (First Edition) (2009)

Peaceful Transitions: Stories of Success and Compassion (2011)

Peaceful Transitions: Plan Now, Die Later—Ironclad Strategy (2011)

My Way Cards for Natural Dying—Living Wills (2011)

Natural Dying Living Will Cards (2011)

Websites with additional information, resources, and media

www.Caring Advocates.org   **www.MyWayCards.org**

Caring Advocates, a 501(c)(3) non-profit organization, is a distributor of these books. A portion of the royalties it receives helps provide Advance Care Planning to individuals who otherwise could not afford it.

Caring Advocates Planning Professionals are located in several American States. Recordings of video interviews as a person sorts **My Way Cards** to generate a **Natural Dying—Living Will** can be conducted over the Internet.(See www.InterviewByInternet.com.)

My Way Cards are currently available in Spanish, Chinese, German, and Dutch; Thai and other languages are planned. Professionals in any country who wish to learn about the training program to become a Caring Advocates Planning Professional can contact us by calling... U S: 1-800 64 PEAC E (647 3223); UK: 44 20 8123 7106; Australia:, 61 03 9016 4284; anywhere: stan_terman (SKYPE); or by e-mailing DrTerman@CaringAdvocates.org.

Why offer the choices of one or two books, in both print and e-book formats?*

Stories have always been the best way to learn and to change behavior…

Peaceful Transitions: Stories of Success and Compassion (referred to as "**Stories**") is *Section ONE* in the combined book. Its goal is to inform readers and to motivate them to become diligent "Advance Care Planners." Completing the process of Advance Care Planning is urgent for those who already have some impairment in thinking or memory, a life-threatening diagnosis, or certain risk factors. Yet anyone can suffer an unexpected brain injury; for instance, in a car accident. The book presents all legal end-of-life options to consider when designing a plan to prevent the *two most feared end-of-life scenarios*: **A)** days to weeks of unbearable, unending end-of-life pain and suffering; and **B)** months to years of dependency and indignity (as the planners themselves define), and unrecognized and untreated pain and suffering—the risk of which is increased in Advanced Dementia since these patients will lose the ability to complain. Diligent planning to create an effective strategy is required due to future potential challenges from a diverse cast of increasingly powerful characters who might sabotage their goal to attain a *timely, peaceful transition.*

"How to" books are dedicated to serve a useful purpose…

Peaceful Transitions: Plan Now, Die Later—Ironclad Strategy (referred to as "**PNDL**") is *Section TWO* in the combined book. It has a pragmatic goal: others shall honor your *Known Wishes*. The book begins with a brief overview of several popular Advance Care Planning forms to illustrate how they may be inadequate to attain the goals of avoiding end-of-life pain and suffering, and lingering in Advanced Dementia. The book guides readers through the process of creating an "ironclad strategy" as it explains the rationale for each component. The forms that constitute the "ironclad strategy" can be used along with other forms—for example, "Five Wishes," or your State's form—provided the planner takes the recommended steps to resolve future potential conflicts among these forms. Similar steps can prevent a new kind of hybrid form, the POLST/MOLST (Physician/Medical Orders for Life-Sustaining Treatment) from overriding one's *Known Wishes*. Omitting these steps opens the door for physicians to complete POLSTs of patients who no longer can speak for themselves. These patients are vulnerable, as next-of-kin who have a financial conflict of interest may influence the treatment choices on POLSTs to lead to premature dying. The goal of the "ironclad strategy" forms is to be effective so that others will honor patients' *Known Wishes* for a *timely, peaceful transition.*

Advance Care Planners must also select an effective individual to serve as their future advocate. The book discusses the qualities to look for when selecting a proxy/agent. Finally, the book shows how to make sure all these forms will be available when "that time comes."

Those who have already read the first edition of **Peaceful Transitions**, and those who are already well motivated to engage in Advance Care Planning, can read only **Plan Now, Die Later—Ironclad Strategy**. All the books in this series are available as e-books.

* Condensed from the author's "Searching for a Timely, Peaceful Transition in Advanced Dementia: The influence of autonomy, philosophy, human nature, the law, and survey results," on www.scribd.com/doc/55580643/ .

CONTENTS

Stories of Success and Compassion

The Plan Now, Die Later—Ironclad Strategy

TOPICS:

First, "WHAT" . . . Then, "WHEN?" (Preface to First Edition)

I couldn't live without a little jazz now and then... mostly then. --Louis Armstrong

Louis Armstrong had a great sense of timing: he could distinguish "now" from "then." So it is with life: Most of us will admit that we like to be in control when the goal is to maximize our pleasure in life—now. Yet when it comes to minimizing our *future* potential pain, many of us would rather not think about it. —Particularly when it comes to dying. To be clear: I am referring not to death, but to the *process* of dying. There is little we can do about death, but much we can do about dying. At best dying can be a peaceful transition that provides a precious opportunity to reminisce and to exchange healing goodbyes. At worst it can be complicated by undertreated pain and suffering, prolonged without benefit to anyone, and plagued with guilt and conflict—only to leave our survivors with grief and remorse, and possibly bankrupt.

If you agree that such a tremendous difference is worth the effort, then engage in "Advance Care Planning." This process of shared decision-making has the potential to reduce our own suffering, to provide our family members with the gift of knowing what we want, and to facilitate a fairer allocation of scarce medical and financial resources. How will Advance Care Planning work in the future? If the time comes when our illness prevents us from being able to speak for ourselves, we will have laid the groundwork so we will still receive **WHAT** treatment we would have wanted... and **WHEN**... because of HOW we chose WHOM to fulfill our well-considered end-of-life wishes.

This book gives you all the information you need to accomplish this goal. It narrows future decisions to be made regarding only WHEN, not WHAT. Now is the time to decide WHAT. This book can help. How? By offering a well-developed set of personal statements for you to consider. If they do reflect your preferences, have a physician sign the accompanying set of orders to prevent the most burdensome of prolonged dying experiences that most people fear. In the future, WHEN "that time comes," the person you selected to trust (either your proxy or your physician) will decide WHEN. Only WHEN. Everything else will have been decided.

The greatest disappointment from Advance Care Planning would be to decide what you want, and to complete your plan but then later, others fail to fulfill your wishes. Formidable challenges may come from well-meaning members of your family, from physicians and institutions who refuse to comply with your requests, or from strangers acting on their moral convictions. This book can be your guide as you strive for an "ironclad strategy" to overcome challenges so that your end-of-life wishes are honored and you can attain a peaceful transition.

The beauty of Advance Care Planning is that after you spend the time to complete your plan, you can feel good that you have done all you can. Then go on with the rest of your life. You do not have to think about this stuff every day. But don't be surprised if you enjoy life even more!

PREFACE to the Second Edition: The real challenge is "HOW."

My **Preface** of two years ago distinguished between WHEN and WHAT. I now clarify the importance of HOW. To attain the **goal** of a *timely, peaceful transition*...

A) **HOW** can you let your future decision-makers know WHEN you will want **Natural Dying**? Learn, decide and express your specific *Known Wishes* in a clear and convincing way.

B) **HOW** can you **make sure others** (especially your future physicians) **will honor your** *Known Wishes*? This is the real challenge. Set in place your own **Plan Now, Die Later—Ironclad Strategy**. Its FOUR PILLARS include forms, a proxy, a physician and a notary.

The need for an Advance Care Plan has become both more compelling and more contentious.[a] Although this is a pragmatic, not a historical book—the consequences of changes in the law, court rulings, evolving clinical practice, and sweeping resolutions by religious leaders all must be considered. The book's new subtitle still has the difficult "D" word. However, at least "Die" modifies "Later"—which can be literally true. The **Plan Now, Die Later—Ironclad Strategy** is designed not only to **prevent *prolonged dying***, but also *premature dying*. It does so in three ways. **1)** *Implicitly:* by describing YOUR own specific criteria for WHEN you would want **Natural Dying**: if you have NOT met those criteria, then you would want to be fed and treated to remain alive; **2)** *Directly:* if you use the optional Advance Care Planning tool, you can indicate for which specific cards/items (**My Way Cards**) you DO want to be fed and to be treated; and **3)** *By explicit choice*: if you trust the strategy will prevent your being forced to linger in a state you feel is "worse than death," you are likely to choose to live longer. British novelist Sir Terry Pratchett said it well:[b] "If I knew I could die at any time I wanted, then suddenly every day would be as precious as a million pounds. If I knew that I could die, I would live."

While the plan described is admittedly not "quick and simple," it is user-friendly. The optional **My Way Cards** tool is readable at the third-grade level. The book now includes eleven line drawings, two photographs, four inserted graphics, and one table.[c] A few stories were added to both sections. The description of the strategy of Section TWO was completely rewritten after improving or replacing some forms in the First Edition.[d] Some **highlights** of new material are:

---

[a] Two examples: 1) The U S Catholics Bishops changed *Ethical and Religious Directive # 58*—from "presumption" to "**obligation**" regarding providing artificial nutrition and hydration to patients who are virtually certain to be **permanently unconscious**. 2) A New York judge set aside a Medical Order for Life-Sustaining Treatment so a Catholic woman who suffered from Advanced Dementia *will* receive tube feeding. The judge even recommended changing secular law so the "sanctity of life" standard will apply to all (unless one "particularizes" his/her wishes).
[b] Richard Dimbleby Lecture, *Shaking Hands with Death*. 2-1-10; BBC One. Youtube.com/watch?v=6qQgWCQESgo
[c] Also a new version of Advance Care Planning tool for religious observers: ***Natural Dying Living Will Cards***.
[d] The extent of changes is enough to consider Section Two, which is also available separately, as a *new* rather than as a *revised* book. Note: the Index was deleted given the ease with which digital searches can now be done.

1. The book consistently emphasizes *preventing premature dying* as well as *prolonged dying*. A new, true story was added to Section ONE. Section TWO reviews your common law and Constitutional right to engage in Advance Care Planning and shows how various Living Wills DO or do NOT deal with people's greatest end-of-life fears. The fears are: **a)** unbearable, unending pain and suffering—for which the book describes a new consent form for *Palliative Sedation* ("sedation to unconsciousness"); and **b)** prolonged dying with pain and suffering in Advanced Dementia—for which the book proposes a solution and cites more clinical evidence that for Advanced Dementia patients, pain and suffering often go unrecognized and untreated.

2. The **Natural Dying Agreement** addresses the two fears above and replaces the previous "Patient-Proxy Contact." This was extensively reviewed by three health care attorneys. This form also includes patient's specific wishes about de-activating intra-cardiac devices. To strengthen the strategy, another form was added: the **Natural Dying Affidavit**. The book explains how all the forms work together and how to complete them yourself (or with help).

3. Given the growing acceptance of Physician's Order for Life-Sustaining Treatment (**POLST**) forms in the U S and other recent developments, the book added: **a)** a true story about a New York judge who set aside orders on such forms based on the teaching of the patient's religion (*in Zornow,* 2010), which makes it compelling to add a clear and convincing Living Will to POLST forms; and **b)** explains how these forms *threaten* to override previously created Advance Directives once a person loses decisional capacity. The book details the strategic steps Advance Care Planners can take to preserve the **durability** of their *Known Wishes*.

4. A guest essay, "A Catholic View on the ***Natural Dying Living Will Cards***," by Reverend Kevin McGovern, Director, Caroline Chisholm Centre for Health Ethics, supports the use of this Advance Care Planning tool and explains why it does NOT conflict with Catholic teaching.

5. The book offers sample arguments and lawsuit citations to consider, if proxies/agents need help to motivate future physicians to comply with a patient's *Known Wishes*.

6. The book refers to a new (optional) consent form for organ donation based on the patients' own criteria of WHEN they would want to donate (e.g., their **Natural Dying—Living Will**) rather than depend on the changing and perhaps arbitrary definition of "death" that happens to be accepted by a future physician, local hospital, or State.

7. To help readers understand how all these forms work together, the book now includes: **a)** a fictional story of someone who overcomes a variety of challenges—from age 45 to age 90; and **b)** a table, "Who Signs What," that summarizes all the needed forms.

8. The book offers new guidelines to readers help choose a health care proxy, an *eight-word job description*—after it compares two styles of relationships: the *covenant* and the *contract*.

9. More important to most readers than the newly revised research diagnostic criteria: a free, quick and private way to test themselves/loved ones for mild cognitive impairment/dementia.

Evidence continues to mount that Advance Care Planning leads to better quality of living in one's last chapter, and less emotional stress and grief for one's survivors. Meanwhile, proposals to reform health care in the U S are intensely debated. One area concerned authorizing insurance payments to physicians for discussing end-of-life planning. Certain politicians intentionally confused the benefits of professional help to diligently consider a plan that could either **accept** OR **forgo** aggressive treatment by instilling fear that a government insurer would use its power to ration treatment that patients *wanted*;. These were the so-called *death panels*. In truth, voluntary end-of-life discussions let patients consider ALL options and then choose what they feel is right for them. It is sound clinical process to ask physicians, who have the knowledge and experience, to help patients make difficult end-of-life choices for themselves, while they still can. As patients learn HOW to plan ahead, discussions that include reasonably fully informed consent should be encouraged—even if some patients decide to forgo life-sustaining treatments *if unwanted and burdensome*, if necessary to attain their preferred goal of a *timely, peaceful transition*—even if this process ***incidentally*** also saves money.

With so much rumbling going on, an ominous fact still looms: the giant-sized "elephant in the room" is dementia. Let me substantiate the numerical claims highlighted on the book's cover:

"14 million U.S. baby boomers will develop dementia."

—The Alzheimer's Association 2010 *Alzheimer's Disease Facts and Figures*, "a statistical abstract of U S data on Alzheimer's disease," estimated that "10 million U S baby boomers will develop Alzheimer's disease." Since 60 to 70% of all dementias are Alzheimer's type, a total of 14.3 to 16.7 million baby boomers will develop some kind of dementia. Recent discoveries of new biomarkers to diagnose presymptomatic dementia and revising the diagnostic criteria are welcome, but they are NOT likely to yield a newly discovered treatment in time to benefit baby boomers.

"One in three of us over the age of 65 years will die whilst having dementia..."

—A 2009 editorial by E. L. Sampson and L. Robinson, entitled, "End-of-life care in dementia: Building bridges for effective multidisciplinary care,"[e] cites as its key reference, an article by C. Brayne and others[f] that reports an

---

[e] Published in the journal, *Dementia 8*; 331-334 (2009).

[f] Brayne C, Gao L, Dewey D, Fiona E. Matthews FE. (2006). Dementia before Death in Ageing Societies—The Promise of Prevention and the Reality. *PLoS MEDICINE: 3 (10)*; 1922-1930. Note: Some US estimates for the prevalence of dementia are lower (one in five for women and one in six for men who reach the age of 55 in California), however the *2009 Alzheimer's Disease Facts and Figures* explain why these estimates may be low: "When one considers the numbers of people with mild to moderate levels of dementia, as well as those with dementia for less than six months' duration, the current and future numbers of people at risk for Alzheimer's

impressive UK 10 year study that followed "approximately 12,000 study participants who had died by the end of the study; just over 2,500 had an assessment for dementia within one year before dying."

Of course, numbers are just part of the story. Sampson and Robinson concluded, "...the quality of end-of-life care received by people with dementia may be less than optimal." This opinion refers to the fact that patients with severe dementia—since they have lost the ability to communicate and thus to complain—frequently experience pain and suffering that goes unrecognized and untreated, or at least, significantly under-treated.

A message to readers: Although research clinicians are trying to develop "objective" instruments to assess pain, answer the question, *Do you want to take the chance that your last physician may not use such an instrument?* Note: Even if your non-research clinical physician does use an instrument to *try* to detect your pain and suffering, your physician may fail to discover you are in pain. Here's why: Research by Drs. Boly, Laureys and colleagues involved giving controlled electrical shocks to patients in the Minimally Conscious State (a condition clinically similar to Advanced Dementia). The PET activation scans showed similar activity as found in normal people. But these patients did NOT manifest the kinds of behaviors that are generally recognized as heralding pain.[g]

So... if you cannot depend on an "objective" approach to detect pain and thus prevent intense and long suffering before you die, on what can you depend? On your *clear and convincing expression* of WHEN you would want your future decision-makers to know it is time for **Natural Dying**; that is, when you would wish to forgo all life-sustaining treatment including tube feeding and *Manual Assistance with Oral Feeding and Drinking*, but still receive all the Comfort Care you need. To attain your goal of a *timely, peaceful dying*, others must honor your *Known Wishes* WHEN that time comes. Yet a cast of diverse characters, whose strength seems to be growing, may present a formidable challenge. How do you overcome their opposition? You need more than to express clearly what you will someday want. You must set in place an effective strategy. That is the purpose of the **Plan Now, Die Later—Ironclad Strategy**.

Stanley A. Terman, PhD, MD
Caring Advocates
Carlsbad, California
June 30, 2011

---

disease and other dementias **far exceed** those stated in the Framingham study." For dying individuals, this is clinically relevant: Must they **suffer** from the *symptoms, losses of function, unwanted behaviors*, and *conflicts with lifelong values* before they die... be it for years, months, or weeks? Also, dementia is about 35% under-reported as a cause of death, according to Wachterman M et al. Reporting Dementia on the Death Certificates of Nursing Home Residents with End-Stage Dementia. *JAMA*. 2008 December 10; 300(22): 2608–2610.

[g] Boly M, Laureys S, et al. (2008). Perception of pain in the minimally conscious state with PET activation: an observational study. *Lancet Neurol. Nov;7(11)*:1013-20. (For additional details, see Page 59.)

FOREWORD

by Thaddeus Mason Pope, JD, PhD

Every twelve seconds, someone dies in the United States. Most of these deaths result from a collaborative, consensus decision to withdraw or to withhold life-sustaining medical treatment. Unfortunately, existing policies for making such life-determining decisions is increasingly at variance with Americans' health care needs. In the absence of instructions to the contrary, the standard approach to end-of-life treatment is to provide aggressive medical treatment—even when such treatment has virtually no chance of achieving a cure or even partially reversing the disease process. Such overtreatment may paradoxically shorten life as it inflicts tremendous suffering on all concerned. This is not the way that most of us want to die. To avoid such a fate, we must affirmatively "opt out" of the technological imperative. Opting out is not difficult if we still have the mental capacity to make our own health care decisions. But few of us will have such capacity as we near the end of our lives.

Over the past three decades, State legislators and clinicians have worked to develop various Advance Care Planning (ACP) documents to address this problem and give us a way to voice our values and preferences after we lose our mental capacity. These include: the Living Will, the Durable Power of Attorney for Health Care, the Advance Directive, the pre-hospital DNR order, and the Physician's Order for Life-Sustaining Treatment (POLST). All strive to declare and preserve our health care choices if, in the future, we become mentally unable to make medical decisions. Unfortunately, a plethora of government and academic studies has confirmed that there are serious and distressing limitations to how well these documents actually work.

Most Americans have not done Advance Care Planning. Of those who have, few can be sure that their physicians will have access to these documents when the need for them is critical. Moreover, even when people have ACP documents and their providers can access them, their instructions are often vague and fail to address clinical realities. For example, almost all ACP documents permit the refusal of only technological interventions like feeding tubes or mechanical ventilators. Yet many very seriously chronically ill patients do not depend on technology for continued existence—especially those millions who are or will be suffering from Alzheimer's and related dementias. The upshot: millions of patients will receive treatment inconsistent with their preferences and values, treatment that may inflict longer and greater suffering. If you do not want this to happen to you, read this book!

Dr. Terman has developed a unique ACP tool that offers substantial advantages over all alternatives. With a deep appreciation of the plight of the cognitively impaired, Dr. Terman has extracted and combined the best elements of current ACP documents to create a new "ironclad strategy" to fulfill our end-of-life wishes. For most of us, the **Natural Dying Advance Directive/Natural Dying Physician's Orders (NDAD/NDPO)** is the most authoritative and durable instrument by which we can avoid unwanted burdensome treatment and avoid lingering with advanced dementia where we would merely exist in a state of total dependency and indignity.

This readable guide shows how we can ensure that our voices are heard at critical points in our future medical treatment. I have been lucky to co-teach with Dr. Terman. He is a true teacher. He combines a thorough knowledge of this subject with the ability to entertain while he communicates. This book provides clear, practical directions to prepare your **NDAD/NDPO**. To assert your personal preferences concerning how and when you die, use this book as your guide to create effective ACP documents. Don't delay. You never know when you might need these documents. Once completed, you can turn your attention to other matters of living, knowing that you have created an effective plan.

Thaddeus Mason Pope, JD, PhD
Widener University School of Law
Wilmington, Delaware

<u>Note</u>: The quote below is from Professor Pope's ***thorough legal analysis*** of refusing food and fluid. It appeared in print and online* just as **Peaceful Transitions** was being published:

Many individuals continue to suffer at the end of life. Patients have the right to refuse life-sustaining medical treatment through an advance directive or through a substitute decision maker. But many ill patients, including a large and growing population with advanced dementia who are *not* dependent upon life-sustaining medical treatment, do *not* have this option. They have the same rights but there is simply no life-sustaining medical treatment to refuse.

These patients have another right, another option by which to avoid suffering at the end of life that enables a good quality death [but it] is widely resisted by healthcare practitioners either because they think that it is illegal or because they are uncertain of its legality. We argue that individuals may refuse [oral] nutrition and hydration just as they may refuse other intrusions on their personal autonomy. This right is grounded in the common law of battery, statutes, state constitutions, and even the United States Constitution. [Exercising this option] does not constitute abuse, neglect, or assisted suicide. Even if exercised through an advance directive or a surrogate decision-maker, these decisions are legal in most United States jurisdictions.

---

* Pope TM, Anderson L. 2011. Voluntarily Stopping Eating and Drinking: A Legal Treatment Option at the End of Life, *Widener Law Rev. 17(2)*; 363-428. http://papers.ssrn.com/sol3/papers.cfm?abstract_id=1689049. Retrieved 7-27-2011. (To improve the clarity of this excerpt that I shortened, a few words were omitted.)

FOREWORD
by Guy Micco, MD

Thinking about death is not a favorite American pastime. At least not thinking about our own death, or that of our loved ones. So, it should be no surprise that planning for life's end is a low priority household item. And, with the amount of time and care that broaching the subject can take, neither is it a surprise that it is infrequently discussed in the doctors' offices. We are woefully unprepared for dying. Perhaps it has always been so in all cultures and times. But recently, there seems to be a move afoot to change this. Death and dying have certainly been "outed"—more and more so since the early Elisabeth Kübler-Ross days. Television, movies, print media: all are putting end-of-life issues ever more frequently in our not-quite-averted faces. We *seem* to want to hear about "the good death." We *seem* not to want the impersonal, high-tech hospital ICU death. And, although I am not convinced this is truly the case, *we seem to want to plan ahead.* If you are in that category, then Dr. Stanley A. Terman—with his immense energy for this issue, his books (including this one), and his websites—is here to help!

First, the strengths of Dr. Terman's project, as evidenced in **Peaceful Transitions**. If you take this book seriously, read through it carefully, consider each point, answer the questions Dr. Terman poses, then I promise, you will have come a long way in planning for a peaceful way for your life to end. But it is not enough—as Dr. Terman tells us—to work through this by yourself. You must share your thoughts and reasoning, your hopes and fears about dying with your loved ones and your primary physician. And you must, in order to fulfill the promise of "ironclad," wade through and complete a few forms. Dr. Terman's optional offering, to sort **My Way Cards**, is an interactive exercise that could be very valuable in helping people consider what is important to them. Will you do it?

This brings me to my concerns. First, in a country wherein completion of an Advance Directive is not generally the norm, how useful is making the process even more cumbersome in order to move toward Dr. Terman's "ironclad" status? Have you done "Advance Care Planning" of any sort? Do you have even the most primitive of "Advance Directive"? If not, what will motivate you to read this book and follow its detailed instructions? Perhaps because of a recent personal experience, you realize the importance of this work. I can only encourage you to keep reading, thinking, and talking about it.

Second, I am especially concerned that people with low educational attainment, those with psychosocial problems, or those for whom English is not the primary language will not be able to go through the rigorous process that Dr. Terman prescribes, even if they wanted to do so. (In one recent study of a county medical clinic population, only 13% of people given an Advance Directive written at a 5th grade level had completed this form at the six month follow-up.*) Is a "peaceful transition, how and when you want it" only for those with the wherewithal to make it through this book and its attendant requirements? Perhaps Dr. Terman will take on the difficult project of making Advance Care Planning available to others besides the well-educated and socially well-connected.

Third, I have "a problem" with the idea of a "Ulysses" contract as presented herein. Briefly, this is a contract that includes a clause whose purpose is to make the contract itself irrevocable. Dr. Terman offers us the option to write such a statement in anticipation of Advanced Dementia. He offers a way to formulate a directive indicating (if we so desire now) that if we were ever in such a state, fluid and nutrition would be withheld. This contract would be binding on our caregivers in the event of such a future. Really "binding"? Even if I had no evidence of suffering? Even if I were *freely* accepting of food and water? For himself, Dr. Terman's answer is "Yes." He would not want to place the physical, emotional and financial burdens on caregivers and society if he reached Advanced Dementia and *appeared* so completely mentally out of it that his only response was an occasional smile when someone put a chocolate covered cherry in his mouth. "No," is my answer. I, along with many others, believe that our current "competent" self cannot make decisions for a future self that is disagreeing, even if that future self is deemed "incompetent." There are good arguments on both sides of this issue. I would encourage readers to seriously consider them before writing such an Advance Directive.

This leads to my fourth concern: Dr. Terman suggests using certain "Criteria of Advanced Dementia" as only a guide. By themselves, several criteria seem to make the problematic claim that a life without (apparent) cognition or memory is a life not worth living. Ditto re: a life of total dependence upon others.... No one is saying that the late stage of dementia will be pleasant; but I will claim, we just don't know ahead of time. A strong lesson from the "disability community" is that the currently able-bodied (and able-mind-ed) cannot well imagine a life without "x"—where "x" is a currently treasured function (like memory or independence)—being worth living. Yet people who lose such abilities often live a good life by their own reckoning, despite, sometimes even because of, such loss. As Dr. Terman quotes Thomas DeBaggio writing during the middle stages of his struggle with Alzheimer disease, "There are days during which I am happier than ever, full of real joy, despite the slow death unwinding itself inside my brain."

In addition, there are the feelings of caregivers to be considered. Such people may well find it better to care for a totally dependent loved one than to see them die from the withholding of, say, food and water. An important proviso here: I am not suggesting that people always and forever be kept alive in pain or in a fearful condition. I am saying that the judgment of what you are like in Advanced Dementia, if such be your fate, should be left to those who care for you most. Treatment decisions should be made by them, contemporaneously. Give them and your physician guidance now, yes. Request (and expect) the best of palliative care for any perceived suffering. But don't tie their hands with a "Ulysses" contract.

My final critical point: please be sure to understand, as Dr. Terman will explain, that "ironclad" does not mean "absolutely for sure." As he wrote, "nothing in life can be guaranteed 100%."

Given the caveats above, I come back to my initial thoughts about this book. We Americans don't like to concern ourselves about dying. We think—if we think anything— it's way in the future; at least it's for another day. As we baby boomers used to say, in some circles, "It's a bummer! Why talk about it now?" But it is certain that if we don't make our wishes known now about end of life care, it will not unlikely fall on others to make difficult decisions for us. Decisions that, perhaps, would be different from the ones we would make for ourselves.

I encourage you to read, consider, and discuss this most thorough, most-important, and perhaps life-altering book. Kudos to Dr. Terman for his monumental efforts in bringing us this work.

Guy Micco, MD
Clinical Professor UC Berkeley - UC San Francisco Joint Medical Program
Director, UC Berkeley Academic Geriatric Resource Center, Center on Aging

---

*Sudore, Rebecca, et. al. Engagement in Multiple Steps of the Advance Care Planning Process: A Descriptive Study of Diverse Older Adults. *Journal of the American Geriatrics Society* 56:1006–1013, 2008

FOREWORD
by Karl E. Steinberg, MD, CMD

As a geriatrician who spends a great deal of time caring for patients in nursing homes and hospice settings, I have seen many unfortunate, unpredictable and heart-wrenching situations involving my patients and their loved ones at the end of life. Dr. Terman's book is an insightful, thought-provoking and ultimately very practical source of much-needed information for people who want to be sure that their wishes for end-of-life care will be respected, and for health care professionals who wish to help their patients achieve this goal. End-of-life issues are challenging, especially when patients and family are faced with the need to make critical and immediate decisions about situations they have never discussed. This is why it is so important to take enough time to consider these literally life-and-death questions, examine your own feelings and beliefs about them, and then do everything you can to ensure that when your time comes, your wishes will be honored.

Certainly, people have passionate and widely varying beliefs about end-of-life matters. No universally right or wrong solutions exist. *Individuals' attitudes may even change over time, although usually not for the most serious of mental and physical conditions, which this book primarily addresses.* Talking to your doctor and to someone you trust, long before you are in your final decline, increases the probability that your wishes will be honored. Memorializing your wishes in written and other recordable media can add credibility to your strategy. Obtaining a formal physician's order is also recommended. Dr. Terman lays out a logical, persuasive and empathetic roadmap to help you complete this process in a way that may stimulate you to consider issues you may have never thought about before. His strategy helps ensure that your end-of-life journey will unfold in accordance with your wishes. Some readers will not take every suggested step, but all should learn what their options are so they can make a truly informed decision about these vitally important issues.

Since I am being accorded a bit of a soapbox here, I will take the opportunity to say a few things I believe are important, but that many people are unaware of, or perhaps disagree with. Thankfully, Dr. Terman does agree.

(1) "Promise me that you'll never put me in a nursing home." This is a truly toxic pledge to extract from a child, spouse or anyone else. If you don't want to go to a nursing home, amass enough assets that you never have to. Sometimes circumstances are beyond our control, and your kids have a life too. I have seen more heartache, guilt, self-reproach and other awful, destructive emotions that result from such a promise than perhaps from any other common family drama, even the *actual deaths* of loved ones. And the guilt is a "gift that keeps on giving," long after the individual patient is gone. Because of my profession, I may be biased in believing that nursing homes are places of great compassion, empathy and caring. But if you really would rather be dead than live in a nursing facility, then there are actions you (and, if you are incapacitated, your loved ones) can take to keep you from winding up there. These strategies are explored in **Peaceful Transitions**.

(2) "Dying of dehydration." Despite its inhumane ring and horrid reputation in the public sensibility, this is a remarkably benign way to exit this life. In fact, most of us could only pray for such a kind and untroubled transition. You get sleepy, maybe pleasantly delirious, your blood pressure drops, and you

drift off to sleep and don't wake up. That is so much better than many of the alternatives we see as people near the end of the line! For example, in dementia patients, they may succumb to aspiration pneumonia or other infectious processes, suffer from pressure ulcers [bedsores], joint contractures, etc. The public really needs to be educated on this. We care for patients dying without nutrition or hydration on a regular basis, in accordance with their wishes, and it is almost invariably an enviable, quiet, non-traumatic experience.

(3) What constitutes an acceptable quality of life for a person is a totally individual decision, and it varies remarkably among individuals. The fact is, other people may feel very differently from the way you feel on this subject, and if they don't tell you specifically, how are you supposed to know? Fortunately, Dr. Terman has devised an ingenious new tool: **My Way Cards**. You and your physician or proxy can sort out your priorities with respect to what behaviors and values you want your future decision-makers to consider, as they determine when it is time for **Natural Dying**. This tool can also prevent the terrible struggling I often see in families when forced to make a decision about forgoing aggressive life-prolonging measures for a loved one whose life may have become truly miserable when s/he has virtually no hope of improvement.

Here are a few examples of important areas that **Peaceful Transitions** focuses on:

- Make sure those who care about you know your values, beliefs and specific wishes.

- Make sure you carefully choose someone you can trust to speak for you. This person should actively try to do whatever is necessary to honor your wishes if the time comes when you cannot do it yourself.

- If you are afraid that someone in your family might try to sabotage your plans because of religious beliefs, unfinished business or any other baggage (including greed), make that clear to others and memorialize it in writing so you specifically exclude them from any future participation in your medical decision-making process.

Dr. Terman's book is full of illustrative and very moving vignettes, wisdom, compassion, and a whole lot of nuts-and-bolts recommendations that will seem controversial to some, but compelling to others. Remember just how different we are from one another, and yet we are all the same in that we have the right to express our beliefs, wishes and goals for end-of-life care, and we all deserve to have them honored. We are blessed to live in a democracy where our freedom to make such decisions is still basically intact. And while there is no way to guarantee absolutely that our wishes are honored, the multiple strategies offered in **Peaceful Transitions** will help us get as close to certain as we can.

Let me conclude by pointing out several areas in which **Peaceful Transitions** is unique among published works that deal with Advance Care Planning, both in content and in probable effect:

(1) It deals in depth with the difficult subject Advanced Dementia and includes the tools for readers to specify the future conditions that they (YOU!) would consider intolerable or incompatible with an acceptable quality of life.

(2) It gives the reader (YOU!) a whole series of sequential, complementary actions (forms, medallions, cards, suggestions for recording interviews, etc.), which combine to provide a guarantee that is closer to 100% than any other Advance Care Planning that his/her (YOUR!) wishes will be honored when the time comes.

(3) It points out numerous potential pitfalls, weaknesses, and horrifyingly plausible scenarios that other, more casual approaches to Advance Care Planning can possibly lead to. (These areas are infrequently mentioned outside of rare case studies in the bioethics or palliative care professional literature—other than the occasional unfortunate legal action that creates a frenzied news media and results in transforming a private patient into a public victim.)

(4) Finally, and perhaps less obviously, **Peaceful Transitions** can prevent readers' anxiety about future serious illness or Advanced Dementia. You don't have to be afraid of dying. And you can live as long as possible, without ending up having to endure years of a horrible existence. The strategies in this book can allow you to reach the point that you yourself have identified as being unacceptable, to receive all the necessary treatment to sustain your life, and to always receive Comfort Care, if that is your goal. Only when you meet the criteria that you yourself have endorsed, and your proxy has, with your physician, determined that you meet, will your Advance Care Planning set the wheels in motion to permit a natural, comfortable, and even peaceful death.

Given the wide range of options this book offers, and the intriguing way it does so, there is—regardless of what specific choices you choose for yourself—one thing about which you can be sure: You will be exposed to many thought-provoking questions. Most likely you will end up feeling confident that you have considered all relevant issues as you contemplate this information in conjunction with your own unique beliefs, values and wishes. The exercise of considering the way you want to die (and the way you don't want to die!) is very likely to be one that adds to the quality and meaning of your life.

So, what should you do with this book? I recommend this: Read it. Appreciate it. Let it stimulate you to think. Use it as a guide to decide what is right for you. Then select the strategies you want to follow, to make sure that others will honor your wishes. While you may begin with the expectation of creating an ironclad strategy, you may also finish with less anxiety about dying and a greater appreciation for what it means to be human, compassionate, and respectful as you enjoy the rest of your life.

Karl E. Steinberg, MD, CMD
Past President, California Association of Long Term Care Medicine
Editor in Chief, *Caring for the Ages*
Medical Director, Hospice by the Sea
Medical Director, Las Villas de Carlsbad
Medical Director, Village Square Nursing Center
Oceanside, California

FOREWORD

by Ferdinando L. Mirarchi, DO, FAAEM, FACEP

Living Wills, Proxy Directives, Prehospital DNR Orders, Physician's Order for Life-Sustaining Treatment (POLST), and now a new, combination form—**Natural Dying Advance Directive/ Natural Dying Physician's Orders (NDAD/NDPO)**. Confused? It could be worse. Your efforts at Advance Care Planning could be ineffective given various State laws and energetic opposition from pro-life groups. And the documents you create may not be safe: If others misinterpret them, you may not receive life-sustaining treatment for reversible conditions you would have wanted, if you could speak for yourself. Warning: Your plan for a peaceful death could lead to a premature death. In fact, little research has been done on safety, yet new untested forms like the POLST are being proposed and adopted even as I read this book and write this Foreword.

My research, which focuses on whether forms are safe, led me to conclude that Living Wills are often misinterpreted as Do Not Resuscitate orders, and DNR orders are often misinterpreted as Do Not Treat orders. How can you prevent such misinterpretations? I propose two solutions:

1) If you still want to receive other kinds of medical treatment but want to refuse Cardio-Pulmonary Resuscitation, add these words in large print to any form that includes a current DNR order: **FULL CODE EXCEPT FOR CARDIAC ARREST**. I recommend this whether or not you are in the hospital, and whether you have one of the older Pre-Hospital (Out-of-Hospital) DNR forms or the newer Physician's Order for Life-Sustaining Treatment (POLST). This cautionary approach is particularly needed for those who receive Living Wills from estate planning attorneys explained in my book that Addicus Books published: **Understanding Your Living Will**.

2) Keep any form that has your DNR order in a safe place until you want to refuse all life-sustaining treatment. Dr. Terman's book offers a **Natural Dying Agreement** with these instructions so that his new form, that serves as the centerpiece of his book, the **Natural Dying Physician's Orders**, is not implemented too soon.

Dr. Terman's book provides the details on how to create an "ironclad strategy" to avoid prolonged dying with end-of-life pain and suffering. The information he provides on voluntary refusal of food and fluids is a legal alternative to Physician-Assisted Dying (Suicide). The book also informs readers about *Palliative Sedation*, so that patients and caregivers will know what to ask for, to reduce pain and suffering in their last days or weeks of life. The book provides the only way I know to avoid lingering in advanced dementia while allowing you to reach that stage so you do not die prematurely. Given the increase in the number of patients who will suffer from Alzheimer's and related diseases, this is a very important contribution.

Whatever set of forms you decide to use, educate yourself on how to create a plan that you individualize to your specific needs. Also: consult your physician if your condition changes.

Department of Emergency Medicine
Hamot Medical Center; UPMC, Erie, PA

FOREWORD

by William C. Fowkes, MD

My first contact with Dr. Stanley Terman was when he asked me to see a patient in the San Francisco Bay Area. He had read the monograph I authored **Prolonged Death – an American Tragedy** (1998, Archstone Foundation), and surmised we were like-minded in our approaches to end-of-life choices. He was right. Our patient was a woman approaching her 90th birthday. Although physically and mentally functional, she did not wish to live any longer. She felt her life had become unbearable. She was plagued by an unusual sensation inside her head. Evaluations by several clinicians failed to reveal a specific diagnosis. She had an additional reason that led her to elect to fast from all food and fluid until she died: she wanted to be sure that she could be in control while she still had her mental faculties. She requested supportive and Comfort Care during this process, not advice regarding whether or not she should pursue this path.

Everyone, including Dr. Terman, her daughter and her son-in-law, and her long-term primary care physicians had tried to talk the woman out of fasting. At least for now. But no one could succeed. The daughter was fearful that she and others – if they helped by providing Comfort Care – might be accused of elder abuse. Dr. Terman was extraordinarily helpful to the patient and family who were reaching out for professional assistance. He diligently interviewed and videotaped the patient to be certain she had the mental capacity to make an informed medical decision to fast until death. He also diligently interviewed three members of the woman's family and contacted her primary physician. Dr. Terman and the organization he founded, "Caring Advocates," have similarly been very helpful for many others patients and their families. I also saw this patient in person, shortly after she began her fast. Her wish, for a **Natural Dying**, was eventually supported by all, including hospice, and was totally peaceful.

Here in California, as of January 1, 2009, we have a newly authorized form, the "Physician Orders for Life Sustaining Treatment," or POLST, which allows individuals to elect or reject certain treatments including cardiopulmonary resuscitation, artificially administered nutrition and hydration, and other medical interventions such as antibiotics and mechanical breathing assistance. POLST is designed to follow patients as they move through the health care system during periods of illness or injury. Providers of health care are protected from liability if they follow the wishes of the patient as expressed in document. There are however, potential problems with the POLST: There is no guarantee that healthcare providers will honor the patient's instructions in Advance Directives. In my experience these previously expressed wishes can be ignored by providers with impunity. Rarely have physicians been sanctioned for intervening with life-sustaining treatments against the patient's wishes.

Dr. Terman has authored a strong alternative to the POLST: the **Natural Dying Physician's Orders** (**NDPO**), which includes significant patient and provider education, and is much more complete in helping individuals make decisions about their end-of-life preferences. He has had the courage to formalize a protocol for patients with Advanced Dementia whose quality of life is extremely low: caregivers would place food at the patient's bedside but would NOT actively assist feeding and drinking—if, when the patient was competent, s/he previously gave consent after being informed of this option, for example by completing the form, the **Natural Dying Physician's Orders**. This innovation is the only one I know of that can prevent many years of existing in Advanced Dementia, while still allowing the patient to enjoy life as much as possible, up to that point.

The **Natural Dying Physician's Orders** form also explicitly lists *"Palliative Sedation"* as a method of Comfort Care for informed consent. This term is, but should not be, controversial. It specifically allows physicians to provide the most aggressive form of palliative treatment—sedation to unconsciousness—if all other modalities of treatment have not been successful to reduce pain and suffering. Here again, this term does not appear on the California and many other State's POLSTs; but it does appear prominently, for both discussion and informed consent, on the **Natural Dying Physician's Orders**.

Dr. Stanley Terman is an authoritative and innovative pioneer in end-of-life issues. I enthusiastically recommend his new book, **Peaceful Transitions**, as well as his previous work, **The *BEST WAY* to Say Goodbye: A Legal Peaceful Choice at the End of Life**. His new book serves as a "How To" guide; the previous one provides the comprehensive basis for the options it offers. Both books have been critically reviewed by clinical ethicists and attorneys. This adds to their credibility and authority.

William C. Fowkes, M.D.
Medical Director, Pathways Hospice, Sunnyvale, CA
Professor Emeritus, Stanford University School of Medicine
Palo Alto, CA

FOREWORD
by Ronald Baker Miller, MD

Many of us say, "If I broke my neck diving into shallow water and was paralyzed, became blind, had a stroke and couldn't speak, had to be on breathing machine, or became demented and did not recognize my loved ones, I would rather die than continue to live." Yet often we make such statements thinking it might happen to a stranger or an acquaintance, conceivably even to a friend or relative, but surely not to ourselves. Thus, we do not seriously complete the "what if" thought by seriously planning as if it might actually happen to us. Instead, we go on to more pleasant thoughts and activities whereas we should document our preferences and name a proxy decision-maker in an Advance Directive. The concept of a treatment directive (commonly called a "living will") began in the late 1960s. In 1976 in a New England Journal of Medicine article, "Personal directions for care at the end-of-life," Sissela Bok anticipated the development of inability to interact with others as a reason not to prolong life. She also appreciated the need for a proxy who would know "how I would weigh incompetence." In 1979 in a New England Journal of Medicine editorial, Arnold Relman noted the living will could be a solution for decision-making for incompetent patients (although he was not specifically speaking of the severely demented). He favored the proxy directive (as do many physicians) which was then the subject of a legislative bill in Michigan and had previously been discussed by Robert Veatch in a Hastings Center Report article in 1977. I list these sentinel concepts in my Foreword as I believe they provided the foundation for Doctor Terman's extraordinary volume, **Peaceful Transitions**.

As many as 70% of seriously ill patients die after physicians decide (guided by patients' preferences and values) to withhold or to remove life-support. But if life has lost its meaning in extreme old age, and particularly if one is suffering but not dependent upon life-sustaining medical technology that could be discontinued (as is so common for patients with progressive dementias such as Alzheimer's), what options are there for such trapped patients? Many well people now hope their state will, like Oregon, Washington, and possibly Montana, legalize physician-assisted dying, to provide another option to hasten dying for those patients who do not depend on life-sustaining treatment that can be withdrawn. Yet many patients are too sick—mentally (such as the demented) or physically (such as the paralyzed)—to ingest a lethal dose of medications without assistance, which is illegal. The physically sick have another option: to refuse food and fluid, which option was explored in depth in Doctor Terman's other book, **The *BEST WAY* to Say Goodbye: A Legal Peaceful Choice at the End of Life**.

Physician-assisted dying can never be a solution for people with dementia since the patient must be competent right up until the time of ingesting the lethal medication. For individuals who fear they will develop dementia and would prefer that food and fluid be discontinued when dementia is advanced, they must have so indicated while competent. Many terminally ill patients, especially those with wasting from cancer, spontaneously forgo nutritional and even fluid intake and die. Other patients can purposely discontinue intake of food and fluid, and then usually die within two weeks. This was called the "voluntary refusal of food and fluid" (VRFF) by Doctor Terman when he conceived the term a decade ago and the "voluntary stopping of eating and drinking" (VSED) by Gert and Bernat, Quill and Byock about the same time and by Judith Schwartz more recently, and "stopping eating and drinking" (STED) by Boudewijn Chabot most recently. Dr. Linda Ganzini reported nurses' observations of relatively peaceful deaths of such patients. Doctor Terman not only described a variety of ways to assuage thirst, but also courageously fasted himself on two occasions, once for four days, another for five. He wanted to be certain that he was not recommending something that would be unpleasant for patients at the ends of their lives. He also emphasized that for the first several days of such fasts, many patients are lucid and can communicate loving and meaningful goodbyes as well as demonstrate that their resolve to end life is not impulsive (since they could, if they wished, simply resume eating and drinking). In contrast, once a lethal dose of medication has been ingested, it is too late for the patient to change his or her mind.

Perhaps the most important contribution of Doctor Terman and this book is the innovative combination of an Advance Directive (authorizing one's physician and/or proxy to withhold food and fluid after one has lost decision-making capacity) with a set of contingent physician's orders that make it possible to honor the individual's preferences for end-of-life care even years later if s/he developed advanced dementia. Doctor Terman recalls his idea to use an irrevocable ("Ulysses") contract for patients with dementia was the successful use of such contracts in the practice of psychiatry.

Some readers have direct experience with the devastating disorder of dementia and the burdens incumbent on caregivers while others do not. Few of us imagine what it would be like to be demented much less understand the impact the coming epidemic of dementia will have upon our society and our healthcare system. Doctor Terman provides important insights in these matters. He not only educates us about the clinical facts, but also about the human tragedy that is dementia. His description of the criteria of advanced dementia should be extremely helpful to patients in early dementia and their family members in anticipating what is to come so that they may be motivated to plan accordingly. Doctor Terman also provides poignant glimpses of what dementia is like as it relentlessly progresses. His book includes descriptive writings of authors Richard Russo and Thomas DeBaggio, as well as several composite memoirs. Having elucidated the nature of the problem and its extraordinary magnitude, he then proposes a practical, pragmatic solution.

Doctor Terman's "ironclad strategy" can provide assurance for a legal, peaceful transition at the end of inexorable illness and suffering or at the end of meaningful sentient (conscious) life that has been destroyed by dementia or loss of consciousness. Ingeniously, he couples a specially designed Advance Directive with a set of **Natural Dying Physician's Orders**. These orders are similar to the Physician Orders *for* (really, *about*) Life-Sustaining Treatments (**POLST**) that began in Oregon in the early 1990s. The POLST approach is only now spreading throughout the country—by legislation, regulation, or by sufficient clinical utilization—to become a standard of practice. Like POLST forms, this book's recommended Physician's **Natural Dying Physician's Orders** (**NDPO**) form converts a patient's preferences into actionable orders that apply across treatment settings. Some advantages of **NDPO** include a recommendation for the implementing physician to consider important safeguards, specific mention of (and consent for) *Palliative Sedation* (the most intensive form of comfort care for pain and suffering that cannot otherwise be relieved), and allowing patients to discontinue oral as well as medically-administered nutrition and hydration. These safeguards and options are not generally available in current POLST forms yet they are critically important for people in pain or with dementia.

A leading European country passed legislation seven years ago enabling a competent person to request (at an earlier time) an end to life (at a later time) if dementia subsequently developed or progressed. This Advance Directive option has rarely been effected, for four reasons. The first reason is that the majority of physicians believed dementia was not a sufficient moral basis for actively ending life (unless the patient had a life-threatening illness, they would withhold life-sustaining treatment). The second reason is that some believed patients with dementia do not have unbearable and hopeless suffering because of anosognosia (impaired insight about their loss of cognitive function). Yet some studies revealed that one-quarter of patients with dementia had unbearable suffering. The third reason is the sense of responsibility and moral distress of the physician, the proxy decision-maker, and the family in complying with a patient's Advance Directive to end life. The fourth reason is to comply with a mandatory standard of care requiring patients' contemporaneous competent requests with "reciprocity" (shared understanding between patient and physician) if life is to be ended. This attitude is not unique in that there are respected bioethicists in the United States (e.g., Leon Kass and Rebecca Dresser) who refute the advisability of precedent autonomy in favor of the concept of "best care for the person now here" as described in President Bush's Council on Bioethics' report, **Taking Care: Ethical Caregiving in Our Aging Society**. The contrary view—that we should respect precedent autonomy in the form of an Advance Directive created while the patient was competent, even years later when dementia has progressed to an advanced stage—is based upon the compelling presentation by Ronald Dworkin in **Life's Dominion: An Argument about Abortion, Euthanasia, and Individual Freedom**, a tenet fundamental to Doctor Terman's strategic approach.

To ensure that patient preferences are honored and that physician orders are durable, Doctor Terman has thought of innumerable potential barriers for which he has devised strategic solutions. These include a proxy-patient contract to supplement the patient's Advance Directive and a physician-patient contract within the physician's orders. Another is the option of an irrevocable (Ulysses') contract, which patients can choose to add to their **NDPO**. Doctor Terman illustrates how typical barriers can be overcome in real and hypothetical stories of patients. The goal is to increase the likelihood of assurance that others will follow the preferences of the individual who expressed his or her preferences prior to losing the ability to make decisions. Dr. Terman's ingenious solution allows the implementation of critical orders years later, when the patient has Advanced Dementia and can no longer make decisions for him or herself. Thus, Doctor Terman's "ironclad strategy" is not only of extreme importance for all of us as individuals, but it will also help protect our healthcare system—even the entire US way of life—from the economic disaster of the Alzheimer's epidemic.

Doctor Terman writes with compassion, passion, clarity, and expertise. His patient stories are compelling and illustrative. He has been responsive to several of his and my critical colleagues whose combined clinical, legal, and bioethical expertise is invaluable and who, along with me, seriously challenged his enthusiastic pushing of the envelope. The result is an extraordinarily practical, logical, legal, detailed strategy for advance health care planning. Using this book, readers can effectively anticipate and deal with the most difficult of problems: disabling, debilitating dementia, unrelievable pain and suffering, and even the ennui of advanced age following the loss of spouse, friends, and innumerable contemporaries—all after having completed one's life work.

Doctor Terman has repeatedly noted that when one has the knowledge to be able to control the end of one's life, often s/he chooses to live longer. He advocates strongly against ending life prematurely. The book shows how this is avoided whether by one's own timing or by a proxy authorized in a previously created Ulysses' contract [where the contract itself make the agreement irrevocable]. Ironically, then, a book about how to end life is really one that empowers readers to prolong meaningful and enjoyable life.

Ronald B. Miller, MD, FACP
Clinical Professor of Medicine Emeritus,
Founding Chief of the Renal Division
Founding Director of the Program in Medical Ethics,
Past President, Emeriti Association,
Department of Medicine, University of California Irvine

Acknowledgments: Stallion, Elephant, or Bloodhound?

As I sat down to write these Acknowledgements, two images initially came to mind. Stallions, under normal conditions, use their magnificent muscular physique to defend and protect their herds, and are capable of daunting gallops. But the one I imagined had its four feet tied close together and could not run or defend itself from the pack of wolves snapping at its loins. The contrasting image was the well-known elephant around which six blind men were meticulously examining different parts. To put these strong images into perspective, they represent only my reactions to the best intentioned criticisms; let me explain:

About a year ago [2008], I became quite discouraged after I sent out an initial draft of this book and received comments from several colleagues whose opinions I hold in high regard. The sum of their formidable concerns led me to nearly abandon this project. At that point I identified with the stallion. Yet as I recovered my courage and analyzed all of their remarks, I realized something: each professional had severely critiqued one area while omitting any mention of the others. Now I identified with the elephant being examined by blind men each of whom seemed oblivious to the concerns of the others. So my task was clear: I would attempt to satisfy each critic in his particular area of concern. As I was finishing this book, a third image came to my mind—that of a Bloodhound—which I will explain below. First, I acknowledge appreciation for all my colleagues, unfortunately limited by the requirement for brevity.

Ronald Baker Miller, MD's critical mentoring was not limited to this book. He introduced me to many of his colleagues, attended my presentations, and supported my vision. He "planted the seed" for this work: as part of his long-term professional commitment to reduce suffering from unwanted attempts at cardio-pulmonary resuscitation, he invited me to comment on his early proposed drafts for California's Physician Orders *about* Life-Sustaining Treatment. Many of his ideas were eventually incorporated into this book's centerpiece: the **Natural Dying Physician's Orders**. His recommendations about this form, and the accompanying **Natural Dying Advance Directive**, strived for perfection through dozens of revisions. If these forms succeed in achieving their goal, it will be due in large part to his tireless input. Dr. Miller read every word of the First Edition (some words, many times) and never failed to stimulate the clarity of its presentation and the reasoning of its arguments. A stickler for crediting earlier contributors to ideas and research, Dr. Miller refined my appreciation of "doctor-as-teacher" and enlightened me about the difference between well-informed benign caring and moral paternalism as it applies to shared decision-making between patients and physicians. Dr. Miller supported me about the importance of this project, despite significant political challenges. I am deeply indebted to Dr. Miller: he helped me create a work that is my best.

I wish to thank Michael S. Evans, MSW, JD, who for a decade, has been my mentor on California's Probate Code and has joined me in scrutinizing newly proposed and passed legislation. Together, we discovered the significant power of "and". Attorney Evans focused my attention on the difference between the "power of a form" and "trusting people we empower by using forms." More generally, he tempered my tendency to let my passion promise more than what we as fallible human beings can realistically expect, given his extensive professional experience with "the best laid plans."

Can two passionate professionals be diametrically opposed to each other's beliefs systems and still have great respect for the other's opinions? In the case of Guy Micco, MD, and me, the answer is "Yes." Exceeding even our own expectations for endurance, we thrashed out several issues, two of which were: Should we use the term, *"Palliative Sedation,"* or just provide the best palliative care possible and invoke the "Double Effect" doctrine if and when it is necessary? And, Do we or don't we have the right to make life-or-death decisions for the cognitively diminished persons we may ourselves someday become? As I think about my intense dialogues with Dr. Micco, what emerges most prominently is the magnificent example he serves as an empathic and responsive physician and teacher. Often I thought, if all physicians were as sensitively tuned in and as skillful in applying their skills as he, much of this book would be unnecessary. Still, for many situations, there will remain an ethical tension between honoring a patient's wish to exercise self-determination (sometimes via an appointed proxy), and the need for the practices of medicine and law to foster the safety of vulnerable people by providing guidelines and protocols. Also, one must have humility in presuming we know what is going on in the minds of those with diminished cognitive capacity. Dialogues with Dr. Micco stimulated my writing a story about "shared decision-making" (page 80).

Thaddeus Mason Pope, JD, PhD, repeatedly challenged the core of my strategy by asking, "How will this really work?" I tried to meet his challenges by describing in adequate detail how to implement each step of the proposed strategies. Attorney Pope's pragmatic legal perspective emerged as we engaged in several long dialogues to discuss, for example, if sanctions to motivate physicians to change their behavior were adequate. We agreed on this reality: When laws lack "teeth," professionals often ignore them. Attorney Pope never underestimated the urgent need to avoid unwanted burdensome treatment (his specialty is "futile treatment") and lingering in advanced dementia. Of his many suggestions, here are two examples: Include several States when comparing Advance Care Planning forms, and add an additional layer of authenticity to people's expressed wishes by giving them the opportunity to rewrite them in their own handwriting on the agreement.

Dr. Ferdinando Mirarchi impressed me with the difference between what is written ("Do Not Resuscitate") and what is interpreted ("Do Not *Treat at All*"). He urged my strategy include focusing on this dangerous gap that can occur between what patients really intended, and how healthcare professionals interpret their wishes—as stated in their Living Wills and orders written by other physicians. Mistakes in interpretation can determine the difference between life and death.

Karl Steinberg, MD, generously shared his extensive clinical, administrative, and editing experience. (He is board certified in Family Medicine, Hospice and Palliative Medicine, and by the American Medical Directors Association, (now, Past) President of the California Association of Long Term Care Medicine, and editor, *Caring for the Ages*.) He offered significant comments on the clinical details of the book's patient stories and, thankfully, could not refrain himself from applying his skills as an astute copy-editor!

William C. Fowkes, MD, offered his wisdom, advice, and support as some of the clinical cases reported in the book unfolded in real time. In a sense, my book is one way to implement the compelling arguments he made in the pioneering book Dr. Fowkes authored a decade ago: **Prolonged Death—An American Tragedy**. I also learned from him, the need to provide *Palliative Sedation* to patients who have unbearable "existential" or mental suffering.

Thanks also to: Jeffrey Abrams, MD, who continued to volunteer his personalized online research service, bringing medical journals and new services to my e-mail; Ronald Koons, MD, whose support, clinical feedback, and frank opinions helped greatly; Rob Gibson, JD, PhD, whose refreshing critical clinical and legal comments on topics that overlapped his fields of expertise: psychology and law; Sidney Spies, MD, for encouraging me to leave out more than I was willing to at first, and for excellent suggestions on how to revise the Criteria of Advanced Dementia; to Stephen Jamison, PhD, for enlightening me with his extensive experience; to Linda Lozanoff who not only helped diligently on so many details including Internet research but also suggested the strategy of using a sworn Affidavit; and to Jeremy Stone, who encouraged me to officially empower proxies to demand "Against Medical Advice" discharges if there is no other option to fulfill a patient's *Known Wishes*. I have similarly learned from many dozens of patients, colleagues, and lecture/workshop attendees who have shared their personal stories, insisted that I clarify my instructions, or otherwise challenged my evolving ideas.

I greatly appreciate Bob Burke's willingness to identify himself as he shared the sad story of his father. While other patients wished to preserve their confidentiality, they still shared more both during and after certain events because they knew I would be writing about their experiences. One daughter even copyedited an early draft of her mother's story. When one works in the end-of-life field, it is common for the noblest of human qualities to emerge; in this case, altruistic efforts to reduce the suffering of others.

The image of the Bloodhound emerged as I considered the goal to reduce end-of-life suffering is one I could not accomplish alone. The analogy is, in the search for a missing person, a single Bloodhound who trails by using its sense of smell is equivalent to 100 human trackers who form a line search. Similarly, in the search for a Peaceful Transition, certain key people have led the way. Here I have space to mention very few: Drs. Joanne Lynn, Sherman Frankel, Linda Ganzini, and Boudewijn Chabot, and attorneys Barbara Coombs Lee and Kathryn Tucker.

Two decades ago, Joanne Lynn published **By No Extraordinary Means: The choice to forgo life-sustaining food and water** (1986, Indiana U. Press). It remains today a superb source of clinical details in support of how peaceful dying can be by fasting. Over a decade ago, Dr. Frankel's article, *The Dementia Dilemma*, in *Perspectives in Biology and Medicine* (1999; p. 174-178), anticipated many obstacles that my "ironclad strategy" tackles, including: "Can one arrange to exit life as gracefully as one tried to live it, and spare our family and caretakers the attending trauma?" He stated these needs: standardized durable Advance Directive forms that can be stored in a safe database, knowledgeable proxies, and a dementia rating scale.

Dr. Ganzini was the first to publish a formal survey of clinical observation. She alerted the medical community that dying from medical dehydration can be peaceful. Dr. Chabot's PhD research thesis and compact book, **A Hastened Death by Self-Denial of Food and Drink** revealed that 83% of bedside observers considered this method of dying dignified; symptoms of fasting are treatable; the time to death depends much on how much liquid patients ingest. Since such basic information is rarely taught in healthcare training programs, Dr. Chabot aptly calls dying by refusing food and fluid, "the 'Cinderella' of end-of-life teaching research."

Attorneys Barbara Coombs Lee and Kathryn Tucker of Compassion and Choices have a long history of political advocacy. Their Comment about the "Provider Conscience Rule" of to Health and Human Services (January 19, 2009) is eloquent. The Rule prohibits federally funded healthcare institutions from discrimination based on an individual's refusal to perform or assist in any service or activity that is contrary to their religious beliefs or moral convictions. This Rule has "teeth": institutions violating its terms risk loss of **all** federal funding. Compassion and Choices voiced these concerns in their Comment:

> "...the Rule could be read to remove a Health Care Entity employee's obligation to inform patients of all of their treatment options (counseling) or to refer patients to other providers if those patient request treatment options with which the employee does not personally agree. The very notion of denying patients access to any such information runs afoul of the fundamental healthcare principles of autonomy and informed consent. This is particularly worrisome for patients at the end of life who are often unaware of their options, hesitant to initiate conversations with their providers about certain of those options, and often unable to remove themselves from their current health care setting in order to seek treatment elsewhere. When dying patients are suffering in the final stages of terminal illnesses, they should be able to receive counseling regarding the full range of information about end of life options, thereby empowering them to make fully informed medical care decisions, including the legal and medically accepted options of opiate pain management, *Palliative Sedation*, and voluntary stopping of eating and drinking (VSED).... by refusing to provide counseling or referrals to patients that may not be aware of all of their options, or able to seek care elsewhere, access to certain forms of healthcare for those patients will be limited. As just one example, consider the case of *Palliative Sedation*...."

The Comment by Compassion and Choices strongly urged, "At a minimum, and in order to maintain at least some level of autonomy, patients would need to have notice that a facility or provider might refuse to provide information or referrals regarding certain types of treatment based on the provider's personal moral or religious views."

Compassion and Choices' statement explains: "Without prior notice, an end-of-life medical emergency could leave patients in agonizing pain or gasping for air." Another possibility is prolongation of existence that the patient would not want. (See Sara's story, page 59.) Unfortunately, these and other excellent Comments did not change the Bush administration's proposed Rule; worse, their responses confirmed the intention to broaden their applicability from abortion to end of life and to reverse State laws that now require physicians to refer patients to other providers if they have a religious or moral conflict.

The Obama administration is striking this Rule (2011) but the laws on which it is based remain, as will the strong opposition whose goal it is to impose its moral view of behavior on others; in this case, directly encouraging the rights of providers to refuse to provide treatment that can reduce suffering—without any balancing considerations for the rights of patients to receive treatment they need and have a right to receive, that could reduce their end-of-life suffering.

Obviously, patients cannot choose an option about which they are unaware. In a recent letter to the *Journal of Palliative Medicine* (*12*: 119-120; 2009), about how uninformed terminally ill patients are about their end-of-life options, Kathryn Tucker could not even estimate the percentage who knew about voluntarily stopping eating and drinking.

To sum up, despite some moments of feeling discouraged, I am now very appreciative for all the provocative support I received, both directly and indirectly, from the efforts of others, to further the goal of this book: to reduce end-of-life suffering. This is a challenging task, but one that is extremely important. Our success can affect every one of us directly, as well as every person we love. It is thus worth our most diligent and persistent efforts.

This book begins an effort to encourage widespread, effective Advance Care Planning. As I try to simplify, however, I will keep in mind these words of attorney/philosopher Ronald Dworkin:

*The greatest insult to the sanctity of life is indifference
or laziness in the fact of its complexity.*

Stanley A. Terman, PhD, MD
Board Certified in Psychiatry
Medical Director and President
Caring Advocates, Carlsbad, California

Peaceful Transitions

Notes:

Peaceful Transitions is available both as a combined book and as two separate books, and both are available in print and e-book versions.

This combined book has two parts: **Stories of Success and Compassion** and **Plan Now, Die Later—Ironclad Strategy**. To make it easier to refer to other versions, this book follows these conventions:

The first part of this combined book (pages 1-101) is "**Stories of Success and Compassion.**" It refers to the book's second part, **Plan Now, Die Later—Ironclad Strategy**, by using the shorthand, "<u>PNDL</u>."

The second part of this book, which begins on page 102, is "**Plan Now, Die Later—Ironclad Strategy.**" It refers to the book's first part, **Stories of Success and Compassion**, by using the shorthand, "<u>Stories</u>."

From page 102 on, the print version of this combined book's page numbers are 100 greater than in the separate print version, but the numbering of the footnotes is the same since the footnotes begin again at number 1, on page 2 or 102.

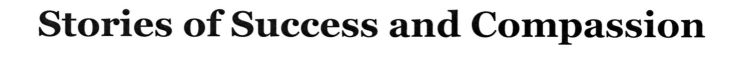

Stories of Success and Compassion

Of Leaves and Life... O. Henry's short story, "The Last Leaf"

"The Last Leaf" is a charming short story by O. Henry.[1] Its three characters are: Johnsy, who is near death like many victims of a current pneumonia epidemic; Sue, her best friend who is now her caregiver; and an old alcoholic painter, who has yet to paint his life's masterpiece.

Sue asks Johnsy why she is counting backwards. Although she initially calls it "nonsense," Sue takes Johnsy's explanation quite seriously: "Leaves. On the ivy vine. When the last one falls I must go, too. I've known that for three days. Didn't the doctor tell you? ... I'm tired of waiting. I'm tired of thinking. I want to turn lose my hold on everything, and go sailing down, down, just like one of those poor, tired leaves."

Sue complains, "Think of me, if you won't think of yourself. What would I do?" O. Henry then narrates: *But Johnsy did not answer. The lonesomest thing in all the world is a soul when it is making ready to go on its mysterious, far journey. The fancy seemed to possess her more strongly as one by one the ties that bound her to friendship and to earth were loosened... the lone ivy leaf clinging to its stem against the wall... with the coming of the night the north wind...*

Sue asks Johnsy to promise to close her eyes so she can paint a model, but what she does next is to ask a skeptical alcoholic to paint a leaf on the wall outside Johnsy's window. The next morning, after a fierce night of wind and rain and a bit of snow, Johnsy looks outside. "Something has made that last leaf stay there to show me how wicked I was. It is a sin to want to die." Later she states her life's goal: "Someday I hope to paint the Bay of Naples."

After Johnsy recovers, Sue reveals that the old alcoholic died of pneumonia after creating his masterpiece: "He painted [the ivy leaf] there the night the last leaf fell."

O. Henry's story has at least five lessons:

1. Our fear of the "mysterious, far journey," can lead us to trade anxiety (when will we die?) for certainty (when the "last leaf falls"), but the cost is dear: *premature dying*;

2. *Premature dying* is tragic because life is sacred, precious, and should not be wasted;

3. People live in a web of relationships; whether they live or die makes a tremendous difference to others;

4. To make life worth living, one must find meaning and something to look forward to;

5. To change a person's behavior: rather than argue that his/her belief is foolish, create a strategy that embraces this belief system and can bring about change consistent with it.

---

[1] This story is available online at http://www.literaturecollection.com/a/o_henry/226/

Timely, peaceful transitions respect the sanctity of life

The goal of this book is really to *live well*; not merely to *die well*. The most compact way to state the goal is this: *to attain a timely, peaceful transition.* "Timely" means neither *premature* nor *prolonged*. It is tragic to die prematurely if you can still enjoy life. Life is sacred; you should strive to maximize your joy of living for whatever time can possibly remain. But it can also be torturous if you are forced to endure treatment that prolongs dying, which is accompanied by unending, unbearable pain and suffering. "Peaceful" means dying with the minimum possible physical and emotional pain—for both you and your loved ones.

What makes this book unique? It strives for a way to die *peacefully* that is NOT *premature*.

This book helps you find an effective way to avoid the two greatest end-of-life fears:[b]

- Being forced to endure **unbearable pain and suffering** as you die from a medical illness (such as cancer)—for **days to several weeks**; or

- Being forced to endure **indignity and dependency** (as you define it) as you die from Advanced Dementia (such as Alzheimer's)—for **months to several years**.

What is even worse? Some conditions may combine both fears. Consider this sad example:

> "The woman, who was in her 90s, had lived for **several years** at the Ecumen Sunrise nursing home in Two Harbors, Minn., where the **staff had grown accustomed** to her **grimaces and wordless cries**. She took a potent cocktail of three psychotropic drugs.... In all the time she'd lived at Sunrise, she hadn't spoken...."

> The woman recently participated in "an experiment to see if behavioral rather than pharmacological approaches could help wean residents off antipsychotic medications... the *Awakenings program*.... With reduced medications, the woman...was able to speak—haltingly and not always understandably, but enough to communicate.... And what she let [staff] know, **after years of being virtually nonverbal**, was that **she was suffering physical pain, the cause of her crying out**."[c] {Emphasis added.}

Psychotropic drugs do "calm" behavior. Often, they reduce anxiety and lift depression. But they definitely do NOT relieve pain. Unfortunately, patients who suffer from Advanced Dementia lose the ability to tell doctors what bothers them. Their physicians may therefore fail to diagnose their pain and suffering. In that case, they will not receive adequate treatment—perhaps for years. Recent research is summarized in Chapter 4 of this book, and is just beginning to illuminate the extent of this serious problem.

---

[b] A third fear is also covered: being subjected to burdensome intensive treatment including hospitalization that has no potential to improve your overall quality of life, which is called "futile" treatment.
[c] Span, P. "Clearing the Fog in Nursing Homes." New York Times, February 15, 2011.

One way to avoid the risk of unrecognized and untreated pain and suffering as well as the burdens and indignities of being dependent in Advanced Dementia is to end your life before you reach the stage of Advanced Dementia. Let me emphatically state that the philosophy underlying this book considers *premature dying* an anathema. Instead, the book urges this alternative: maximize your enjoyment of whatever time remains, but also set the stage so that treatment will not force you to exist in a state you consider "worse than death." You must inform others WHEN you would want your *timely, peaceful transition*, and you must make SURE your future physicians and others will honor your wishes. This book names this means, the **Plan Now, Die Later—Ironclad Strategy**. It appreciates one of life's greatest ironies:

Knowing you can control *when* you will die, can —and often does—lead to choosing to live longer.

If you cannot trust you will have a *timely, peaceful transition*, then you may consider yourself an ***involuntary sufferer***, may experience depression and anxiety, and may decide to end your life *prematurely*. But if you can trust you will have a *timely, peaceful transition*, then you can consider yourself a ***voluntary survivor***, can make the best of each day, and can find meaning in your life until you get to "that point." (The book "**Stories**" illustrates both.)

Planning a successful, *timely, peaceful transition* is not easy for two reasons. First, most Advance Directives (Living Wills and Proxy Directives/Durable Powers of Attorney for Health Care) do not consider Advanced Dementia[d]. Second, the means to control WHEN you die is controversial: opponents may challenge your plan. That is why you need an effective strategy.

This book presents step-by-step details so you can create a successful, compassionate strategy for life's final challenge. The goal is practical: invest *two to three hours* in Advance Care Planning now to prevent being forced to endure *days to several weeks* of unbearable pain and suffering (if you suffer from a terminal illness such as cancer), and to avoid lingering *months to several years* restrained by chemicals or straps in a bed, confused, fearful, and unable to communicate to others that you are in pain (if you suffer from Advanced Dementia). If you complete the recommended forms and you empower people you trust to speak for you if you cannot speak for yourself, you are likely to experience the peace of mind that comes from knowing you have done all you can so you will live the last chapter of your life as *well* as possible. Once accomplished, you can put this strategic planning task aside and continue to enjoy living every day, perhaps with even greater appreciation and meaning.

---

[d] Reasons: In the 1970s and 1980s, as they created statutes for the first Living Wills, legislators were conservative. The New Jersey Supreme Court ruled that physicians were NOT committing "murder" when they disconnected Karen Ann Quinlan's ventilator. Lawmakers included only patients very close to death (terminally ill, unconscious, and sometimes Permanent Vegetative State patients) but they did NOT consider Advanced Dementia. In the mid-1970s, there were only 500,000 demented patients. Unless there is a research break-through, by 2050 there may be 16 million demented patients. This would be a 30-fold increase in just one lifetime.

Introduction
Do you consider these physician's orders *outrageous*?

Terminally ill patients who are enduring extreme pain and suffering sometimes request these physician orders. So do those patients with Advanced Dementia if they plan ahead for when they cannot interact with others, are totally dependent and suffer indignity as they define it, and may experience unrecognized and untreated pain and suffering.

Consider all four orders (referred to as **A**, **H**, **F**, and **R**). Then rate your opinion of each using the scale below, where **0** = **not outrageous at all**, and **10** = **extremely outrageous**.

←Not outrageous at all								Extremely outrageous→		
0	1	2	3	4	5	6	7	8	9	10

A: Physician-Assisted **Auto-Euthanasia**: Physician sets up an intravenous system to deliver poison into the vein of a competent, terminally ill patient and then instructs: "If your untreatable suffering is so unbearable *now* that you desire a peaceful death, push this button." Note: Some people worry that this method may permit unauthorized others to push the button.

H: Physician-Assisted **Hastened** Dying: Physician writes prescription and then instructs the patient: "Most likely, you will die within six months. Fill this prescription for a lethal dose of medication. Take the pills to hasten your dying, if the time comes when you want to avoid unbearable suffering." Notes: Patient must be mentally competent when physician writes the prescription and must be physically able to ingest the pills without assistance from others.

F: Assisted **Feeding** per physician's order: "*Always* provide food & fluid by mouth if medically feasible." Notes: Physician knows assisted feeding may prolong the dying process and may increase pain and suffering, but still follows the culturally accepted norm for people who are NOT dying, or the interpretation of the law or *benevolent-sounding* guidelines. Physician does not consider the ethical need to ask patients or their surrogate decision-makers for their informed consent to indefinitely continue *Manual Assistance with Oral Feeding and Drinking*.

R: **Refusal** of all feeding per physician's order: "Respect patient's preference to stop *Manual Assistance with Oral Feeding and Drinking* and tube feeding *in the future*—if patient's condition meets the criteria the patient had previously specified." Notes: It is not common for physicians to write orders *more than a year before* the time implementation is anticipated. While withholding/withdrawing tube feeding is now becoming common, it is not yet common for physicians to write orders to stop *Manual Assistance with Oral Feeding and Drinking*.

Answer online at www.surveymonkey.com/s/Are_these_physician_orders_OUTRAGEOUS.
See how I answered on the next page:

A:	Physician-Assisted **Auto-Euthanasia** (patient starts poison Dr. put in vein):	9
H:	Physician-Assisted **Hastened** Dying (patient takes Dr.-prescribed lethal dose):	5
F:	Assisted **Feeding** (always feed orally if feasible, even if it prolongs suffering):	8
R:	**Refusal** of feeding (order includes oral; written years before implementation):	1

My ratings are of course based on more information than indicated above. Actually, I wrote a book on this subject: **The *BEST WAY* to Say Goodbye: A Legal Peaceful Choice at the End of Life** (2007). Many readers asked me to write a step-by-step approach to accomplishing its goal: a *timely, peaceful transition.* —This is one reason I wrote this book.

Will your physician comply? S/he might, but many are resistant, uninformed, or lack the time or interest to help Advance Care Planning, a service for which insurance companies rarely pay. As I wrote this book, an alarming movement was underway to deliberately obstruct patients' ability to learn about certain legal options that can reduce the duration and intensity of end-of-life pain and suffering. This movement increased the need to inform patients more fully about all reasonable legal options for peaceful transitions. —My second reason for writing this book.

New research findings worried me: As noted in Chapter 2, one out of six physicians object to *Palliative Sedation* (sometimes the ONLY way to relieve unbearable pain and suffering) based on their religious/moral conscience. About half of the objecting physicians also indicated they would not refer their patients to other physicians or institutions to reduce patients' suffering—even though law and ethics require referrals in such situations. Legislative efforts in California to encourage physicians to inform their patients of ***all*** reasonable legal options failed in 2008. Physicians who object are protected. The Bush administration passed a new federal regulation threatening to *withdraw **all** federal funding* unless institutions accommodate health care workers whose *conscience* prevents them from providing certain services. (This regulation may change in 2011.) These and other actions lead to this worry: patients who are NOT informed or who are NOT referred to willing providers may suffer greatly as they die. To attain the goal of a *timely, peaceful transition,* you may need the components of the **Plan Now, Die Later— Ironclad Strategy** (as detailed in the companion book with this subtitle) so others will honor your wishes, treat you with compassion (as you define it)—so that you receive the treatment you DO want and do NOT receive treatment you do NOT want.

Specific Disclaimer regarding the term "ironclad strategy"

Courts of law ultimately determine the legal effectiveness of strategies. But the most successful strategy not to prolong your dying is to avoid litigation. Too often, lawsuits result in *To Delay is To Deny.* Success in fulfilling the goal of a *timely, peaceful transition* depends on **1)** Effective forms you completed with diligence that motivate physicians to comply with your clearly expressed *Known Wishes.* **2)** A designated proxy/agent whom you can trust to put forth enough effort to make sure others will honor your *Known Wishes.* By themselves, the forms may just sit there. Without the forms, an earnest, energetic advocate may lose no matter how hard s/he tries to overcome the opposition. You need both. The stories in this book point out common pitfalls of Advance Care Planning and indicate the qualities to look for, when selecting someone as your proxy/agent. Success in fulfilling your end-of-life wishes may also depend on other variables such as: limited finances, restricted health care resources in your geographical area; few or no personal and professional people available to help; and additional restrictions imposed by your State's laws. Members of ethics committees and judges sometimes have idiosyncratic convictions. Bottom line: Placing a sheet of iron around a wood ship made it virtually impenetrable to being sunk by cannons, but it was still vulnerable to, for instance, fire. This book shows you how to avoid "fires"; but nothing in life comes with a 100% guarantee.

Conflict of Interest Statement: I personally developed and tested the methods this book describes, learning from my colleagues in medicine, bioethics, and the law, with feedback and outcome from my patients and others. I have been a board certified Psychiatrist since 1980. In 2000, I founded a nonprofit 501(c)(3) organization Peaceful Transitions® that became Caring Advocates® in 2005. Currently, I am Caring Advocates' Medical Director and CEO, and a member of its professional team. Someday I may derive financial benefit from this organization for performing my administrative duties. I now receive reasonable compensation in the form of fees and honoraria for performing professional psychiatric and educational services. I share a portion of my royalties from the sale of books, DVDs, forms, Medallions, and My Way Cards with Caring Advocates. I receive no incentives or samples from manufacturers of pharmaceutical agents, whose products I refer to generally in this book and list as thirst control aids. (These products control the symptoms of dry mouth and provide general Comfort Care.) Caring Advocates may in the future apply to agencies and foundations to support its educational and research efforts, and if funds are awarded for these purposes, I may benefit from them as an investigator.

This book explains how professional teams can help: For example, Caring Advocates' Planning Professionals can use the interview technique, "Show & Tell," to help document decisional capacity for the task of sorting **My Way Cards**. Caring Advocates offers Thirst Reduction Aid Kits to its members to augment the Comfort Care they receive from **hospices** and **palliative care physicians** with whom Caring Advocates works closely, usually insisting that patients enroll in hospice. Caring Advocates emphasizes research, education and patient services; it does not conduct political campaigns to change laws. One reason: all the MEANS to attain our goals are currently legal in most of the world. A possible exception is the law in Victoria, Australia: it forbids a person's *Advance Directive* to refuse in advance, the OFFERING of oral food and fluid. The well-meaning intent was to prevent suffering and maximize Comfort Care. The obvious way around this law, and also local regulations of skilled nursing facilities, is to accept OFFERING, but to refuse PROVIDING.

Caring Advocates embraces a policy of cooperation rather than competition with similar organizations. For those organizations who wish to take advantage of our knowledge and experience, Caring Advocates offers "Affiliated Memberships" to members of other organizations so they can benefit from our approach to Peaceful Transitions. No change in name or leadership is required. For more information, call 1 800 647 3223.

Do you need to be a member of an organization? No. If you follow the step-by-step instructions in this book, you can create a *strategic plan* to achieve the goal of attaining a *timely, peaceful transition* without help from organizations or Planning Professionals. This *IS* a "do-it-yourself" book. (A common mistake is to think you need an attorney to create a Durable Power of *Attorney* for Health Care, but you do not.) However the plan does require a discussion between you and your current personal physician who should sign three forms. When the time comes to implement your *Known Wishes*, your proxy/agent (or their alternates) may still appreciate support and advice from an organization similar to Caring Advocates.

Hospice: Caring Advocates usually insists that all patients enroll in hospice. Some hospices expressed appreciation for the extra expertise we provide since patients and families frequently need additional advice and support when the patient has chosen to avoid a prolonged dying by *Manual Assistance with Oral Feeding and Drinking* (voluntary medical dehydration).

General Disclaimer: Although I am grateful to my attorney colleagues for the advice they provided, the statements and opinions about the law in this book are from my point of view as a medical physician and psychiatrist, not an attorney. As a clinician, I try to navigate the fine line between respecting the ideal of **patient autonomy** on the one hand and prudent practices that offer patients needed **protection and safety** on the other.

Information in this book is limited to general comments on general principles; it cannot offer specific guidance to specific individuals. Neither the author nor the publisher of this book is engaged in rendering medical, legal, or other professional services by distributing this book, although the book may serve as a resource for those who do render such services. For specific advice, readers must consult with professionals who have knowledge, experience, training, certified qualifications, and appropriate licenses to provide specific advice in the reader's legal jurisdiction. Such advice can then be specifically tailored to the reader's particular needs and circumstances. Caution: Statements in this book about laws in certain States may not apply to other States. Readers who wish to follow the book's general guidelines must check with legal experts who know and can apply the law within their jurisdiction. In one sentence: **This book is not a substitute for professionally delivered medical or legal advice**.

Stanley A. Terman, PhD, MD
Caring Advocates, Carlsbad, California
June 30, 2011

Overview:
A Book for Our Last Season... Designed for Several Types of Readers

Woody Allen famously said, "I'm not afraid of dying, I just *do not want to be there* when it happens." Sadly, he and millions of others might actually get their wish—if they suffer from dementia as they die. Why sad? Because their minds will "not be there" to speak for their bodies—if their suffering is so severe and so long that they would want to refuse any treatment that will only prolong their dying. Trapped, they may suffer more and longer since their pain may go unrecognized and untreated. While non-demented terminally ill patients may be able to communicate to some extent, 70% to 95% cannot make medical decisions before they die.

The only solution is to learn what dying can be like, to make your decisions, to inform others, and to take the necessary steps so others will honor your wishes. Your last chapter of life is similar to any other: you strive to maximize pleasure, to minimize pain, and to honor your relationships. But it is very different in one significant way: to attain the goal of a *timely, peaceful transition*, you must diligently plan ahead. This is called *Advance Care Planning*.

This book enlightens and thus empowers. If you follow its recommendations now, then—if your future medical or mental condition prevents you from being able to speak for yourself—you will have set the stage so others *will honor your last wishes*. This "stage" includes **A)** a set of instructions—your Living Will, and your signed informed consent on a set of Physician's Orders (your *Known Wishes*); and **B)** other forms that legally authorize your future advocate—your proxy/agent—to make sure others will honor your *Known Wishes*. Why do your Advance Care Planning now? You can always revise your plan if you are competent. But you cannot predict when your plan will be needed, if you have a sudden medical crisis or car accident.

Part ONE of this book has illustrative stories. They should motivate you to diligently set up a strategy effective enough to overcome a powerful opposition. Part TWO details how.

Experienced teachers realize that the less students initially know about a subject, the more they can learn. For you, what kind of books will **Peaceful Transitions: Stories of Success and Compassion; Plan Now, Die Later—Ironclad Strategy** be? It depends on your and on your physician's present state of knowledge. The books can serve a number of purposes:

1. **Peaceful Transitions** is a *self-help book*. Read it to decide what you DO or o NOT want, as your life ends. Sorting **My Way Cards**, which this book introduces, is an optional, complementary, new Advance Care Planning tool. If you start with the cards, you can send the non-profit organization Caring Advocates your sorting/deciding results. They will send back, your **Natural Dying—Living Will**. This form can function as a standalone expression of your end-of-life wishes if you attach it to your state-approved Advance

Directive. It can also serve as the centerpiece as you discuss your end-of-life wishes with your physician, proxy/agent, and loved ones. The best way to use this Living Will is as the first form in your **Plan Now, Die Later—Ironclad Strategy**.

2. **PT** is a *guide book*. It provides step-by-step instructions on how to complete all the recommended forms for the **Plan Now, Die Later—Ironclad Strategy**. It also explains who should sign what and when; if you need a notary instead of qualified witnesses; how you can store everything in a national registry so that authorized people can request them, immediately when needed; and when and why you might choose to wear an alert medallion.

3. **PT** is an *informative book*. It will increase your knowledge about essential end-of-life options to avoid end-of-life pain and suffering, or total dependency and indignity (as *you* define it, after you learn what it is like to live in the stage of Advanced Dementia). It also informs you why and how the opposition may even challenge *your right to know*.

4. **PT** is a *motivational book*. Stories illustrate the *benefits* of following its strategies: peaceful transitions compared to the *burdens* of prolonged pain and suffering—if you do NOT.

5. **PT** is a *political book*. It explains why others may vehemently oppose your wishes and it considers some strategies to change policies to overcome their challenges.

6. **PT** is a *manual for professionals*. For physicians, physician assistants, nurse practitioners, psychologists, social workers, family counselors, pastoral counselors, and estate and elder attorneys—Section TWO, the **Plan Now, Die Later—Ironclad Strategy** especially—can enhance their ability to help patients/clients in the task of Advance Care Planning. (Professionals can also take advantage of supplemental videos and personal training.)

7. **PT** is *NOT a comprehensive treatise* on the emotional, practical, clinical, legal, moral, ethical, spiritual, religious, and political aspects of refusing food & fluid; these subjects are in **The *BEST WAY* to Say Goodbye: A Legal Peaceful Choice at the End of Life**.

8. **PT** does *NOT present detailed arguments for social change*, but some statistics—about the greatest epidemic we will ever see—are presented to urge readers to exercise individual choice. My next book will present some arguments for social change. Its tentative title is: **An Outrageous Proposal for Advanced Dementia: *REQUIRE* Natural Dying**.

9. **PT** can be an *interactive workbook* as you *make your own decisions*.[e] Readers can *memorialize* their personal thoughts and feelings by writing notes, especially if the book asks questions, such as the Survey in the Introduction. *Now you may wish to write down an answer to:* Considering the present state of your end-of-life planning, what do you expect from this book will help you attain the goal of a *timely, peaceful transition*?

---

[e] Note: If the practice in your culture is to designate an authority figure to make life-determining decisions for patients, it may be appropriate to give a copy of this book to that person.

Chapter 1

A Problem. Its Solution. Why Others may Challenge it.

Everyone has the right to expect compassionate treatment. Those who are dying should not be forced to endure a prolonged dying if they are suffering. It takes energy to fight for any right, however. If we wait until we are close to death, we will be too weak to fight. We must thus be proactive while we still have the mental ability to express our preferences about our future treatment.

The best way to attain our goal—to achieve a peaceful transition—is to complete strategically designed forms as we discuss our last wishes with our physicians, our proxies and our loved ones. Once we accomplish this task, we can turn our energy toward enjoying a full life with less anxiety about how long and how much we might suffer, feeling confident that others will honor our final choices.

A Well-Intentioned Hell

What motivated Bob Burke (his real name), a successful general insurance agent, to sell long-term care insurance? It was living through the ordeal of his father's prolonged dying from Alzheimer's disease. The Burke family was lucky in some ways. Although Bob's father did not have long-term care insurance, he did have several sources of income: Social Security plus $30,000 per year from his retirement savings and $12,000 from rental income. He also lived in a region of the country where residing in a Skilled Nursing Facility cost *only* $54,000 a year (in 2002 dollars). (In large coastal cities, the cost can be twice as much.) Bob learned that most families with a member who suffers from Alzheimer's disease are not so lucky; many declare bankruptcy. The statistics are appalling and getting worse. Every year, an increasing number of adult children and spouses lose their entire life savings as their parents or spouses require long-term care for Alzheimer's and related dementias.

Sheltered from financial strain, Bob could mentally sort out where his deep feelings of sadness came from: It was from seeing the father he loved, the man who had been so strong all his life... just slip away... slowly. So slowly that it took eight years from the time of initial diagnosis until his death. The worst time, however, was the last two years.

As commonly happens, the problem was not recognized until several months after symptoms began. One day, Bob's father called and complained, "A lot of different people are phoning me, but I don't understand why." Bob promptly visited his father's home. There he found mounds of disorganized mail including several months of unpaid bills. The utility companies were about to shut off all services. Hence the phone calls. Bob's father had always been responsible about paying his bills. Something had to be wrong... After several visits to a few doctors and a series of tests, the cause was given a diagnosis: Dementia, probable Alzheimer's type.

With expert help from his father's family doctor, Bob set up a plan of care through a home health care company. In-home assistance sufficed for three years. When Bob's father needed more help, he entered an assisted living home. When his behavior subsequently became unmanageable, which is quite common as Alzheimer's disease progresses, he had to be transferred to a skilled nursing facility (nursing home).

For the last 2 years, there was nothing left to remind Bob of who his father was, other than the physical resemblance. In retrospect, Bob's father eventually met the *Criteria of Advanced Dementia* listed in Chapter 4. They include not being able to recognize family members, express wishes or thoughts, or remember important life values and events.

Given his father's dramatic decline, Bob discussed the situation with other members of his family. They wondered, "How long can he go on this way?" All agreed, "What's the use of Dad's continued existing?" Bob's siblings empowered him to request the doctor to administer only those medications needed for comfort, to stop any medication that could prolong his dying, no tube feeding. If the time came when he couldn't eat, they would *let Nature take its course.*

The doctor replied with an air of professional authority as he made this pronouncement: "Okay, no tube feeding. But I insist: We must continue *Manual Assistance with Oral Feeding and Drinking* for as long as he can swallow. Otherwise, I'd lose my license."

> Comment: *The doctor was wrong: he would not lose his license. But Bob had no basis to doubt him or to ask for a second opinion. Since the doctor previously earned Bob's confidence by offering prudent advice about in-home care, Bob followed his advice.*

Manual Assistance with Oral Feeding and Drinking became more difficult and less efficient and despite efforts by skilled nursing facility staff, Bob's father could not be encouraged to ingest as many calories as his body needed. Over two years, his weight dropped from 180 to 70 pounds.[6] Throughout this time, Bob's father was not able to express any feelings or thoughts, let alone voice complaints of hunger or pain. Looking back, it seems obvious that he died of extremely slow starvation—a process of dying that very likely, caused him great suffering.

> *With malnutrition Bob's father, like so many other frail patients, may have suffered from unrecognized, untreated pain. Some clinicians (especially in Europe) treat demented patients with pain medications for symptoms such as irritability and anger, since these clinicians are convinced that severely demented patients still experience pain after they lose the ability to complain, and the source of pain may not be obvious.*

---

[6] I appreciate Bob Burke's willingness to provide these specific details.

Bob's father finally died of pneumonia, which his then-treating doctor finally agreed not to treat with antibiotics or hydration. The infection lasted a week and Bob's father suffered from symptoms of untreated pneumonia—including high temperature that makes patients feel toxic; desperate struggling to breathe; and repeated spasms of coughing that tax a severely weakened state. In 1898, Sir William Osler said, "Pneumonia is the old man's friend." This statement was true for most of the Twentieth Century, but may not be true now. Nor was it true for Mr. Burke.

Neither Bob nor his father had been informed about another, more peaceful way to die. Instead of suffering from starvation for two years, and then from symptoms of untreated pneumonia for a week, Bob's father could have experienced a peaceful transition by ceasing *Manual Assistance with Oral Feeding and Drinking*. Dying by medical dehydration usually takes one to two weeks. It rarely causes hunger due to the euphoric effects of breakdown products called ketones. Thirst—the symptom of dry mouth—can be effectively treated with Comfort Care.

> *One cannot make a prudent choice unless one is fully informed about all available options. This is why the medical profession endorses the ethical practice of striving to provide "Fully Informed Consent." It is below the standard of professional care to inform patients about two options for treating cancer if three options are available. A physician should inform you about all options—even if s/he specializes in only one area.*
>
> *Politics and religion can create controversy in end-of-life clinical care. Sadly, you cannot assume your **current physician** will fully inform you about and offer you all your legally available options. You also cannot be sure your **future physician** will honor the preferences you expressed in your Living Will—unless you take other steps.*

As I sadly pondered Bob's father's prolonged starvation, I recalled a religious description of eternal punishment: In Hell, the fires slowly burn sinners' flesh every day. Guards give sinners just enough water so their flesh is not totally consumed—to permit them to survive so they can continue to exist and thus endure further suffering of their flesh as it burns the next day... day after day... year after year. This image prompted the title of this story.

Why was Bob's father forced to endure this two-year hell? Possible reasons include:

A) His physicians might not have known how peaceful it can be, to die by medical dehydration after ceasing *Manual Assistance with Oral Feeding and Drinking*;

B) His physicians might have erroneously feared they could lose their license to practice medicine or lose a malpractice lawsuit if they provided ONLY Comfort Care to a patient whose family all agreed the patient would prefer to die by medical dehydration;

C) Well-intentioned skilled nursing facility staff might have naïvely but wrongly considered providing oral nourishment as necessary for humane comfort. It IS, for people who are well. It is may NOT be, for dying patients. It is definitely not, for patients who have stated their *Known Wishes* and explained why this is exactly what they do NOT want.

D) The bylaws of the facility might have reflected the religious view of Pope John Paul II: the withholding of nourishment—even for patients whose doctors expect them never to be able to recover consciousness—is a sin: specifically, "euthanasia by omission";

E) The skilled nursing facility's administration might incorrectly fear being cited, fined, or sued for neglect/abuse or lose their "five-star rating" for not providing nourishment; or,

F) The skilled nursing facility's decision-makers might have had a self-serving economic incentive to keep Bob's father existing: to keep his bed filled for as long as possible.

Our wishes will prevail only if we create an effective strategy for anticipated future challenges.

Advance Care Planning:
so others will honor your end-of-life wishes

The fact that we are mortal has this inevitable consequence: if we do not die of one disease, we will certainly die of another. This principle is called, *Substituted Dying*. Physicians do not really "save" lives; they only postpone deaths. Of course, with the help of "modern medicine," they make possible more decades of quality living. With few exceptions, we want to live as long as possible. One exception plagues psychiatric patients who have temporary, but treatable emotionally based impulses to commit suicide. More commonly, *almost all of us* can imagine living in a condition we deem "worse than death." Since we have no direct knowledge about "death" itself, we really mean this: If our physicians predict we will die before we recover any pleasure in living, there are certain conditions in which we would prefer **not to prolong our dying**. Almost all of us would NOT want to continue to exist if we are permanently unconscious, in the Permanent Vegetative State, or suffer from Advanced Dementia. *Almost all of us*—but *not all.* Consider this statement of US Conference of Bishops: "Life is our first gift from an infinitely loving Creator... A society that devalues some people's lives, by hastening and facilitating their deaths, will ultimately lose respect for their other rights and freedoms." [http://www.usccb.org/toliveeachday/bishops-statement-physician-assisted-suicide.pdf; 6-16-11.]

The **problem**: Modern medicine has made it "possible" for more than 40% of us to die *slowly*, from a chronic, progressive illness, and many of us will not be able to express our treatment preferences for a long time before we die. A large study published in 2010 reviewed data of people who died over the age of 60: 7 out of 10 lacked the capacity to make their own medical decisions, and more than 4 out of 10 required critical end-of-life decision-making. Thus, more than one-quarter of patients had *both* lost the ability to make medical decisions themselves *and* needed critical life-or-death decisions made.[7] For patients who cannot speak for themselves, how will their physicians and loved ones know what treatment they do, or do not want at the end of their lives? They must decide and tell those concerned, ahead of time.

---

[7] Silveira MJ, Kim SY, Langa KM. Advance directives and outcomes of surrogate decision making before death. *N Engl J Med.* 2010;362:1211-8. Other studies show about 95% of critically ill adults cannot make medical decisions.

The **solution**: Advance Care Planning is the process of learning, discussing, and deciding on what we want, which results in legal forms that inform and empower our proxies and future physicians so they can fulfill our end-of-life preferences for medical treatment. Its steps are:

➔ First, we must learn about the end-stages of diseases so we can decide for **what** specific mental and medical conditions we would NOT want to prolong our dying.

➔ Second, we must describe these conditions so **well** that our future physicians can understand our *Known Wishes*. The way we express our wishes should meet the highest standard for proof of evidence in civil law: our **criteria** should be *clear and convincing*.

➔ Third, we must understand the peaceful and legal treatment option of **Natural Dying** (which includes stopping *Manual Assistance with Oral Feeding and Drinking*).

➔ Fourth, we must designate proxies we *trust* to help decide **when** we meet our criteria to want **Natural Dying**, and will try hard to get others to honor our *Known Wishes*.

➔ Fifth, we must create **effective** legal forms that **empower our proxies** so they can garner the strategic cooperation of some, and overcome the challenges of others.

Four Benefits of *Effective* Advance Care Planning

1. You can relieve your loved ones from the anguish of wondering what you really wanted in the last chapter of your life, which in turn can reduce their subsequent guilt and grief;

2. You can prevent others from forcing you to endure a prolonged process of dying with unbearable pain and suffering if you are **terminally ill**;

3. You can avoid **burdensome non-beneficial** ("**futile**") medical interventions that are **NOT** likely to be **effective** to restore you to an acceptable state of overall health; and,

4. You can indicate you want **to live as long as possible** until you reach the stage of **Advanced Dementia**, defined by criteria you previously selected, and then avoid the indignity, dependency, and risk of unrecognized and untreated pain and suffering.

Benefit 1 can be a real gift—if you make the effort to give it! *Benefit 2* reflects a compassionate view that has motivated the movement to legalize Physician-Aided Dying (Suicide), however Voluntary Refusal of Food and Fluid is a legal and peaceful alternative. *Benefit 3* is important: make sure your Advance Care Planning says you refuse futile treatment and consider wearing a medallion with these words engraved: "Do not hospitalize unless needed for Comfort Care."

Benefit 4 recognizes that patients with Advanced Dementia often have no life-sustaining high technology treatment to withdraw. Thus, our options to NOT to prolong our dying are limited.

Consider a *science fiction device* that exists only in the creative mind of Philosophy Professor Margaret Battin. Early Alzheimer's patients, if still competent, could choose to have an **implanted delayed-release device** inserted painlessly below the skin. Ahead of time, patients must set the time for when the device will release a lethal dose of medication to bring about a peaceful death. For example, a person with early dementia who had capacity could set the time to be 3 to 5 years hence. As long as patients are competent, their decision is reversible; patients can request removal of the implant. After memory becomes impaired and patients forget about their implant, the device will cause death—unless they die from another cause.

In theory, this device could honor patients' wish to avoid lingering in Advanced Dementia "without forcing them to waste 'good' life" [Battin's words];[8] that is, without requiring *premature dying*. Battin's goal included NOT involving other people in deciding WHEN, or in participating in the final act. But can we predict WHEN, years in advance? A bad guess can lead either to missing some years of good living, or to lingering some years in a miserable, undesired state. Battin's device has a legal obstacle: Even in the two European countries where euthanasia is legal, their protocols would not permit it: patients must have a discussion with their physician where both agree **death** is the only alternative to avoid unbearable *current* suffering.

This book's solution is legal and practical but you must appoint others (your proxy and/or your physician) to determine WHEN your condition meets your criteria for **Natural Dying**. You thus need to know enough about Advanced Dementia to describe those criteria. Compared to the universal experience of pain and suffering, many people are in the dark about what living with Advanced Dementia is like. This is due in part to the phenomenon, "closet-within-a-closet." (Alzheimer's disease is the outer closet; the advanced stage is inner closet.) One way to illuminate this information gap is to sort **My Way Cards**. Each has an average of 23 plain words with almost no medical terms, and a clarifying line-drawing illustration. For example:

I cannot say or show what I want—by using words, moving my hands, or changing the look on my face.

Imagine how frustrated this patient must feel. He wants something urgently, but cannot say or show what it is. If his difficulty in communication is long-term, even caring professionals may not pay attention to him.

His condition could be even worse. Patients who cannot complain about pain or suffering may not be adequately diagnosed or treated. ➔

---

8 Battin, MP. (1994). **The Least Worst Death. Essays in Bioethics on the End of Life**. Oxford Univ. Press.

I have severe pain. But I cannot say what bothers me.

Doctors don't see my pain. They do not treat my pain.

The patient illustrated above is more fortunate than many. His doctor does not know what is going on, but at least is trying to figure it out. Physicians may fail to recognize and treat pain and suffering. Some may use chemical or physical restraints for violent or aggressive behavior. But antipsychotics medications do NOT relieve pain and physical restraints make patients feel *worse*.

Does specifying your selected criteria for **Natural Dying** always hasten your death? No, but some people challenge **Natural Dying** by citing this undeserved criticism. Actually, saying WHEN you want **Natural Dying** can extend your life. By selecting certain specific criteria, you will have simultaneously expressed your wish to live *as long as possible*—UNTIL you meet your specific criteria. Some **My Way Cards** insist on specific treatment to try to extend life. (See the illustration on the left and the words, below.)

First I can enjoy things like eating, sing-alongs, finger painting, and being touched. Then I get very sick. Ask my doctor if I might get better. If "Yes," TREAT me.

The **My Way Card** on the previous page shows treating a patient with antibiotics, hydration, and a *temporary* ventilator. "Full Treatment" often cures pneumonia in a *reasonable time* (a couple of weeks). If successful, the patient can again enjoy some simple pleasures of life.

LIFE is PRECIOUS so tell others precisely what you want

Sometimes, physicians and well-meaning family members make a joint decision NOT to treat a potentially curable pneumonia for patients in the *middle stage of dementia*. Their reasoning is typically this: A) The patient's disease is **irreversible** and **progressive**; and B) It could be years before another "**opportunity**" occurs where they can *let Nature take its course*.

Suppose you felt life was still precious in the *middle stage of dementia* and you did not want to die. Then choose "Treat & Feed" for this **My Way Card**. Your preference will become part of your *Known Wishes*. If a future physician is aware of your wish but still lets you die, s/he risks a malpractice suit. Note: **1)** Being informed sets the stage for the *power of specific Advance Care Planning* to help you **live as long as you want**. **2)** Sorting the **My Way Cards** can help you precisely define those states in which you DO, or do NOT want treatment.

Question: Is diagnosis and prognosis enough to let someone die if they can still enjoy living? Many people think not. Many religious people and humanists argue that cognitively intact people have *NO right to judge the lives of patients in the middle stage of dementia as not worth saving*. They argue: the patients' *values* about life have changed. Some philosophers go even further. They say the Advance Care Planner him/herself has *no right* to refuse treatment in advance for his/her "future demented self." The reason: the demented patient is a *new, different* person who is not even related to the former person, the Advance Care Planner.

Many patients *refuse* treatment for pneumonia for their "future demented self" in the *middle stage of dementia*? If I interview them, I discuss this choice in depth. I point out many patients in the middle stage of dementia are **happy** based on their *new set of values*. Like many disabilities, people can accommodate to conditions they initially doubted they could. Most important, I make sure they realize the "ironclad strategy" makes it unnecessary to wait years for another life-threatening illness to present "an opportunity" for *Nature to take its course*. They can define now, the precise criteria WHEN they will want **Natural Dying**. Some Advance Care Planners still say they would not want to "live like that" or "be a burden." I then ask if they will—for this card/item *only*—allow their proxy to make this decision in the future—when that time comes. If they still do not agree, I must respect the law and honor their wishes.

Comment on sorting **My Way Cards** versus reading this book: **My Way Cards** have few words but offer this advantage: you can consider one card at a time and discuss your choice with others, as you sort. The book has more words about each card plus stories and explanations and thus lets you think more deeply about certain key choices.

A Challenge to Relieving End-of-Life Suffering

Some devoutly religious people never want to risk unintentionally hastening death by using high doses of medications—even if such doses are required to relieve extreme pain and suffering. Yet most people do not want to suffer if that is all life then has to offer. Surveys reveal the vast majority of people similarly do not want to remain on feeding tubes if there is no hope of regaining consciousness.[9] This includes most religious and disabled people. Yet a highly vocal and powerful opposition prefers to **maintain biologic existence** indefinitely even if there is no hope of regaining consciousness—not only for themselves, which is of course their right, but also for others. They base their arguments on: **A)** the duty of the State to protect vulnerable people, and **B)** "conscience" laws or regulations that permit professionals to refuse to provide medical procedures that conflict with their religious or moral convictions.

In his allocution of 2004, Pope John Paul II stated that withholding food and fluid from people in the Permanent Vegetative State is *euthanasia by omission*. Pope Benedict XVI strengthened this position in 2007 by stating it applied even to those patients whose physicians all agree will never regain consciousness. In November, 2009, the US Congress of Catholic Bishops voted to strengthen *Ethical and Religious Directive* #58 by using the strong word, "obligation": "This **obligation** [to provide food and water] extends to patients in chronic and presumably irreversible conditions (e.g., the 'persistent vegetative state') who can reasonably be expected to live indefinitely if given such care." The only exceptions to continuing feeding were **A)** if the patient is close to dying or **B)** if complications from feeding "become excessively burdensome."

This view has also diffused into the secular arena. A New York judge set aside a patient's Medical Orders for Life-Sustaining Treatment based on her religion. (See *In the matter of Zornow*, discussed on Chapter 5.) Consider two quotes below from the President's Council on Bioethics 2005 report[10] and a quote from one of its prominent members:

Quote 1: "Can individuals really know in advance that such a life [with dementia] would be worse than death? And, more fundamentally, do we possess a present right to discriminate against the very life of a future self or—even more problematic—*to order others to do so*, on our behalf?" {Emphasis added.}

My critical questions about this first quote:

A) Is it even *possible* for a person to discriminate against him/herself? Why assume that others can make better decisions about what I will want in the future, than I can decide for myself, now—as long as I am adequately informed?

---

[9] Example: 93% of 61,000 polled by America Online agreed with the decision to remove Eluana Englaro's feeding tube. http://news.aol.com/health/article/after-long-battle-woman-allowed-to-die/326594; retrieved 2-11-09.
[10] **Taking Care: Ethical Caregiving in an Aging Society** is available at http://www.bioethics.gov.

B) What about honoring the federal Patient Self-Determination Act (1990)? It requires all federally funded institutions to inform all admitted patients that they have the specific right to create Advance Directives to make such future *requests*?

C) What about the 1990 U S Supreme Court ruling *in Cruzan* that embraced and thus established this personal right: every competent adult has the right to refuse any medical treatment, even if their choice might hasten dying?

Quote 2: "We emphasize both the singular importance of seeking to serve the life the patient still has and the moral necessity of *never seeking a person's death* as a means of relieving his suffering." {Emphasis added.}

My critical questions about this second quote:

D) What about accepted medical ethics? *Document E-2.20* of the American Medical Association's Council on Ethical and Judicial Affairs states: "The social commitment of the physician is to sustain life and relieve suffering. Where the performance of one duty conflicts with the other, the preferences of the patient should prevail" [2005].

E) How do we define "death"? In 1968, a consensus of professionals met at Harvard to define Death by Neurological Criteria ("Brain Death"). Yet the definition of *death* continues to be tweaked; in part so more transplantable healthy organs can save the lives of more patients. The practice of "Declaration of Cardio-Circulatory Death" (**DCD**) permits clinicians to pronounce "death" after they remove life-support and wait to see if the heart will resume beating without resuscitative efforts. *They wait before declaring death has occurred. How long?* The Institute of Medicine standard is 5 minutes; the University of Pittsburgh: 2 minutes; Denver Children's Hospital: 75 seconds.[11] Professor Robert Veatch asked if it violates the "Dead Donor Rule" to use the criteria of "irreversibility," if the same heart is started in a recipient patient.[12]

There are no easy answers here, but consider the perspective of Christian medical ethicist, Nick Yates, M.D., who embraces organ donation as a "gift of life." He states that the *moment of death* is clearly "a *stipulated* point in the dying process."[13] (Legally, "stipulated" means: agreed to, as required by a contract.)

Based on these considerations, if you prefer to define WHEN *you* want to donate organs rather than to let the words "Upon my **death**" be *stipulated* by a future doctor or institution, consider a **Natural Dying Organ Donation Consent Form**.

---

[11] Boucek MM et al. (2008). Pediatric Heart Transplantation after Declaration of Cardio circulatory Death. *N Engl J Med. 359*: 709-714. "DCD" also means "Donation after Cardiac Death." See also Sanghavi D. When does death start? New York Times Magazine. Dec. 16, 2009. Retrieved on 12/20/09.

[12] Veatch RM. (2008). Donating Hearts after Cardiac Death--Reversing the Irreversible. *N Engl J Med. 359*: 672-673.

[13] Yates, FD. (2007). Donor after Cardiac Death: What is the Christian's Response? Retrieved on 12/11/08 from http://www.cbhd.org/resources/healthcare/yates_2007-02-02.htm

Quote 3: Professor Gilbert Meilaender, a member of The President's Council on Bioethics, previously wrote: "The principle that governs *Christian compassion* is *not [to] 'minimize suffering.'* It is [to] 'maximize care.' ... The suffering that comes is an evil, but... *we are called simply to live out our personal histories*—the stories of which *God is author*... Even God does not really 'solve' or take away the problem of suffering; rather, God himself lives that problem and bears it. *His way is steadfast love through suffering.*"[14]

My critical questions about this third quote:

F) Must everyone be forced to suffer? —Even those who do not believe that God is the author of their life story, who are not comforted that God suffers with them, and who do not believe in the redemptive value of suffering as necessary to enter Heaven?

G) Does Professor Meilaender speak for all Christians? Consider physician/bioethicist John T. Dunlap, MD's interpretation of Paul's message to the Philippians (Philip.1:20-26): "If I am to live in the flesh, that means fruitful labor for me." According to Dr. Dunlap, when Paul "was trying to decide whether to hope to live or to die"... "his response was...to hope to live [only] if he could continue to serve others in their spiritual walk..." Paul recognized "to depart and be with Christ was the natural end of a life spent serving others, and he would hope for that, if he were no longer able to serve." Dr. Dunlap concluded that, in today's era of high tech medicine, it is "a reasonable expectation to be able to serve others as an *indicator* of *when* to forgo burdensome life-sustaining technology."[15] According to the U S Bishops' statement of 6-16-11, the goal of palliative care is to "allow patients to devote their attention to the unfinished business of their lives, to arrive at a sense of peace with God, with loved ones, and with themselves." If this goal is unattainable, is it time for **Natural Dying**?

The Successful, Compassionate Strategy

If you do not want to endure extreme suffering or to prolong your dying if disease has destroyed your brain so you have virtually NO values (as opposed to new, different values), and if the essence of the person you *were* is virtually gone... and you feel you have the right to "stipulate [your own] point in the dying process," then consider **Natural Dying**.

> **NATURAL DYING** means to receive all necessary Comfort Care, but NO life-sustaining treatment and NO *Manual Assistance with Oral Feeding and Drinking*.
>
> Refusing life-sustaining treatment includes DNAR (Do Not Attempt Cardio-Pulmonary Resuscitation), no ventilator to assist breathing, no tube-feeding, no dialysis, no blood transfusions, and no antibiotics—unless needed for Comfort Care.

---

[14] Meilaender, G. (1996). **Bioethics: A Primer for Christians**. W B Eerdmans Pub.

[15] Dunlap, JT. (2007). *A Good Death*. From http://www.cbhd.org/resources/endoflife/dunlop_2007-07-20.htm.

The Urgency to Complete Advance Care Planning

An obvious truth: The hardest thing to predict is the future. Specifically, we never know when a situation will arise for which an Advance Directive will be needed. To save ourselves from suffering and to save our loved ones from prolonged anguish, *we must complete our forms in advance.* Three U S women did not and, in their twenties, they lost the ability to respond to the environment: Karen Ann Quinlan, Nancy Beth Cruzan, and Terri Schiavo.

Completing Advance Care Planning forms is particularly **urgent** for patients who have...

- A cancer that recurred and might spread;
- A progressive neurological disease like multiple sclerosis, Lou Gehrig's disease (ALS);
- Had a previous minor stroke and fear that the next stroke might be devastating;
- Suffered several infections but now wish no further intrusive burdens from treatment;
- Fallen and now worry about serious complications if they fall again; and especially,
- Experienced significant memory loss or thinking ability and dread getting an irreversible, progressive dementia.

Completing forms is especially **urgent** for patients who have the diagnosis of **early dementia**, **mild cognitive impairment**, or **Parkinson's disease** (for which the risk of developing dementia in 10 years is nearly 80%[16]). Patients must memorialize their preferences regarding end-of-life medical treatment before their finite window of mental capacity closes forever.[17]

Seven Safeguards that Respect the Preciousness of Life

1. Clinicians must evaluate patients to see if they possess the **mental capacity** to make **voluntary** end-of-life **medical decisions** before they complete any forms.
2. Clinicians must discuss other reasonable, available legal options with their patients and patients must **sign consent forms** if they decide certain options reflect their end-of-life wishes. These importantly include consent to refuse CPR,[18] to receive *Palliative Sedation* if needed, and to forgo *Manual Assistance with Oral Feeding and Drinking.*
3. Patients' signatures must be **witnessed** by qualified individuals or a **notary**, and in some cases, by a person who has no conflict of interest (an Ombudsman)—to make sure the decisions the patient is making are voluntary and free of duress.

---

[16] Aarsland D, et al. Prevalence and Characteristics of Dementia in Parkinson's Disease. An 8-Year Prospective Study. *Arch Neurol. 2003;60:*387-392. (Of the dementias, Lewy Body/Parkinson's is the second most common.)

[17] Recommended: to avoid future challenges based on the patient not possessing decisional capacity, sort **My Way Cards** as a Planning Professional conducts and records an interview on audio or video.

[18] In contrast, the policies of many hospitals allow physicians to write Do-Not-Resuscitate (**DNR**) orders without obtaining the patient's or the proxy's signature. Some States allow physicians to just explain their order in the chart on the basis of the patient's prognosis. Others require physicians to write a note in the patient's chart to document their discussion with the patient or proxy. A few States require these discussions to be witnessed.

4. The **Natural Dying Physician's Orders** form prompts physicians to write their initials after they ask physicians who treat pain and suffering or psychiatric symptoms— to make sure the patient received maximum benefit before implementing its orders.

5. The **Natural Dying Physician's Orders** form prompts physicians to inform patient's family members, close friends and significant others—before implementing its orders.

6. The default option is to err on the side of life so others will hand feed demented patients who request food or fluid *after* they met their criteria for **Natural Dying** and cannot make medical decisions. Note: patients can change this option to increase the effectiveness of the "ironclad strategy," if they desire, as detailed in "**PNDL.**"

7. Patients who have capacity and their legally designated proxies (for patients who lack capacity) can revoke any order *to accept* any treatment for its *life-sustaining potential.*

No person should feel compelled to hasten death *prematurely* by dying when s/he *still can.* Instead s/he should die when s/he *will want.* LIFE is PRECIOUS. This book's goal is a *timely, peaceful transition. Accept* life-sustaining treatment *when it can restore health. Refuse* such treatment *if it will only prolong dying*— with minimal benefits and great burdens. Burdens can either be direct (such as food entering the lungs that causes pneumonia) or indirect (such as increasing the risk of unrecognized and thus untreated pain and suffering). Thus for certain conditions/situations, a particular treatment may become extraordinary and disproportionate.

Not all Advance Care Planning forms will be effective. Some are obviously vague; for example, "Allow me to die as gently as possible." Others omit important provisions that, to my knowledge, only this book offers: **A)** a way that always relieves unending, unbearable pain and suffering, which is called "sedation to unconsciousness" (*Palliative Sedation*); and **B)** a way to avoid lingering for years in Advanced Dementia by waiting until one gets a life-threatening illness for which life-sustaining treatment is then withheld. The "way," called **Natural Dying**, includes refusal of spoon/hand feeding (*Manual Assistance with Oral Feeding and Drinking*).

How many of us will need *Palliative Sedation*? The estimate is between 5% and 35% of hospice patients will experience intractable severe pain and other symptoms in the last week of life.[19]

How many dementia patients might want **Natural Dying**? The number will be huge:

Dementia: an Epidemic of Staggering Proportions

- Fourteen million baby boomers are destined to suffer from dementia (10 million from Alzheimer's dementia, and 4 million from other dementias).[20]

---

[19] Quill, T. E., Byock, I. R. (2000). Responding to intractable terminal suffering: the role of terminal sedation and voluntary refusal of food and fluids (for ACP-ASIM End-of-Life Care Consensus Panel). *Ann Intern Med.* 132:408-414. (The number varies, depending on the kind of patients cared for, and how hard the physicians may have looked.)

- Add to these 14 million, those who are presently older than baby boomers. Some experts estimate that for those 85 or older, 47% suffer from some stage of dementia.

- The life-time risk of dementia increases with advancing age. For Californians who reach the age of 55, the risk is 1 in 6. For U K residents who reach the age of 65, the risk of dying in some stage of dementia is about 1 in 3.

- Of those who will suffer from dementia, 43% will "need a high level of care, equivalent to that of a nursing home."[21]

- By 2025, California may have 660,000 cases of dementia; Florida, about 590,000; Texas, about 470,000; New York, 340,000; Illinois, Ohio, Pennsylvania, North Carolina, each over 200,000. The "one-new-case-every-70 seconds" will increase by a third.

- Deaths from Alzheimer's disease in the U S increased 66% between 2000 and 2008. It is "now the sixth leading cause of death and the only one in the top ten that cannot be prevented, cured, or even slowed." Yet fewer than 9 percent of people between the ages of 55 and 64 own long-term care insurance.[22] One survey revealed 44% *incorrectly* believed that Medicare or private insurance will pay for long-term care. About 70% had no long-term care plan at all.[23]

- The cost to care for an Advanced Dementia patient who resides in a skilled nursing facility will exceed $100,000 year. From 2010 to 2050, the cumulative total cost of Alzheimer's disease to the U S is predicted to be $20 trillion. Thus "Alzheimer's disease could become the social and economic sinkhole of the modern era," according to Harry Johns, President and CEO, Alzheimer's Association, who presented at the Aging in America Conference in San Francisco, California, on April, 28, 2011.

Of all developed countries, the United States is one of very few that has no enforced savings plan for long-term care. We are totally unprepared for the impending *"gray tsunami"*—the epidemic of Alzheimer's and related dementias. Some people will prefer not to bankrupt their families and then be "warehoused" and to suffer for years in a Medicaid-funded nursing home.

To consider your options and to decide what you want requires time and effort. Others will honor your choices only if you have an effective, legal strategy. Once your plan is in force, you can *worry less* about how you will spend the last chapter of your life. Free from this source of worry, you can *enjoy the rest of your life even more (*and *die later)*. Planning now for how you will *die* can make your *living* feel even more precious, more enjoyable, and more meaningful.

Conclusions: Individuals, families, and society will face difficult choices in the future. The wise will plan ahead so that their preferences will be honored.

---

[20] **Alzheimer's Disease: Facts and Figures**. 2010. Alzheimer's Association.

[21] Brookmeyer R, Johnson E, Ziegler-Graham K, Arrighi HM. (2007). Forecasting the Global Burden of Alzheimer's Disease. *Alzheimer's and Dementia, 3*:186-191.

[22] news.yahoo.com/s/usnews/20110411/ts_usnews/5reasonsyouneedalongtermcareplan. Retrieved 5-5-2011.

[23] http://todaysseniorsnetwork.com/ltc_week_procliamed.htm. Retrieved 5-5-2011.

Chapter 2

Advance Care Planning . . . or Advance Care HOPE?
Formidable Challenges to Fulfilling Your End-of-Life Wishes

As I wrote this chapter, I recalled the excitement about the groundbreaking Patient Self-Determination Act that became law in 1991. This law required institutions that accepted federal funds to inform all newly admitted patients about their *right* to indicate their end-of-life preferences. Yet today, more than two decades later, only 30% of adults have completed Living Wills or Proxy Directives (Durable Powers of Attorney for Health Care).[24] Why so few?

- Could it be too hard to contemplate the way we might die?
- Do we not consider it important to avoid end-of-life pain and suffering?
- Do we not care about how long our process of dying will take?
- Do we not want to reduce the emotional burden for our loved ones by leaving them clear indications about what we want?
- Do we not want to avoid lingering after our existence has ceased to have meaning and our lives have lost all quality, especially if unrecognized and untreated pain is likely?
- Do we not want to protect our devoted families from devastating financial expenses?

Of course we do. Then why do only 30% of adults create Advance Directives?

Human nature certainly includes the qualities of procrastination and psychological denial. Yet we buy life insurance and we create last wills and testaments. We also read voraciously about dying. Recall the best sellers, *Tuesdays with Morrie* and *The Last Lecture*. Most of us intensely tracked newspaper and TV accounts as the Terri Schiavo saga unfolded. Many of us frequently read reports about how end-of-life medical expenses are rising. On a more personal level, who among us does not have deep feelings about the death of someone close to us?

So once more I ask: Why do so few of us proactively plan for how we will die?

> ### Could this reason be why few people complete
> ### Living Wills and Proxy Directives?
>
> ### They are NOT CONVINCED these forms will be EFFECTIVE.

---

[24] *Poll: More Americans Have Living Wills.* Pew Research Center poll. Retrieved on 12-11-08 from http://archive.newsmax.com/archives/articles/2006/1/5/125608.shtml. Older people and certain population segments have higher percentages of completing Advance Directives, yet most of these documents consider only terminal illnesses, Permanent Vegetative State, or irreversible loss of consciousness. Rarely is Advanced Dementia mentioned, even though it is now the **6th most common** and **only incurable cause of death** in the top ten.

Many people are skeptical. If they are not convinced Advance Care Planning will ultimately work, why bother grappling with such an unpleasant subject? This book presents reasons why its strategy will succeed. In addition to the listed "Benefits" in Chapter 1, Advance Care Planning can prevent premature, violent, and criminal dying. Consider for example two who suffered from early dementia and one who suffered from cancer, below.[25]

- Michigan, 1990: Days before 54-year-old Janet Adkins died in an old VW van, she played a full set of tennis with her son... and won, although she had to ask her son to keep score. She suffered from early dementia. At Dr. Jack Kevorkian's trial, medical experts estimated Janet could have enjoyed another two to three years of quality life had she not caused her death by pushing a button to infuse a lethal drug into her veins.
- California, 2001: Bob Stern, 77, made a home movie to explain that he feared complications from cancer surgery might leave him brain-damaged. Since he could not trust any family member to facilitate his Peaceful Transition, he shot himself.[26]
- Maryland, 2004: Maryland Supreme Court Judge Robert Hammerman died violently from a self-inflected gunshot wound to the chest. He died across the street from the nursing home where he feared confinement, given his probable diagnosis of dementia.

Research results are fueling the public's *growing distrust* of Living Wills—directly and indirectly. "Indirectly" refers to physicians who learned Living Wills have flaws[27] so they do not encourage their patients to engage in Advance Care Planning. Dr. Fred Mirarchi's research[28] raises serious concerns about the dangers of misinterpreting Living Wills: if health care providers incorrectly see a Living Will as a DNR order, the result can be *premature dying*.

Two line drawings on the next page illustrate that a Living Will cannot enforce itself and that a physician may still say "No" to an authorized proxy's treatment REQUEST. Physicians who say a proxy's request conflicts with **their** moral conscience or religious beliefs are protected by State laws. But what is "morally right" for Bob Burke's father? **To deny him Natural Dying and insist on "Comfort Feeding Only"?** This course of action *conflicts with the goal to reduce his suffering.* It also prolongs his dying—from two *weeks* of peaceful dying to two *years* of starvation. *Question:* Would you let those who prioritize the *sanctity of biologic life* exercise their *power* by imposing *their view of morality* on you? Or would you insist on **Natural Dying** as a compassionate way to reduce your suffering after you meet your own criteria? If you choose **Natural Dying**, follow the **Plan Now, Die Later—Ironclad Strategy**.

---

[25] For additional details, see **The *BEST WAY* to Say Goodbye**. Examples of criminal actions are on page 41.
[26] His daughter expanded his video to an award-winning documentary, "The Self-Made Man" [2005].
[27] Fagerlin A & Schneider CE. (2004). Enough! The failure of the Living Will. *Hastings Cent Rep 34(2)*: 30-42.
[28] Mirarchi FL. (2006). **Understanding Your Living Will—What You Need to Know Before a Medical Emergency**. Addicus Books. Mirarchi FL. (2008). TRIAD I: The Realistic Interpretation of Advance Directives. *J. Patient Safety 4*: 235-240. (2009). Mirarchi FL, et al. TRIAD II: do living wills have an impact on pre-hospital lifesaving care? *J Emerg Med*. Feb;36(2):105-15.

Terman and Blochwitz 2005

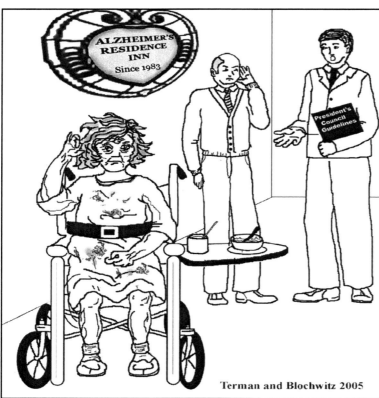

Terman and Blochwitz 2005

Fiction: a piece of paper—your **Living Will**—tries to convince your physician to honor your written end-of-life wishes. It magically raises its voice and shakes its fingers. In reality,

Living Wills are **not self-enforcing**.

Physicians have power to write orders about life-sustaining treatment. Some physicians are biased by their own values and preferences.

Other physicians or the hospital's risk management department may weigh the risk of a lawsuit for withholding life-sustaining treatment *versus* the risk of a lawsuit for not honoring your previously written end-of-life wishes.

A proxy asks but the physician says, **"No! Your request conflicts with my morals."** Here, he cites the 2005 *President's Council on Bioethics'* report on "Best Care," and the State's "Provider Conscience" clause.

Is this *Moral Paternalism*?

Proxy Directives *authorize* another person to speak for you if you cannot speak for yourself... but they *cannot guarantee* your future physician will honor your proxy's request.

Fortunately, Proxy Directives can be crafted to empower your proxy/agent to fire one physician and to hire another—hopefully, one who **will honor** your end-of-life wishes.

Living Wills and Proxy Directives share a significant hurdle: Even the *best written* forms and the most *highly motivated individuals* have limited power. The best they can do is to *request* your future physician honor your wishes. Between when you express your *Known Wishes* and designate your proxy/agent, and when a critical decision must be made, your future physician may say "No" and deny your end-of-life preferences. "**PNDL**" offers a strategy to overcome this obstacle. This chapter explores the opposition's underlying motivation, impressive power, and several recent actions that resulted in **keeping secret**, the two most important options: **Palliative Sedation**, to eliminate your pain and suffering; and **Natural Dying**, to prevent your prolonged dying. This chapter also shows various ways physicians and institutions may deny your legal requests and maintain the status quo instead of encouraging you to become informed so you can initiate your own autonomous choice. To introduce these challenges, I share a story from my youth, when I dealt with another "formidable obstacle."

Moving Targets

Naïvely, I responded to a magazine advertisement that guaranteed a solution to the common problem of house flies. The mailman delivered a small box a week after I sent in my check. Inside were two 1.5-inch wood blocks and one piece of paper with these printed instructions:

> **Rid your home of flies:** You have in your hands, a 100% effective method, when used as directed:
>
> 1. Place a fly on one of the two wood blocks.
> 2. Hit the fly firmly with the other block.
> 3. Repeat steps 1 and 2 until all flies are gone.

I re-read the words, "when used as directed," several times. I felt more disappointed in myself than in this simplistic technology. I was too embarrassed to ask for a refund. I wasn't even sure I *could* ask for one. Several decades later, however, I had this flash of enlightenment:

Flies are moving targets...   **So are physicians!**

Let me explain. Your mind might be sound right now, but you still cannot predict the future. Few of us can be sure who our *last* physician will be. Even patients who are terminal ill may find that their physician has taken a weekend vacation just when it is time to implement their final set of Physician's Orders. A new form, the **Physician Orders for Life-Sustaining Treatment** (POLST) is especially good for revising the level of Limited Levels of Care, with periodic reviews of your medical condition. It is also designed to provide continuity of care as you transfer among treatment settings. But when you are admitted to a new institution, your new physician must take responsibility for you. This means re-evaluating your medical condition and writing new orders, which *should but may not always* honor your end-of-life wishes. Physician's orders have ultimate authority, but a new physician can change the orders.

Example: Suppose you resided in a skilled nursing facility and you previously gave your consent to a willing physician for *Palliative Sedation* with no artificial nutrition or hydration—in the future, if you were terminally ill and your pain and suffering became unending and unbearable. If you broke your hip and Emergency Medical Personnel transported you to a Catholic hospital, you would need to transfer to another hospital to honor your *Known Wishes*.

A 2007 survey revealed that one out of six physicians would refuse to provide *Palliative Sedation*, based on their moral/religious conscience, and less than half of the objecting physicians would refer you to another physician or institution that would provide *Palliative Sedation* to relieve your pain and suffering.[29] You may not want to exist indefinitely if sedated, but a Catholic hospital might still insist on continuing your artificial nutrition and hydration.

When conflicts arise, most State laws require an objecting physician/institution to make *reasonable* efforts to transfer you to a non-objecting physician/institution so you can receive the treatment you want. But these laws rarely define "reasonable" and sanctions are modest and rarely have been imposed. Bottom line: a significant percentage of physicians do not feel obligated to transfer such patients. As mentioned before, between 5% and 35% of hospice patients have intractable symptoms in the last week of life.[30] If you do not want to suffer, you need to provide your proxy with an effective strategy to motivate your future physician either to provide the Comfort Care you want, or to transfer you to an institution/physician who will.

Worse: Many patients and family members are not even aware of the Comfort Care option,

Palliative Sedation. A new California law requires physicians to inform terminally ill patients about *some* legal end-of-life options—if they ask. But the initial bill, AB 2747, was "gutted" in July, 2008. One of the bill's opponents, Attorney Wesley Smith, used the word "gutted" along with this photograph in his post on his blog, "Second Hand Smoke," to gloat over this perceived "win." The revised bill also removed the legal option, Voluntary Stopping of Eating and Drinking (VSED).[31]

---

[29] Curlin, FA, Lawrence, RE, Chin, MH, Lantos, JD. (2007). Religion, conscience, and controversial clinical practices. *N Engl J Med. 356*: 593-600.

[30] Quill, T. E., Byock, I. R. (2000). Responding to intractable terminal suffering: the role of terminal sedation and voluntary refusal of food and fluids (for ACP-ASIM End-of-Life Care Consensus Panel). *Ann Intern Med. 132*:408-414.

[31] The original bill, AB 2747, would have offered a terminal patient this "menu" of choices for end-of-life care: "442.5 (5) The patient's right to comprehensive pain and symptom management at the end of life, including, but not limited to, adequate pain medication, treatment of nausea, palliative chemotherapy, relief of shortness of breath and fatigue, and **VSED [voluntary stopping of eating and drinking]**, and **palliative sedation.**"

"Gutting" had this result: If a terminally ill Californian asks a physician about her end-of-life options, the physician is not required to **mention**, **discuss**, or **obtain informed consent** for *Palliative Sedation*! VSED, which opponents mischaracterized as "self-starvation" or "backdoor to Physician-Assisted Suicide" need not be mentioned as a way to avoid lingering in Advanced Dementia for those who wish to avoid *premature dying*. (Note: the similar Palliative Care Information Act (New York, 2010) lists no specific interventions; hence none could be struck. While NY physicians are supposed to initiate the conversation, how will an uninformed patient realize her physician omitted informing her, so that sanctions can be levied? For both Californians and New Yorkers, who will tell patients that they have the right to be informed?

Federal regulations about protection from discrimination: In 2008, to support a new Bush era regulation, U S Health and Human Services Secretary Mike Leavitt said (L. A. Times, 8-22-08), "People should not be forced to say nor do things they believe are morally wrong" [so] "Healthcare workers should not be forced to provide services that violate their own conscience." David Stevens of the Catholic Medical Association, asserted the regulation covered "...any type of morally objectionable procedure and research activity." The harsh penalty for not accommodating objecting workers' "personal, moral or religious grounds" was **loss of all federal funding**. In February 2011, Obama's administration began to rescind the regulation.

A Powerful Opposition: Certain Religious Organizations

Ideally, compassion should strive to reduce patients' suffering and physicians should provide information about all legal options so patients can make informed choices. Yet professionals who claim "discrimination" can deny patients treatment. Why? So they can view their behavior as "moral" or "religious" (in their opinion) as they choose which teachings of their church leaders to follow. (Note: sections of the Catholic *Ethical and Religious Directives* conflict with Centuries of tradition in applying the compassionate principle of *Proportionality*.) Unfortunately the typical outcome of conflicts between professionals who want to view themselves as moral or religious *versus* suffering, terminally ill patients is this: **patients lose**.

How powerful is this vocal minority, including the Catholic Church? Five of the top seven richest non-profit hospital systems are Catholic based. Note cash and investments, as of 2008:

Ascension Health	**7.43 billion**	(Catholic)
Partners Health Care System	**5.60 billion**	Harvard
Catholic Health Initiatives	**5.57 billion**	(Catholic)
Catholic Healthcare West	**5.19 billion**	(Catholic)
Trinity Health	**4.32 billion**	(Catholic)
U. Pittsburgh Medical Center	**3.35 billion**	(Presbyterian)
Providence Health Services	**3.02 billion**	(Catholic) [32]

---

[32] Carreyrou J, Martinez B. Nonprofit hospitals, once for the poor, strike it rich. With tax breaks, they outperform for-profit rivals. April 4, 2008; Page A1 http://online.wsj.com/article/SB120726201815287955.html

About one in five US hospitals (a total of 636) is Catholic based. One in six US patients was cared for in a Catholic hospital. Catholic hospitals admitted over 5.6 million patients 2009. In addition, Catholic Health Association and Charities have nearly 700 skilled nursing services, nearly 400 assisted living/residential care programs, nearly 600 other housing programs, including senior, low-income and special need housing, over 170 adult day care programs, over 300 home care programs, and nearly 400 hospice programs. Catholic tradition emphasizes compassion and caring, so these numerous institutions must do much good for very many!

The **Alliance Defense Fund** (ADF) is a formidable organization. Founded in 1994 by more than 30 Christian ministries, it promotes conservative Christian principles. In 2007, it spent almost $4 million defending "Christian legal issues" by strategizing and coordinating with hundreds of lawyers. They won almost 3 out of 4 cases. On their website near their report of this great success rate, they cite *John 15:5*: "I am the vine; you are the branches. If a man remains in me and I in him, he will bear much fruit; apart from me you can do nothing."[33]

Another Powerful Opposition: Leaders of Disability Groups

Some self-appointed leaders of the disability community claim they speak for all people who have disabilities. One group, *Not Dead Yet*, submitted an *amici curiae* (friends of the court) brief in the case of Terri Schiavo in 2003.[34] They argued, "The denial of medical care based on cognitive disability constitutes illegal differential treatment," and "the proposed dehydration and starvation violates Titles II and III of the **Americans with Disabilities Act** (ADA), 42 U.S.C. §§ 12131 et seq. & 12181 et seq." They also argued, "**Absent proof that it is truly the person's decision**, withholding medical care based on the belief that he or she would rationally want to die because of a disability is **discriminatory**." Their statements revealed a profound distrust of physicians. For example: "Because of **bias against disability** and **ignorance** about the support systems and successful coping strategies that preserve autonomy, meaning and pleasure in life, **some physicians have decided that some deaths are more rational** than others and that ill and **disabled people do not deserve** the same type of health care that 'competent' people would receive." {Bold emphasis added.}

Just as parents' overprotection may harm children, apparently well-meaning arguments of organizations like *Not Dead Yet* could sentence disabled persons to burdens they do NOT want to endure, including longer and more intense suffering at the end of life. Note: The key to overcoming their global statement is to PRESENT "proof that it truly is the person's decision."

Not Dead Yet does not speak for all disabled persons. For example, Attorney Andrew Batavia was quadriplegic and helped write the landmark 1990 ADA, yet he favored legalizing physician-

---

33 http://www.sourcewatch.org/index.php?title=Alliance_Defense_Fund#_note-0

34 Retrieved on 11/10/2008 from www.notdeadyet.org/docs/schaivobrief.html, dated February 21, 2003. (Notes: The URL above misspells "Schiavo." Congress passed the Americans with Disabilities Act in 1990.)

assisted dying. He urged to "shift the emphasis from questions of whether [patients with certain diagnoses] have a **minimal quality of life** to questions of whether these individuals are **'alive' at all**, in the sense of maintaining the essential characteristic of living human beings."[35] He rejected ADA's definition of "disabled" as applying to the Permanent Vegetative State, coma, and anencephaly (congenital absence of brain). He wrote,[36] "**consciousness** is the most critical, moral and constitutional standard for determining **personhood.**" He endorsed proposals for the **neocortical (higher brain) definition of death**. One version listed "no self-awareness" and no ability to "respond behaviorally... to the environment."

Professor James Werth explained why some people with disabilities fear the danger of *Palliative Sedation* even more than Physician-Assisted Dying.[37] Once a physician sedates a patient, the patient (typically) does not have a further opportunity to change her mind before she dies.[38] In contrast, laws for Physician-Assisted Dying require competent patients to make the final decision. On behalf of patients too ill to make their own medical decisions, disability groups worry that physicians might impose their values, underestimate their quality of life, or inconsistently apply the standards of futile medical treatment—as they make life-or-death decisions supposedly in the patients' "best interest." The flaw in this argument, like the flaw in Sarah Palin's "death panel" allegation, is this: the best way to honor patients' wishes is for physicians to inform their patients of all available options and discuss them openly so patients can feel free to ask questions, express their feelings, and *decide if they wish to consent—or not.*

How can disability advocacy groups reduce their fear of inappropriate sedation? One possible way is to try to keep this option of *Palliative Sedation* a secret—even though it is a legal, recognized protocol routinely offered by palliative care and hospice physicians. Perhaps this is why they supported "gutting" the term from California's "Right to Know Act." Note: the term *"Palliative Sedation"* does not appear on California's Physician Orders for Life-Sustaining Treatment or similar forms in other States, such as MOLST and POST. The danger of withholding information is that it forfeits the American right to provide informed consent necessary for patients to exercise their autonomous choice. When one discusses something and asks for consent, the patient or surrogate decision-maker can refuse. When you hide

---

[35] Batavia, AI. (2002). Disability Versus Futility in Rationing Health Care Services: Defining Medical Futility Based on Permanent Unconsciousness—PVS, Coma, and Anencephaly. *Behav. Sci. Law 20*: 219–233.

[36] Attorney Batavia noted some reasons why courts are currently reluctant to apply such a standard: "out of respect for life and respect for religious beliefs, concerns that an erroneous decision would not be reversible, reluctance to impose a duty to die, and disability discrimination." He predicted an increased number of permanently unconscious patients will lead society to pass new laws to ration scarce medical resources based on two premises: 1) dead people have no right to consume life-sustaining technology, and 2) physicians should not provide medically futile treatment. Despite this prescient view, Attorney Batavia omitted any consideration of the enormously larger increase—by millions—of those who will suffer from Advanced Dementia.

[37] Werth JL. (2005). Concerns about decisions related to withholding/life-sustaining treatment and futility for persons with disabilities. *J Dis Policy Stud*. 16: 31-37. ("Terminal Sedation" is the original, more negative term.)

[38] Unless the patient is informed about and chooses *Respite Sedation*. See "**PNDL**," TOPICS 5 and 22.)

something, there may be more risk that it will be applied inappropriately. Ignorance may lead to more suffering for all patients... non-religious and religious; abled and disabled.

The need for informed consent: To deal with the greatest end-of-life fears—unbearable pain and suffering, and prolonged dying in Advanced Dementia—one needs to know about these two options: *Palliative Sedation* and **Natural Dying** (which includes "Voluntary Stopping of Eating and Drinking"[39]). One way of becoming informed about these options is to sort **My Way Cards**. The resulting **Natural Dying—Living Will** suggests that patients discuss these options with their physician using the **Natural Dying Physician's Orders** form (discussed in detail in "**PNDL**"), which includes places for physician and patient to sign for informed consent after they discuss these options. These forms include safeguards so they may *serve* rather than *scare* the community of disabled people. If so, *they*—not their politically motivated leaders or their physicians—can make informed choices based on what they diligently decide is right for themselves.

Danger: "Do Not Attempt to Resuscitate" (DNR) Orders

Fear of our "last" physician's power is justified. In many jurisdictions, physicians can write unilateral DNR orders without a witnessed discussion or a patient/proxy signature.[40] Both common law and Constitutional law are clear about *receiving* treatment: physicians must first obtain our competent, informed consent. Yet the U S Supreme Court has not explicitly ruled on any case that hinged on the unilateral *withholding* of CPR. For individual patients, Dr. Constantine Manthous views "truly unilateral DNR, in which a single practitioner withholds CPR from a patient without disclosing to the patient, [is] unethical because it is potentially arbitrary, deceitful, and ignores patient autonomy."[41] Professor Paul Biegler argued that the right to receive CPR is included "under a positive liberty formulation of autonomy... Doctors have a duty to act in their patients' best interests at all times... [hence] the withholding of a treatment that would be in the patient's best interests to receive, harms that patient."[42] While true for many patients, there are important exceptions. Interestingly, Dr. Manthous thought a carefully orchestrated process crafted ahead of time by consensus, could ethically permit unilateral DNR orders. She also wrote they are inevitable, but provided no specific examples.

For Advanced Dementia patients, Drs. Volandes and Abbos proposed a change in the default assumption to offer CPR. They argued that CPR is far more likely to harm patients significantly

---

[39] Actually, **Natural Dying** ceases *Manual Assistance with Oral Feeding and Drinking*, and "feeding" is not "eating," and it may not be voluntary since the patient may not have given informed consent. See TOPIC 8.

[40] The State of New York is one exception: either patients must sign, or the discussion providing consent must be witnessed. It is common for States to require patients' signatures on Out-of-Hospital or Pre-Hospital DNR orders, but defer to the hospital's/institution's policies regarding the requirements of inpatient signatures.

[41] Manthous CA. (2007). Counterpoint: Is it ethical to order DNR without patients' consent? *Chest 132*: 751-754.

[42] Biegler, P. (2003). Should patient consent be required to write a do not resuscitate order? *J Med Eth'cs 29*: 359-363.

than to prolong quality living.[43] They proposed that patients can still opt for CPR, but if not expressed in their *Known Wishes*, clinicians should assume patients do NOT want CPR. This **flips** the **present default**. Proposing a similar argument for assisted oral feeding and drinking—that the default for Advanced Dementia patients should change to provide oral food and fluid only for those patients who previously signed specific consent forms—is consistent with the First Principle of Medical Ethics, DO NO HARM and the goal of social justice. Yet this proposal may sound Draconian to many. The "ironclad strategy" leaves the default unchanged but informs Advance Care Planners about their options and asks them to sign consent forms they can understand, as witnessed by qualified individuals to help ensure consent is voluntary.

The Opposition is Becoming Stricter

In 2004, the pope required tube feeding for PVS patients in part because *some* might be misdiagnosed and hence recover. Today, many U S Catholics interpret recent teachings as requiring tube feeding for patients whose physicians expect they will *never recover consciousness* (and Advanced Dementia patients are conscious). The Westchester Institute for Ethics and the Human Person, whose mission is "anchored in the classic perennial and Catholic view of the human person," issued a White paper in 2010 to explain the Fifth Edition of the *Ethical and Religious Directives* revised on November 17, 2009, at the U S Conference of Bishops.[44] Unless the patient is imminently dying, not able to absorb food, or lives in a remote area where tube feeding is not available, Artificial Nutrition and Hydration (ANH) is always *obligatory* except in "**rare**" instances where ANH *itself* causes the patient "excessive burden" such as significant physical discomfort—as determined (contemporaneously) by others such as proxies, loved ones, attending physicians and a priest or ethicist trained in the Church's moral teaching on these matters. The White Paper concluded: "It would be immoral for [Catholics] to indicate in their living wills or advance medical directives an across-the-board desire to forgo or have withdrawn—without any further consideration—the provision of food and water if they should suffer some severe cognitive impairment."

Important note: the U S Conference of Bishops speaks only for the U S; and not all U S Catholics agree. In other countries, use of feeding tubes for Advanced Dementia patients is rare and it is considered moral for Catholics to use Advance Care Planning to refuse tube feeding. As two examples, see the essay by Reverend Kevin McGovern, who leads a center for ethics in Australia: *A Catholic View of **Natural Dying Living Will Cards*** ("PNDL," TOPIC 10). Dr. Keri Thomas, lead physician of Gold Standards Framework in U K, not only emphasizes the importance of Advance Care Planning in nursing homes (which her work helped increase four-

---

[43] Volandes AE, Abbos ED. (2007) Flipping the Default: A novel approach to CPR in end-stage dementia. *J Clin Ethics (summer):* 122-139.
[44] Fr. Thomas Berg. Catholic Teaching on Assisted Nutrition and Hydration. Jan 26, 2010. http://www.westchesterinstitute.net/resources/white-papers/491

fold), but also trains staff not to send their patients to hospitals, since hospitals are where feeding tubes are surgically implanted. Still, U S Catholic teaching influences what happens in the U S; for example, the New York court case, *in the matter of Zornow* (in Chapter 5).

Planning *or* Hoping?

The opposition is based on religious teachings, moral conscience, fears about discrimination, worries about other undervaluing their lives, confusion about government regulations to provide adequate nutrition and, of course, greed. There are also institutional regulations, new standardized forms, and judges who may override your Known Wishes. (Note: this is the short list.)

Now you can appreciate this chapter's title: "Advance Care Planning... or Advance Care HOPE?" Formidable challenges from powerful opposition groups require strategically designed forms if your plans are ambitious: to obtain relief from unbearable end-of-life pain and to avoid a prolonged dying in Advanced Dementia. Completing and signing typical Living Wills and Proxy Directives are good initial steps, but they may leave you with only hope... hope that your future physician will honor your end-of-life wishes. But hope, when you can no longer argue for what you want, is NOT adequate. Even clearly expressed requests may be inadequate unless they are combined with a strategy that can effectively overcome a powerful opposition.

After you decide on your specific end-of-life preferences, this is reasonable: **A)** For the last chapter of your life, you want others to honor your wishes so your transition will be peaceful and timely; **B)** From now and until that time, you want to feel sure that (**A**) will happen. The process to attain this goal is to create your "ironclad strategy" that "**PNDL**" describes.

Chapter 3 explains **Natural Dying**. Chapter 4 gives you a glimpse of what it is like to live with Advanced Dementia. Chapter 5 has stories that illustrate successes and failures, with and without this strategy. These chapters should motivate you to learn about and then implement your own **Plan Now; Die Later—Ironclad Strategy** that "**PNDL**" describes.

There are options presented along the way. For example, you can summarize your feelings about the *Criteria of Advanced Dementia* using the list in Chapter 4, or you can sort **My Way Cards**. You can take a "do-it-yourself" approach to the detailed recommendations of "**PNDL**," or you can ask an organization such as Caring Advocates to recommend a Planning Professional to help you with some of the logistics.

For your peace of mind now
And for your peaceful transition later,
You decide if it is worth the effort...
Given the potential benefits to you
And to your loved ones who will survive you.

Chapter 3

Natural Dying: Advantages and Safeguards

Many people are surprised to learn that the experience of dying after one refuses all food and fluid can be peaceful if *Comfort Care* is adequate. Dr. L. Ganzini led a study where experienced hospice nurses were asked to rate the quality of dying for their last competent patient who refused all food and fluid. Nurses rated the patients as experiencing a *good death* and their average score was **8**, where **9** was the highest.[45] Dr. R. Pasman's study of severely demented patients showed their *discomfort decreased* as they approached death from "medical dehydration."[46] My first book presents more studies and several personal stories.[47] Two new videos are available: one offers a loved one's perspective: "At the Bedside of a Peaceful Transition"; another is my own experience of *temporarily* refusing all food and fluid.[48] The bottom line is that **Natural Dying** can lead to a peaceful dying, typically within two weeks (depending on the initial nutritional status of the patient and how much fluid s/he continues to take in). Hunger is rarely reported as more than a brief problem. Symptoms of dry mouth, including thirst, are problems that can readily be solved. A convenient way: obtain a Thirst Reduction Aid Kit (TRAK) from the non-profit organization, Caring Advocates. Another way: get the individual, (non-prescription) components from local drug stores.

For patients who meet their *Criteria of Advanced Dementia* based on their Advance Care Planning, what does **refusal** of *Manual Assistance with Oral Feeding and Drinking* look like?

Food and fluid are never withheld from patients who still have the mental ability to eat and drink independently. Competent patients with physical limitations who so request will always receive help with the mechanics of eating and drinking. But patients who suffer from Advanced Dementia typically forget what to do with a bowl of puree and a spoon, or a cup and a straw—even if they are placed near them. Their devastating brain damage leads to **Natural Dying**.

Some Advance Care Planners want food and fluid placed near them until they are asleep most of the time. Then, their loved ones will know for sure they did not change their mind or regain the independent ability to eat and drink. Others prefer no food and fluid near them as they fast

---

[45] Ganzini L, Goy ER, Miller LL, Harvath TA, Jackson A, & Delorit MA. (2003). Nurses' experiences with hospice patients who refuse food and fluids to hasten death. *N Engl J Med. 349(4)*: 359-365.

[46] Pasman HR, Onwuteaka- Philipsen BD, Kriegsman DM, Ooms ME, Ribbe MW, & van der Wal G. (2005). Discomfort in nursing home patients with severe dementia in whom artificial nutrition and hydration is forgone. *Arch Intern Med 165(15)*: 1729-1735.

[47] Terman, SA. (2007). **The *BEST WAY* to Say Goodbye: A Legal Peaceful Choice at the End of Life**. Life Transitions Publications, Carlsbad. Some stories and authors are: "An October Morning," by Fran Moreland Johns; "I'm still telling others how well this worked for my mother," by Dr. David Eddy; and "A Peaceful End to a Beautiful Life," by Dr. Ronald Baker Miller.

[48] My video, "Fasting: A Legal Peaceful Way to Avoid Prolonged Dying," and others at: www.CaringAdvocates.org.

so they will not see or smell food. Either way, the **Plan Now, Die Later—Ironclad Strategy** reduces or eliminates the chance that your "future demented self" can sabotage your goal of a *timely, peaceful transition.* If you point to a bowl or cup and grunt—so that others might interpret your future wish as requesting help with feeding or drinking, you can empower your proxy so that others will honor your previously expressed *Known Wishes.*

Some institutions insist their staff at least "offer" their patients food and fluid. After discussing this issue, providers/institutions will usually agree on this acceptable way to OFFER: Show the patient food and fluid and ask if s/he wants them. Unless the patient indicates s/he does want them, remove the food and fluid. Almost as good: place food and fluid in front of patient for an hour and then remove them if untouched. The instructions below should also be followed.

Specific instructions for Natural Dying: How to OFFER food and fluid

Place a bowl of food and cup of fluid within eyesight and reach of the patient. (For patients who can hear but not see, place their hands on the bowl and cup.) Tell him/her what is in the bowl and cup. Tell them that they must eat and drink without help from another person. Then wait...

1) *Do NOT put the straw in the patient's mouth;*
2) *Do NOT spoon-feed the patient;*
3) *Especially do NOT put puree at the rear of the patient's tongue to evoke his/her swallowing reflex;*
4) *Do NOT use "techniques" to start chewing and swallowing such as sing-alongs, tickling the chin, or rubbing the neck;*
5) *Do NOT role-model eating; and,*
6) *Do NOT encourage eating and drinking by verbal or nonverbal gestures.*
7) *However **DO** repeatedly state verbally that food and fluid are available and they have been placed right in of them, if the patient desires them.*

Occasionally, a brain-injured patient will experience improvement in mental functioning after some dehydration. Here are some reasons: brain swelling decreases so the brain functions better. Fluid in the lungs drains off so more oxygen can be absorbed. Less blood volume makes it easier for the heart to pump. Improvement in heart and lung functioning delivers more oxygen and other nutrients to the brain. Whatever the reasons, if a patient can again eat and drink independently, the caregivers should stop **Natural Dying**. Caregivers may provide *Manual Assistance with Oral Feeding and Drinking* again, if patient subsequently needs help.

IMPORTANT: **Natural Dying** NEVER includes the withholding of food and fluid from patients who can eat and drink by themselves *without* manual help from others—a clear ethical and clinical line. However **Natural Dying** will allow Nature to take its course if disease has destroyed the brain to such an extent that the patient no longer knows how to eat or drink.

Forced feeding can be difficult to distinguish from intense encouragement to eat and drink. Some nursing home workers perform their job vehemently. While being interviewed on radio, a listener called in. After she found her mother's tooth missing, she arranged to observe the staff feed her. Then she insisted they be less aggressive. Consider this line drawing and words:

I cannot eat in the usual way. I forget to swallow so food stays in my mouth. Helpers place very soft food at the back of my tongue—so I SWALLOW by REFLEX. This is forced-feeding.

In 1997, U S Supreme Court Chief Justice William Rehnquist heard a verbal argument about not allowing hunger strike prisoners to die, to which he gave this response: "It seems odd that your bodily integrity is violated by sticking a needle in your arm, but not by sticking a spoon in your mouth. I mean... how would you force-feed these people in a way that would not violate their bodily integrity?"[49] Rehnquist's statement blurs the often-made distinction between medical treatment and basic care. To many, it seems obvious that spoon feeding MUST BE an intrusion into a person's bodily integrity—IF the person previously indicated s/he did NOT want it.

There are two logistic problems: **1)** Patients in Advanced Dementia no longer have the mental capacity to refuse anything; and, **2)** Except for the plan in this book, patients were **rarely asked** if they wish to refuse *Manual Assistance with Oral Feeding and Drinking* if they reach the stage of Advanced Dementia. **Rarely asked**—both in terms of total numbers and relative to inquiring about CPR: many more Advanced Dementia patients will receive unwanted spoon feeding than unwanted CPR. It is *urgent* to ask patients who recently received the diagnosis of early or mild dementia, or mild cognitive impairment, yet *all patients* who engage in Advance Care Planning should be given this informed choice. Many well-meaning people including clinicians make this **wrong assumption**: **"If she can swallow, she wants to swallow."**

---

[49] *Vacco v. Quill*, 117 S. Ct. 2293 (US 1997); www.oyez.org/cases/1990-1999/1996/1996_95_1858/argument

"Wrong" is based on no one who sorted the **My Way Cards** has yet chosen to receive spoon feeding when given this choice. When Advance Care Planners understand *Manual Assistance with Oral Feeding and Drinking* will only prolong their dying and may increase pain and suffering, they choose **Natural Dying**. The uninformed may think it cruel not to assist feeding patients who are willing to swallow what is put in their mouths. Yet not assisting is actually compassionate, kind, and consistent with the First Principle of Medical Ethics, DO NO HARM.

While our culture places high values using food and fluid to celebrate life, and on helping the needy get the nurturance they need (which is instinctual, in the case of infants)—these values must be reexamined in terms of the specific needs of dying patients. Advanced cancer patients typically decide to stop eating and drinking. Some totally lose interest in food and fluid; others will suffer more if they eat and drink. No one challenges these decisions. Actually, the law does not require competent patients to justify their decision to refuse all food and fluid. All competent adults have the right, by Constitutional law and common law right, to determine what enters their bodies. Still, when patients *can* eat and drink but choose not to do so, some opponents criticize their choice and call it, "*backdoor* Physician-Assisted Suicide"— especially if a doctor is providing *Comfort Care*. Yet these patients would want to live were it not for the extreme burdens of continued living that typically include unbearable pain and suffering.

For alert patients who have decisional capacity, it is kinder to ask, "Do you want treatment for your dry mouth?" than to ask, "Do you want something to drink?" Ideally, rehearse this question and review the consequence of each answer ahead of time. "Treatment for dry mouth" means **Natural Dying**. "Something to drink" can prolong dying and increase suffering.

Patients with Advanced Dementia can neither complain about their suffering nor decide contemporaneously they want **Natural Dying**. They need to have specified in advance, what criteria they must meet, to want **Natural Dying**. They also need to have designated someone they trust to decide WHEN they meet these criteria (to consult the treating physician, in a process called, "shared decision-making"). Otherwise others may **assume** they want to receive *Manual Assistance with Oral Feeding and Drinking* for as long as they can still swallow (even *by reflex*). **Natural Dying** is often the only legal method that can prevent a prolonged dying in Advanced Dementia since these patients' continued existence typically does not depend on higher technology that can be discontinued. The alternative—to discontinue life-sustaining treatment earlier, or to stop eating and drinking while still competent—sacrifices precious life. *Premature dying* is NOT necessary with the **Plan Now, Die Later—Ironclad Strategy**.

For competent patients, **Natural Dying** is legal and available to patients even if their medical condition renders them unable to open a bottle of pills and swallow them without assistance from others. (Direct assistance is illegal according to the laws that legalized Physician-Assisted Dying in Oregon and Washington State). **Natural Dying** has several advantages: The last few days can present precious, "last-in-a-lifetime" opportunities to exchange healing goodbyes. (Read: "To live long enough to warm the hearts of others," in Chapter 5.) **Natural Dying** also has important safeguards. One is that patients can change their minds (see the two stories, below). For patients who do maintain their resolve to continue their fasts, all concerned can feel assured that the patients firmly decided that this was their time to die.

She changed her mind twice. She was ready only after she had created her loving legacy.

A 43-year-old Utah woman was diagnosed with Lou Gehrig's disease (ALS) in January 2001. Unfortunately, it was a rapidly progressing type. In May and again in June, she voluntarily stopped eating and drinking with the intention to hasten her death. But both times, after a few days, she changed her mind and resumed intake of food and fluid.

In late July, after the Utah mother had prepared many years of special gifts and written years of personal loving notes for her young daughter, she again refused food and fluid. This time, she maintained her resolve. After several days, she experienced a peaceful transition.

Her husband believes that his wife would have died *prematurely* had she taken an overdose of medication instead of choosing to refuse all food and fluid. Her additional months of living were challenging in many ways, but they were also rewarding. The extra time provided her the opportunity to leave her daughter a personal and loving legacy. As she began her first two fasts, she may have reflected on what possible meaning remained in her life, on what goals she still wanted to accomplish, and on how she could accomplish these goals. So... still conscious, she could and did change her mind. This would not have been possible had she chosen "Physician-Assisted Dying." Yet she was still able to legally avoid a prolonged dying without assistance from others.[50]

"Whose Life Is It, Anyway?"

Ken Harrison is a young sculptor whose freak automobile accident left him quadriplegic. (In the movie adaptation,[51] Richard Dreyfuss plays this role.) After several months, Ken asked to be discharged from the hospital... so he could end his existence. Ken's doctor refused. He argued that it was his professional duty to protect Ken from himself since Ken's judgment was impaired due to a depressive disorder that made him suicidal.

Ken obtained an expedited hearing for a *writ of habeas corpus*—the legal procedure to release a person from unlawful restraint. Initially the judge seemed to be on the doctor's side as he challenged Ken to explain how any decision to die could be reasonable. Ken responded:

---

[50] Based on this article: Jacobs S. (2003). Death by voluntary dehydration: What the caregivers say. *N Engl J Med. 349(4)*: 325-26. Note: due to paralysis, many ALS patients require physical assistance with feeding. It is not legal to assist the administration of a lethal dose of medications to a patient, which may induce caregiver's guilt.
[51] From the 1981 film version adapted by Reginald Rose; directed by John Badham. Adapted from Brian Clark's 1972 television movie and his play ©1974, which was first performed in 1978.

"It is a question of dignity. Look at me here. I can do nothing, not even the basic primitive functions [of] urination [or moving my] bowels [or] turn over [or] act on any conclusions... I find the hospital's persistent effort to maintain this shadow of a life an indignity that is inhumane..." With passion, Ken continued, "If I choose to live, it would be appalling if society killed me... If I choose to die, it is equally appalling if society keeps me alive... Dignity starts with choice. Without it, it is degrading because technology has taken over from human will."

The judge agreed with Ken and gave him permission to leave the hospital. The play ends with an interesting twist that underscores a major advantage of **Natural Dying**.

The doctor asks Ken, "Where will you go?"

Ken answers, "I'll get a room somewhere."

The doctor responds, "There's no need. We'll stop treatment, remove the [IV] drips. Stop feeding you if you like. You'll be unconscious in three days, dead in six at most."

Skeptical about the doctor's sudden change in attitude, Ken asks, "There'll be no last minute resuscitation?"

The doctor answers, "Only with your permission."

Ken says, "That's very kind; why are you doing it?"

The doctor explains, "Simple. **You might change your mind**." {Emphasis added.}

Comment: If Ken's condition included factors that permitted his doctors to consider his medical condition as terminally ill and he lived in a State where Physician-Assisted Dying was legal, then... if his initial passion to end his life led him to receive and ingest a lethal dose of medication, his decision to die might be quick and irreversible. As this play ends, however, his refusal of food and fluid requires that he maintain his resolve for at least three days while he is conscious. During this period of time, it is quite possible that he will change his mind.

Knowledge about Natural Dying
may prevent premature, violent, and criminal dying

Several stories about premature, violent, and criminal dying are in **The *BEST WAY* to Say Goodbye** of which three were summarized on page 26: **Janet Adkins**, **Bob Stern**, and **Robert Hammerman**. The more mysterious story about **Myrna Lebov** is analyzed in the Epilogue of ***BEST WAY***, using "The Seven Principles of Good End-of-Life Decision-Making." At best, her death resulted from her own well-considered request for assisted dying—not by her physician... but by her husband. At worst, it is possible that husband George Delury killed her by committing the worst kind of caregiver abuse: euthanasia against her will. The Epilogue lets readers decide for themselves if Delury was guilty. This sad story illustrates an important, general principle: If the couple had known that dying by refusing food and fluid is both legal and peaceful, there would have been no need to hasten her dying in total secrecy without any professional oversight. With professional input, it is possible that Myrna Lebov would not have died *prematurely*.[52] Whether or not Mr. Delury was culpable, this story illustrates an important point: lack of knowledge exposes vulnerable patients to ultimate harm.

It was 1995 when Myrna Lebov died, yet prosecutions for mercy killing crimes are still occurring throughout the world. Rarely did the people involved consider refusing food and fluid as a legal and peaceful alternative. Consider two examples from California:

- 2007: **Albert Pollock**, 84, was sentenced to 12 years in prison for mercy killing his 88-year-old demented wife. He was probably correct in interpreting her request to die when he strangled her with a towel. Prosecutor Jill Lindberg said, "It was a good marriage... she wasn't going to get any better... He didn't want to put her in a nursing home. He didn't see any other way out." Niece Molly Risak referred to her aunt and uncle as a beautiful, loving couple for 60 years and said, "My family and I want my uncle to know our family forgives him. We support him and we bear no ill will toward him."

- 2009: **James Wheeler**, 84, was married 64 years. For the last five, he was devoted to taking care of his wife. She suffered from dementia and could no longer recognize him or her children. "The kindly old man [] gently guided his ailing wife on walks around the block every day." He tried but failed to kill both his wife and himself by carbon monoxide poisoning. He thus faced possible life imprisonment for attempted murder. Deputy District Attorney Mary Barron argued, "From her perspective, she had absolutely no say in the matter... What gives someone the right to take the life of another person just because she had dementia?" The galvanizing case ended with a sentence of three years of probation and 100 hours of community service, in addition to the 7 days he had spent in prison.[53]

The needs of patients, including the prevention of *premature dying*, may overlap with the needs of loved ones. In England, 46-year-old multiple sclerosis sufferer **Debbie Purdy** went to the Royal Courts of Justice, hoping to receive assurance that her husband would not be prosecuted if he assisted her travel to Switzerland, where she can legally receive assistance to die. Switzerland is the only European country that allows foreigners to receive physician-assisted dying, which in

---

[52] To reflect my deep concerns, I would rename the title of George Delury's book *from*: **But What if She Wants to Die? A husband's diary** [Birch Lane Press, 1997] *to*: **But what if *HE* wants her to die?** In his book, the author revealed a secret that he did NOT disclose while engaged in plea bargaining, which (successfully) led to his spending only six months in prison. When the available hoard of prescribed pills his wife took did not cause her death by *overdose* "soon enough," he put a plastic bag over her head to cause her death by *suffocation*. After her death, Delury cut up the plastic bag and flushed the incriminating evidence down the toilet. His book relates no prior discussion with his wife in which she agreed to this alternate plan.

[53] LA Times, 9/23/08, A3, and 9/26/09: http://latimesblogs.latimes.com/lanow/2009/01/act-of-love-or.html.

England is punishable by up to 14 years in prison. Ms. Purdy argued she wanted to live as long as possible and that without legal assurance, she must travel alone when she is healthier and therefore will be forced to end her life earlier. Her first two requests were denied,[54] but in the summer of 2009, the Director of Public Prosecutions issued these practical guidelines: if the patient is over 18, has no mental health issue or learning difficulty, and there seems to be no financial motive to assist, then the act might be permissible. The Swiss government considered tightening their guidelines to make it obligatory to "present two medical opinions declaring their disease incurable, that death is expected within months and that they have made their decision of sound mind and fully aware of their options." Founder of Dignitas Dr. Ludwig Minelli described these proposals as "outdated and patronizing." Others thought they were reasonable safeguards.[55] In May 2011, Swiss residents voted to continue offering "suicide tourism." In June 2011, Sir Terry Pratchett accompanied a patient to Dignitas. The suicide was shown on BBC TV.

To further the political cause to define when assistance in dying might not be prosecuted, Ms. Purdy and her advisors never mentioned the alternative of **Natural Dying** by refusing all food and fluid. Yet if her multiple sclerosis became end-stage, and Ms. Purdy opted for **Natural Dying**, she likely could enjoy *living even longer* because she would NOT *need* to travel at all. She could remain in the comfort of her own home and never worry whether her husband could legally be by her side. But she might have to specify while still competent, the precise behavioral condition for which she would someday want **Natural Dying** (perhaps by sorting **My Way Cards**). This protocol offers a more secure way for her to avoid a prolonged and undignified dying. Why? Because professionals at Dignitas may refuse to perform euthanasia if by the time she arrived, she was no longer competent. Her Living Will (Advance Decisions in the U K) would still be honored however, provided the form was specific and clear and convincing and properly signed. Such practical considerations lead to an interesting **question**:

Why has no organization like Britain's *Dignity in Dying*, or any similar activist US organization suggested the alternative of **Natural Dying**? Why instead do such organizations support patients like Debbie Purdy as they try to legalize physician-assisted dying... as if it were the only other option? I cannot be sure, but there is one *possible* reason: "*It is difficult to get a man to understand something when his salary depends upon his not understanding it.*"[56]

Bottom line: Knowing about the **Natural Dying** option can help people avoid the tragic outcome of *premature dying*. It can also save loved ones from punishment for acts of love. Sadly, the cause is not attractive to "activists" because it requires absolutely no change in the law. There is no cause 'to fight for" other than to advocate the education of people about this available legal and peaceful end-of-life option.

---

[54] "Ask parliament, not courts, whether your husband can help you end your life." Retrieved from: http://www.guardian.co.uk/society/2008/oct/30/assisted-suicide-law.

[55] http://www.timesonline.co.uk/tol/life_and_style/health/article6894726.ece

[56] Attributed to the author Upton Sinclair in "I, Candidate for Governor: And How I Got Licked" (1935). Repr. Univ. California Press 1994, page 109.

Chapter 4

What is it like to live with Advanced Dementia?

To make the ultimate existential decision—either to continue existence *versus* NOT to prolong the process of dying—one should be informed about both states. The previous chapter provided a glimpse of what it is like to die by **Natural Dying**. Many people have scant knowledge about Advanced Dementia, which this chapter and the optional **My Way Cards** have as their goal, to remedy. The chapter ends by comparing these two alternatives and providing an opportunity for you to express your end-of-life preferences by taking a short questionnaire.

As mentioned, Advanced Dementia is "the closet within a closet," which feeds into our tendency for psychological denial so we can avoid thinking about unpleasant topics. It is more appealing to emphasize the positive, especially for fund raisers: First choice is prevention; second choice is cure; third is effective treatment; fourth is support when the first three have failed... But nowhere in this regression of goals is there a proactive strategic plan to deal effectively with the longest, most cruel, painful and burdensome end stage of this disease.

Organizers of fund-raising meetings usually present patients who can articulate their appreciation for the help they received or express hope for a future cure. Audiences would be outraged if presented with a patient for even ten minutes, if he was strapped into a wheelchair, merely stared into space, or worse, cried from confusion or yelled in horror. It just doesn't happen. Until recently, it was hard to find videos depicting patients in Advanced Dementia; however this is changing slowly. WGBH offered a new video and HBO offered a miniseries in 2009.[57] Yet knowledge is essential to make prudent decisions. Drs. Angelo Volandes and Muriel Gillick showed that a two-minute research video made a tremendous impact. Of those who viewed the video, 90% opted for "Comfort Care Only" compared to only 50% if they only heard the narration about Advanced Dementia, but did not see the patient and her daughters.[58]

We begin with two views of Advanced Dementia: the "objective" observations of a spouse who lived with an afflicted patient and the "subjective" experience of a patient who is struggling to articulate his thoughts and feelings as he suffers from diagnosis through moderate dementia. You can use the *Criteria of Advanced Dementia to Consider* **Natural Dying** to inform your

---

[57] **Alzheimer's Disease: Facing the Facts**. WG43199 of Program, Motion, Inc. © 2009 WGBH Educational Foundation and the HBO series, **The Alzheimer's Project**, www.HBO.com/Alzheimers. The full length films **Iris** (2001, British) and **Song for Martin** (2001, Swedish) portray Advanced Dementia much more realistically than **Away From Her** (2007, U S) and **The Notebook** (2004, U S). Other films are: **Firefly Dreams** (2001), **One Special Night** (1999), **Age Old Friends** (1989), **Noel** (2004), **A Time To Remember** (2003), **The Savages** (2007), **Aurora Borealis** (2006), **Barney's Version** (2010), and **Win Win** (2011).

[58] Volandes AE, et al. (2007). Using Video Images of Dementia in Advance Care Planning. *Arch Intern Med. 167:* 828-833. Their two-minute video is viewable at www.MyWayCards.org (if you scroll down).

future decision-makers how you feel—if someday they must decide WHEN you would want **Natural Dying**. (The alternative is to sort the optional interactive deck of **My Way Cards**.)

A loving husband's observations about living with dementia[59]

"Within two short years, Ann would go from confusing similar-sounding words to not communicating at all."

"As her condition worsened, she became more confused, frightened, and angry than she'd ever been." ... "Even worse than Ann's failures of memory were her brief periods of terrible lucidity." [Once,] as her husband tried to help her dress, "she turned on him in a fury and said, 'Why don't you just shoot me?'"

Her husband "began to understand the link between memory and identity, that we are all, in a sense, not so much the sum of our experiences as the sum of our memories of them."

"Though she was no longer really Ann, the body that had once housed Ann's mind, her memory, her spirit, soldiered on and would continue so for years."

"Ann lived for nine years after she was diagnosed, but after three she was gone, her identity stolen."

"For the [last] three years [husband] Lee visited Ann in Houlton...sometimes one of the kids would go with him, but they all came to the same reluctant understanding: Ann never knew."

[Reflecting on the husband's decision to place her in a nursing home:] "[Lee] knows that he couldn't have done anything more without losing himself in the bargain, and knows that neither Ann nor his love and devotion to her demanded that sacrifice."

Comment: When they are well, couples often make mutual promises never to send each other to a nursing home. Much later, when the burdens of home care reach an enormity they cannot handle, which neither anticipated they might imagine this *ethical* (*but impossible*) scenario:

> Temporarily restore the sound mental judgment of the afflicted spouse and let her observe the quality of her life and weigh the benefits and burdens to herself and to others—if she continues to reside at home. Inform her about her prognosis; for example the high risk she will fall and break a hip at home, which may result in pain and restricted mobility. Then ask the patient to inform others what her decision is: Does she want to remain at home or does she want to reside in an environment that can offer greater safety? (Once she makes the decision, she must return to her demented state.)

---

[59] Reproduced with permission from the author, Richard Russo, from his memoir, "You know who you are," in Russo, R. (2008). **A Healing Touch: True stories of life, death, and hospice**. Down East Publications.

When others imagine what decision patients would make for patients who did NOT previously express their *Known Wishes,* they are using "Substituted Judgment," an accepted ethical practice. It is not easy for one person to make "tough" decisions that may determine when someone dies. Several concerned family members can each sort a deck of **My Way Cards**—pretending to be the patient, *WHEN WELL.* This process may be comforting for the designated decision-maker (if there is one) and may be more accurate than putting all the responsibility on one person to make a difficult decision. If sorters do reach a consensus of opinion, they can feel supported by the others that the decision they made is what the patient would have made, if s/he could.

If *Known Wishes* are not available and others' appreciation about the patient's general values and other preferences do not suffice to make a decision, then relatives and physicians must decide based on what they believe is in the patient's "Best Interest." Sometimes this means "what a reasonable person would want, under similar circumstance." (The problem is that there are many versions of "reasonable.") These decisions can be morally difficult and may be plagued with guilt of paralytic proportions. Why? Part of the answer is that the decision-making spouse is the same person who will receive the most relief from the reduction in emotional, physical, and financial burdens. About one-third of decision-makers experience significant negative burdens lasting months or years. Most common were stress, guilt, and uncertainty about the decision they made. A study provided data to recommend reducing surrogate's emotional burdens by providing comprehensive, specific Living Wills that give clear guidance to decision-makers so they can feel sure they are carrying out the patient's wishes.[60]

Some ethnic groups have strong cultural norms for traditional nurturing and may impose moral sanctions for abandoning elders in need. Many people still fail to realize that the needs of the dying are different. Just like it can really be an act of kindness to place someone in a locked facility where they are less likely to fall, get lost, or be confused without help, it can also be kind to cease providing *Manual Assistance with Oral Feeding and Drinking* to patients if it would only prolong their dying and possibly increase their physical and emotional suffering.

When a conflict of interest is *possible,* that does not by itself mean necessarily that the *decision to institutionalize* is wrong. Similarly, **Natural Dying** is not necessarily wrong if there is a potential conflict of interest. Still, a practical question remains: Where exactly should one draw the line? Patients have their good and bad days. Caregivers struggle with feelings of commitment and responsibility while they attempt to balance frustration with hope. Many caregivers find it easier to make decisions based on a set of criteria ahead of time lest they, like the proverbial frog, experience the water gradually get hotter until they have exhausted all emotional, physical, and financial resources. It can help to consult professionals experienced in guiding families make difficult, heart-wrenching decisions. Consider the *Criteria of Advanced*

---

60 Wendler D, Rid A. Systematic Review: The Effect on Surrogates of Making Treatment Decisions for Others. *Ann Intern Med.* 2011;154:336-346.

Dementia to Consider **Natural Dying** or the **My Way Cards**. Also view movies and read about this devastating disease. In the next few pages, you can learn from an afflicted person.

Thoughts and feelings about Dementia, from Thomas DeBaggio

Thomas DeBaggio was a unique human being. Before he was diagnosed with Alzheimer's disease at the age of 57, he was a journalist and writer. He put privacy aside and devoted much of his remaining life to articulating as best he could (with help from others), his thoughts and feelings as the disease relentlessly chipped away at his memory and his ability to communicate.

I heard his story from interviews of him and his wife on National Public Radio.[61] I consider his first book a *must listen*: one can hear Thomas' voice utter haiku-like poems dispersed among longer passages of professional narrations. In this first book, Tom provides insight into what it is like to receive, and then to live with the devastating diagnosis of Alzheimer's.[62]

The material below, excerpted from Thomas' second book,[63] is emotionally difficult. I hope the selected passages will broaden Tom's audience and achieve these goals: to enlighten readers about what millions of people will go through, and to motivate patients and family members of patients who recently received the diagnosis of dementia to engage immediately in diligent, strategic Advance Care Planning—before their finite window of mental competence closes forever. While Thomas was in the middle stages of dementia, he provides a glimpse of what would inevitably come in the advanced stage. Such information is important to consider when deciding whether or not to forgo life-sustaining treatment, if one reaches the advanced stage.

To express himself, Thomas noted he struggled long to express himself and it is likely that some ideas were expressed earlier, when his ability to construct sentences and recall words were less impaired. Mr. DeBaggio could not author a third memoir to reveal the experience of Advanced Dementia,[64] since by then he could no longer communicate. His perspective provides insight into the consequences of memory loss, the loss of sense of self, confusion and loss of control, and a multitude of emotions—yet he was still able to express one positive reflection. Overall, the awesome impression is Thomas' angst over losing his sense of himself.

---

[61] For links to the programs on "All Things Considered": http://www.alzforum.org/eFAD/profiles/debaggio.asp.

[62] DeBaggio T. (2002). **Losing My Mind: An Intimate Look at Life with Alzheimer's.** Free Press of Simon & Schuster. Both this book and DeBaggio's second book are recommended for much valuable information.

[63] DeBaggio T. (2003). **When It Gets Dark: An Enlightened Reflection on Life with Alzheimer's**. Free Press of Simon & Schuster and Thorndike Press Large Print Basic (2004).

[64] Tom died on February 22, 2011. He lived with Alzheimer's disease for 12 years. The last NPR interview was on June 16, 2010. This nine-minute audio is extraordinarily frank: it includes examples of the patient's minimal verbal output. When the interviewer asked his wife how she then felt about her husband, Joyce introspectively remarked that she couldn't believe she had just referred to him as "it." Possibly, in her mind, her husband had passed the point where she still considered him as possessing the qualities of personhood. Listen, to hear and to decide yourself: http://www.npr.org/templates/story/story.php?storyId=127857149&ps=rs .

I re-sequenced excerpts from the book to place them into these four categories:

Overview: Thomas' goal to share his thoughts and feelings.
Memory: Why Thomas felt memory was so important; what it felt like to lose it.
Emotions: Thomas' feelings about living in the state of moderate dementia.
Death: Thomas' thoughts about dying.

Overview

Despite the poverty of words, and a memory chewed by Alzheimer's, I intend to open my inner life and at the same time reflect on everyday simple things, as death's shadow falls across my dwindling days.[59]

This is a story of a crippled man imprisoned within himself.

I am alive but lost.

This is my long good-bye.

About Memory

My head used to be full of ideas and memories. Now hardly a moment of yesterday waves its flag at me. Upon my shoulder sits a vessel emptying itself of life.

Words tell us who we are and where we've been. Words make us sad and happy. To lose word-making skills is to compromise a large part of what makes us who we are. Words provide details of the world in which we live and a way to understand what goes on. At some point, not far off, I will not be able to kiss Joyce or enjoy Francesco's jokes.

Memory is the most intimate of the muses, particular to each individual. Its loss empties the mind and leaves one forever a cripple and soon a corpse.

It takes longer almost every day to remember the makeup of my breakfast. Before long everything will have to be labeled for me as I lose my mind.

Simple things are difficult and every minute is a frustrating struggle. I worry I will drive off and forget where I am going and why I am in the car.

I want to crawl out of my body and disappear into a world I can understand, move to a country where language does not sizzle before my eyes and flicker in the midnight dark.

Sometimes I think I have the mind of a baby and I slip into a world of unfamiliar streets. At other times, I float in a place of opulent emptiness.

Almost any memory disappears as fast as it comes to life. I live in a world of surprises and fogs of fear.

Memories float to the top of consciousness, swirling and diving. I try to catch them but they slip away and I am left empty and in tears.

My mind is a-twitter with echoes of spent words that persist in bobbing to the surface of my consciousness and licking the edge of memory. Yet in a few seconds it is flashed away, leaving bewildered emptiness.

In unguarded moments, I am robbed of memories every day, severing me from my life.

Heavy clouds move in and leave me stumbling and lost in the thick fog of my mind.

The chaos of my mind is like a drunkard in a story, tipsy and wandering.

More than sweet recollections are at stake when memories begin to lose their leaves.

Yesterday has no meaning anymore. Events of today flee from memory before day concludes.

My brain is full of forgotten memories. The few remaining memories are scars of long ago.

I live in the moment now. I remember I had a past but it is vacant now in a time of sorrow.

What happens when memory is gone? Alzheimer's finishes you off.

How long will it be before I am imprisoned here, trembling, forgetful and without the memory of who I am or who I used to be?

About Emotions

I have become emotional and find tears on my cheeks when I least expect them.

Tears come without warning, choking speech. Things I cannot find quickly grow into uncontrollable explosions. The world is slipping from my grasp. Frustration is abundant and I am filled with anxiety.

My days are full of anxiety and searching, for what I no longer remember.

I become agitated easily from frustration over little things. It was easily handled a few years ago, but now a bomb swells inside me until I explode.

What remained of the frightening event were tears drying on my cheeks and Joyce's bewildered arms around me, trying to understand how a body so familiar can explode suddenly in the pyrotechnics of a brain slowly destroying itself.

This fight with a failing brain brings tears to my eyes and exhausts me physically.

Alzheimer's eats me away in little increments, stealing here, bombing there, until there is little left to enjoy in life.

My life is dissolving into an unhappy scream as I slide into a time of anger at little, helpless things I can no longer control.

Now I am sick, wary and full of uncertainty. I am possessed by stuttering dreams and lackadaisical memory.

So barren is my life now that you will find me looking at the world through a furtive slat in the bathroom shade like a spy in a tree.

Every minute I breathe I am on the edge of tears.

Anguished days of confusion and unreadable secrets puff up time and bring sudden yelps and rainbows behind my eyes where the tears live.

I am almost useless except to make others angry with me while the hopes of a lifetime disintegrate into unhappiness and whispers.

I seethe with private anger I dare not expose except in private moments alone.

I go inside to hide and cry with frustration. I find an empty house and let go an angry bark directed at the loneliness in which I live and the helplessness of having within me a dying brain.

All day I wrestled with the feeling of being empty, a man drained of humanity and meaning who stares into the void in helpless anger without courting comprehension. I have slowly become a useless vessel in the hands of Alzheimer's.

All pleasure has disappeared; even the idea of enjoyment is gone. In its place there is numbness.

There is no joy in my life, only difficulty slings at me.

There are days during which I am happier than ever, full of real joy, despite the slow death unwinding itself inside my brain.

I wake up, tears streaming from my eyes. A strange sound comes from my mouth: a dry half cry for help, half chant of death.

About Dying

Most people don't take time to think about death... With Alzheimer's there is plenty of time to ponder death, too much really. It makes me want to be run over by a fancy car.

It is not the sepulcher where the hurt lives wagging its finger at me; it is the twisting mental messages that cause the worst bewilderment.

Death is a challenge for beings who can feel their own demise squirming in a deteriorating body.

Fire scours the brain, disabling mind and body and squeezing what is left of life hanging on a tombstone.

So this is the way my world ends, fighting shadows, wrapped in fear, trembling to remember who I am and where I am headed.

After you feel death crawling inside, and watch it scamper over hallucinating dark night walls, there is no reason to have fear. In the end, death does not matter; it lightens the earth's load, and enriches those who follow.

Using the *Criteria of Advanced Dementia* for Natural Dying

The *symptoms, unwanted behaviors, losses of function,* and *conflicts with lifelong values* listed on the next two pages are commonly seen in Advanced Dementia; some are seen earlier.

HOW TO USE THIS LIST for Advance Care Planning: First read just the underlined <u>eight areas</u>. Then read all the items; since there are many, you might want to re-read them. Then decide how you feel about the items. Note: you do not need to complete this at one sitting; you can finish another day. (The interactive process of sorting **My Way Cards** may be easier.[65]) To make decisions about each item as a guide to inform your future decision-makers:

1. ***Cross out*** an item if you do **NOT** want your future decision-makers to consider it as they decide if it is time for **Natural Dying**. If you suffered from only these items, you would be **treated and fed**.

2. ***Circle*** any item you feel will cause **enough suffering—*by itself*—**for **Natural Dying**. You would want **Natural Dying** if you had any one of these items.

3. Future decision-makers will consider all remaining items together for **Natural Dying**.

4. Repeat the process of crossing out and circling in two to four weeks, using a fresh new list. Compare your two lists, make any necessary final changes, and write explanations.

5. Attach your "Final Version" to your other Advance Care Planning forms. You can always modify your selections if you are still competent. Revisit your list in about a year; make any changes and write why, or write that you did not change your mind. Following this protocol may help your proxy/agent prove that your choices were consistent over time.

List of *Criteria of Advanced Dementia* for Natural Dying

1. <u>About myself</u>: I cannot recall or appreciate the important past events of my life. I cannot recall my life-long values. I am not aware of myself. I do not respond to my own name. I do not recognize myself in the mirror. My actions embarrass or hurt my family. I cannot remember my past or what gave my life meaning, but I can still enjoy the simple pleasures of living;

---

[65] **My Way Cards** descriptions average 23 words, are at reading grade level 3, and each has an illustrative line drawing to clarify its meaning. The *Criteria* above are at about grade level 10. The cards are interactive and allow making a decision about each item, one at time. You sort twice to place each card into one of three stacks. **My Way Cards** were created since initially, few people followed this suggested protocol. Yet it may work for some people and if so, could be more time and cost efficient. The **Natural Dying—Living Will** from Caring Advocates is still the recommended form to guide future decision-makers. (See also: www.MyWayCards.org.)
The *Criteria* above were modified from **My Way Cards**, which were in turn modified from the *Behavioral Preferences to Permit Natural Dying* in **The *BEST WAY* to Say Goodbye** (2007; pages 397-398).

2. <u>Expressing my wishes to increase my pleasure and decrease my pain</u>: I cannot say or show what I want by using words or gestures. My utterances and gestures do not consistently indicate "Yes" or "No." I cannot make or carry out plans to get what I want. I do not understand how current actions lead to future goals. I can think but cannot express myself in any way and being "locked-in" makes me feel socially isolated, lonely and sad. Since I lost the ability to complain, my doctors do not know I am suffering or in pain so they do not treat me effectively;

3. <u>Relating to others</u>: I cannot recognize family members or cherished friends. I seem puzzled by who they are; or I identify them incorrectly. I utter no words or sounds and make no gestures, as others enter and leave my presence. I do not initiate social activities. I do not express feelings of love or affection. I cannot feel spiritual, pray to, or relate to a Supreme Being;

4. <u>Dependency and Dignity</u>: I am totally dependent on others for basic care. I cannot bathe or dress myself. I am incontinent times two and others must change my diapers. My behavior no longer reflects my life-long values. My confusion makes me resist help I need. If I could see my future behavior now, I would conclude that I have lost my "dignity";

5. <u>My mood, even with treatment</u>: I rarely express joy or pleasure. I am almost always apathetic, despondent and non-responsive... or confused, worried and frustrated. I am plagued by severe fear, horror, panic, or hallucinations or delusions. I am agitated or aggressive without provocation. I need physical restraints or high doses of medication to prevent me from hurting myself or striking others;

6. <u>Burdens versus effectiveness</u>: To keep me alive, I require almost constant basic care or life-sustaining medical treatment that cannot restore my overall quality of life or allow me to live independently without intense medical care that institutions typically provide. The only way to relieve my unending, unbearable pain and suffering is to give me enough sedating medications so I am no longer conscious. Treating me for a reasonable time for potentially curable life-threatening illnesses (such as an infection) might allow me to enjoy life's simple pleasures again, if I previously could enjoy them (as in the middle stage of dementia);

7. <u>Burdens versus benefits</u>: Prolonging my dying provides me no benefit that I can appreciate, but meanwhile burdens on my loved ones are great. Their sacrifices include: depleting their finances, diverting their attention from other important activities and responsibilities of their lives, and suffering from physical exhaustion or mental depression. I have changed greatly but my body still looks like me so prolonging my dying also prolongs the grieving of my loved ones;

8. <u>Regarding food and fluid</u>: I require much help and encouragement to eat and drink. I have lost the *mental ability* to eat and drink. I cannot ingest enough food so I am slowly starving to death. My actions indicate I do not want to eat. Since I forget to chew and swallow, food stays in my mouth unless skilled helpers place thickened puree at the back of my tongue to get me to swallow by reflex. If food slips into my lungs it could cause pneumonia; however tube feeding cannot prevent this or help me live longer or better.

The next story is a "composite" patient. His/her symptoms resemble two litigated cases: stroke victim Brenda Young and Minimally Conscious State patient Robert Wendland.[66] The case is also used for the questionnaire at the end of this chapter that lets you express your treatment preferences. The case is very similar to an anonymous one later reported in the literature.[67]

Is it FEAR? Or, Is it PAIN?
More important: how can we compassionately provide relief?

Edward is 86.[68] Fifteen years ago, after a successful career as a mechanical engineer, he retired. His wife of 54 years died 3 years ago. His one child is a daughter named Julie. Six years ago he was given the diagnosis of dementia, probable Alzheimer's type, which progressed. His dementia is now severe, in the advanced stage. For a year, he has not been able to recognize anyone, including his daughter. He cannot recall any significant event of his life. He requires total care for feeding, bathing, eating, and for bowel and urinary incontinence. He cannot express any wish or feeling, using words or gestures.

A few weeks ago, Edward started screeching loudly. For hours, he calls out, "Mommy! Daddy!" His face is twisted with a fearful grimace. His whole body is agitated as he shakes both fists. The shouting continues until he becomes exhausted. Then he sleeps awhile, but when he wakes up, his horror resumes. Two days ago, Edward struck out and hit his daughter. She was approaching him with a warm soapy sponge. Previously, he enjoyed this caring way of cleaning.

More worried about her father's severe mental anguish than upset at being hit, Julie used this event to request a consultation with Edward's physician.

As the doctor closed the door of the skilled nursing facility's conference room, Julie asked, "For months, my father has seemed totally unable to enjoy any aspect of his life. Do you think he will ever be able to enjoy life again?"

The physician frowned and shook his head. "Extremely unlikely."

"What about eating? He eats. Can he still enjoy eating?" she asked, desperately.

"Personally, I doubt *feeding* him provides much, if any pleasure. He lost the ability to use a spoon or straw months ago... And, even though he still accepts nourishment by mouth—when a

---

[66] Osgood v. Genesys Reg. Med. Ctr. (Mich. Cir. Ct. 94-26731-NH) (1997);
Conservatorship of Wendland (2001) 26 Cal.4th 519 [No. S087265, Aug. 9, 2001].

[67] Lantz, MS. Verbal Outbursts in a Patient with Dementia. (2010). www.clinicalgeriatrics.com/articles/Verbal-Outbursts-a-Patient-with-Dementia. This case was published a year after the questionnaire/survey went online.

[68] A similar situation could exist for a patient named "Edith," who is suffering from metastatic breast cancer.

skilled helper places puree on the very back of his tongue to get him to swallow by reflex—we can give him only thickened puree. Anything else is more likely to go down the 'wrong way' and cause pneumonia. So he doesn't really enjoy chewing or tasting. And, despite our best efforts, he continues to lose weight. He will soon reach the point where his malnutrition becomes so severe that his bedsores cannot heal."

Julie asked, "What about his prostate cancer?"

"His cancer was treated with radioactive implants. He's had years of cancer-free survival. But your father is otherwise healthy. He's survived so long, his cancer has recurred. The longer he lives, the more pain he'll have as his prostate cancer metastasizes to his bones. And that's one real rough type of pain to treat. The problem is that, sadly, he just can't tell us if he's in pain. He could be suffering right now, from something we haven't recognized or treated. I've been meaning to ask you: Would you consent to my ordering him a bone scan?"

Julie thought a while. As her father's proxy, she had to make all his medical treatment decisions. Her tone softened as she asked, "Doctor, first tell me all my father's options, okay?"

The physician nodded. "Instead of a scan, we could just assume all your father's symptoms of agitation—facial grimacing, his crying out, and his shaking both fists—are due to pain. Clinicians in Europe frequently make this assumption. You could consent to my giving him enough morphine to relieve these target symptoms—even if the dose he needs might hasten his dying. Don't be alarmed by the words, 'might hasten dying.' Many Advance Directives use these words, including the one offered by the California Hospital Association."

Julie gave her verbal consent to this treatment plan. Two days later however, the physician called her with an update. "Unfortunately, narcotic-like medications alone have not sufficed to calm your father down. He also needs strong sedatives, like those used in anesthesia. Let me explain. "Sedation to unconsciousness" is a clinically acceptable and legal way to provide the most aggressive kind of Comfort Care. Most clinicians call it *'Palliative Sedation'* although some use the term, 'Terminal Sedation,' since patients often do not wake up before they die. But the goal of treatment is to eliminate extremely distressful symptoms that cannot be treated in any other way. The goal is NOT to hasten death. Since your father does not have a feeding tube, he might die of medical dehydration. This way of dying is actually very peaceful—even for patients who are awake, as long as symptoms of dry mouth are treated. If you choose this form of Comfort Care, we may never know the exact cause of your father's death. Possibilities, in addition to dehydration, include prostate cancer, an undiscovered infection, a stroke, or a heart attack—or some combination. It is even possible, although unlikely, that he might live longer without food and fluid since he is more likely to avoid aspiration pneumonia."

The physician asked Julie to sign a "Consent Form to Obtain Relief from Unbearable Suffering," which gave him permission for rapid and total sedation—but just for a few days. He would then reduce the dose of sedatives, to let her father wake up. He explained: sometimes total relief provides enough rest so patients can again live consciously. Also important: the plan to wake him up distinguished this Comfort Care method (*Respite Sedation*) from euthanasia.

Adding sedatives allowed Edward to finally become peaceful. Julie's anxiety abated initially, but then she had an intense moral pang. She did not want to feel she authorized an overdose to hasten her father's dying. She was glad the doctor had planned to reduce the dose of sedatives. She stood by her father's bed as he woke up. His agitation and facial grimacing returned. This behavior made her sure that continued sedation was the right treatment for her father. Still, Julie felt compelled to remind the physician, "Just be sure you administer only enough medication to completely control his symptoms." The physician reassured her: the dose of sedatives would only relieve her father's suffering, not hasten his death.

After eight days of total sedation, Edward stopped breathing. Julie thanked the physician for his compassionate care. Later, when she thought about her last conversation with the doctor, she recalled having no need to ask him what he thought was the probable cause of death. The only thing that seemed important was that her father's transition had been peaceful.

Comments: Edward's act of hitting Julie prompted his daughter to request a full discussion about his treatment options. Only then did the physician **1)** explain that agitation *might* be due to pain, and **2)** offer *Palliative Sedation (Respite Sedation)*. Many physicians are reluctant to bring up the option of *Palliative Sedation* and some will never do so, because of their beliefs. Similarly, physicians may be reluctant to explain the option to cease *Manual Assistance with Oral Feeding and Drinking*. *Questions*: How many patients are there who have Advanced Dementia and cannot express themselves and so suffer from undiagnosed and untreated pain? How many patients have suffered prolonged dying by continued oral feeding, when they cannot experience any pleasure in life? We don't know exactly, but the number could be huge.

This story can make us ask, do we really want to wait until "the patient's condition has deteriorated to the point that quality of life has become completely absent [to] diminish uncertainty," and to wait—perhaps for years—until a triggering event occurs, such as pneumonia?[69] If your choice is not to wait, you must strive diligently to create an ironclad strategy to avoid treatment that could prolong a horrible last chapter of life plagued by mental and physical suffering. Such a strategy will make it possible for your proxies and family members to make sure that you do have a *timely, peaceful transition*.

Note: Edward/Edith had a possible source of unbearable pain and suffering—advanced cancer. Many Advanced Dementia patients suffer pain that is hard to see, like arthritis and constipation. This literature is new and not yet well appreciated. Here is a brief summary.

---

[69] Caron CD, Griffith J, Arcand M. (2005). End-of-life decision making in dementia. The perspective of family caregivers. *Dementia 4;* 113-136.

Palliative (Comfort) Care for Advanced Dementia Patients

Birch and Draper reviewed 29 articles to conclude: "Patients dying with dementia are often still not given access to Palliative Care services," and "There is an urgent need to improve Palliative Care provided older people with end-stage dementia."[70] Ouldred and Bryant considered three factors as barriers to good palliative care: "dementia is not recognized as a terminal disease; problems in recognizing symptoms; and decision-making conflicts between family caregivers and other health and social care providers."[71] Chang and others recommended training staff to develop improved knowledge and skills to accurately assess pain "owing to the inability of people with advanced dementia to communicate their symptoms."[72] A study by Zwakhalen and others revealed that "nursing home staff respondents showed knowledge deficits about several aspects of pain, even though they [staff] were satisfied about the way pain was assessed and treated at their wards."[73] This last finding is worrisome as it implies caregiving staff is satisfied as they provide care while the patients for whom they are responsible, are in fact suffering.

Sampson and others urged more research about the needs of patients with Advanced Dementia who have "complex needs but often lack capacity to express their wishes," and "have infrequently engaged in prior discussions or planning on handling acute medical conditions."[74] Goodman and others concluded,[75] "Research on end-of-life care for people with dementia has yet to develop interventions that address the particular challenges that dying with dementia poses." Hertog and The[76] recommended we "invest seriously in diverse forms of supportive care for nurses" to overcome the "'intrinsic complexity' of caregiving in this field of palliative care," whose "origin [is] the key problem of dementia, namely the loss of a common shared world of meaning." Voicer described the *Namaste Care* approach, which is designed to honor the **spirit** (essence of the person) beyond the disease.[77] Clinicians should try to avoid what

---

[70] Birch, D., & Draper, J. (2008). A critical literature review exploring the challenges of delivering effective palliative care to older persons with dementia. *Journal of Clinical Nursing, 17*, 1144-1163.

[71] Ouldred E, Bryant C. (2008). Dementia care. Part 3: end-of-life care for people with advanced dementia. *Br J Nurs.;17(5)*:308-14.

[72] Chang E, Daly J, Johnson A, Harrison K, Easterbrook S, Bidewell J, Stewart H, Noel M, Hancock K. (2009). Challenges for professional care of advanced dementia. *Int J Nurs Pract. Feb;15(1)*:41-7.

[73] Zwakhalen SM, Hamers JP, Peijnenburg RH, Berger MP. (2007). Nursing staff knowledge and beliefs about pain in elderly nursing home residents with dementia. *Pain Res Manag. Autumn;12(3)*:177-84.

[74] Sampson EL, Thuné-Boyle I, Kukkastenvehmas R, Jones L, Tookman A, King M, Blanchard MR. (2008). Palliative care in advanced dementia; A mixed methods approach for the development of a complex intervention. *BMC Palliat Care. Jul 11;7*:8.

[75] Goodman C, Evans C, Wilcock J, Froggatt K, Drennan V, Sampson E, Blanchard M, Bissett M, Iliffe S. (2009). End of life care for community dwelling older people with dementia: an integrated review. *Int J Geriatr Psychiatry. 2010 Apr;25(4)*:329-37.

[76] Hertogh, CM The, BA. (2008). [The loss of a common shared world. Ethical problems in palliative care for people with advanced dementia]. *Tijdschr Gerontol Geriatr. Dec;39(6)*:265-72. (English abstract only.)

[77] Voicer (2007). Goals of care in advanced dementia: quality of life, dignity and comfort. *J Nutr Health Aging. Nov-Dec;11(6)*:481.

Tom Kitwood called inducing a "malignant social psychology,"[78] although patients in Advanced Dementia may have a greater need for palliative care than social interventions. Unfortunately, the kind of care patients receive (e.g., tube feeding) may be determined more by the culture, staffing, and financial needs of the institution than by the needs of individual patients.[79]

In contrast to emphasizing palliative care, whose goal is comfort, many nursing homes still continue to refer patients with Advanced Dementia for aggressive curative care, despite the known intrusive and often painful burdens of such medical interventions. They typically send patients to hospitals to treat pneumonia despite Hurley and Volicer's clinical advice: "Hospitalization for pneumonia... does not improve the outcome in nursing home patients but actually results in more frequent death and functional deterioration."[137]

Dementia patients suffer at the mercy of others. The worst example I know of is the sad case of 85-year-old Al Barnes. His younger wife, Lana, made him endure 78 emergency hospital visits between 2002 and 2010. Almost every hospital in The Twin Cities, Minnesota, admitted him. Lana petitioned the court for extra time to find a medical expert to testify who would agree that her husband could survive—after she admitted she had altered her husband's Advance Care Planning forms. Olson reported, "Barnes died while still receiving mechanical help to breathe and eat" on February 14, 2011. His last hospitalization began on Dec. 25, 2010.[80]

Unrecognized, Untreated Pain and Suffering in Dementia

The causes of pain and suffering in patients who suffer from Advanced Dementia may be *observable*, such as cramping, contractures, and bedsores. They may also be suspected, such as cancer. Unfortunately, the source of pain and suffering is not always recognized or treated effectively or adequately and thus pain and suffering may go untreated or under-treated. Unrecognized, untreated pain commonly leads to abnormal behavior. Typical sources of pain are fecal impaction, urinary retention, unrecognized fracture, surgical abdomen, arthritis, old fractures, neuropathy, and malignancy, according to Volicer and Hurley.[81]

A real patient similar to "Edward"/"Edith" presented earlier in this chapter was reported in an article by Dr. Lantz.[82] After screaming began, doctors tried another medication for Alzheimer's

---

[78] Kitwood, T. (2007). **Dementia Reconsidered**. Open Univ. Pr.

[79] Lopez RP, Amella EJ, Strumpf NE, Teno JM, Mitchell SL. (2010). The influence of nursing home culture on the use of feeding tubes. *Arch Intern Med.;170(1)*:83-8.

[80] Olson, J. Wife's Surprise Shakes Barnes Case. Star Tribune. Feb. 2, 2011. www.startribune.com/lifestyle/health/115116219.html?elr=KArksc8P:Pc:UockkD:aEyKUiD3aPc:_Yyc:aUoD3aPc:_27EQU. And" http://www.startribune.com/local/west/116204949.html

[81] Volicer L, Hurley AC. (2003). Management of Behavioral Symptoms in Progressive Degenerative Dementias. *J Gerontol A Biol Sci Med Sci.58A(9)*;M837-845.

[82] Lantz, MS. Verbal Outbursts in a Patient with Dementia. (2010). www.clinicalgeriatrics.com/articles/Verbal-Outbursts-a-Patient-with-Dementia .

disease, then a combination of three medications (which individually are approved for treating depression, seizures, and psychosis). Finally, "the issue of pain was raised as a factor in his calling-out behaviors. X-rays of his knees and hips revealed **moderate-to-severe osteoarthritis**." After "**injections of steroids** into his knees... **episodes of cursing, screaming, and moaning rarely occurred**." So **pain** turned out to be the real culprit.

Several studies report unrecognized and untreated pain and suffering in Advanced Dementia:

A) London, U K: A survey of charts from selected hospitals of patients who died showed that only 9% of patients with a diagnosis of dementia were referred to physicians to provide Comfort Care versus 25% of dying patients who did not have dementia. Patients with dementia were also prescribed fewer Comfort Care medications: only **28% versus 51%**.[83]

B) New York, US: Before and after surgery for hip fractures, over 40% of non-demented patients *complained* about NOT receiving adequate medication and "severe to very severe pain." Patients with dementia lacked the ability to complain; they **received one-third as much pain medication**. Very likely, demented patients suffered much more. Dr. Morrison wrote that this finding "suggests that the majority of dementia patients were in severe pain postoperatively," and "Advanced Dementia patients may be at substantial risk for undetected or undertreated pain."[84]

C) Bergen, Norway: This article posed this question in its title: "Are nursing home patients with dementia diagnosis at increased risk for inadequate pain treatment?"[85] The answer was, "Yes." Dementia patients depended on the observations of nurses to receive medication as needed for pain (called, "PRN"). Patients who suffered from dementia were about **one-fifth as likely to receive PRN pain medication** as similar patients who did not suffer from dementia.

D) Amsterdam, the Netherlands: Physicians trained to treat nursing home patients were interviewed about recent patients who died of dementia if the patient's Advance Directive requested hastened death if they suffer from dementia.[86] "**One-quarter** of the physicians reported their most recent patient *suffered unbearably* to a (very) high degree, and **half** the physicians reported their patient *suffered hopelessly* to a (very) high degree." Suffering was "almost exclusively a result of dementia and its complications," which included pain, breathing difficulties, cramps, contractures, pressure ulcers, vomiting, agitation, confusion, and anxiety.

---

[83] Sampson EL, Gould V, Lee D, Blanchard MR. (2006). Differences in care received by patients with and without dementia who died during acute hospital admission: a retrospective case note study. *Age Ageing 35*; 187–189.

[84] Morrison RS, Siu AL. (2000). A comparison of pain and its treatment in advanced dementia and cognitively intact patients with hip fracture. *J Pain Symptom Manage 19*; 240–8.

[85] Nygaard HA, Jarland M. (2005). Are nursing home patients with dementia diagnosis at increased risk for inadequate pain treatment? *Int J Geriatr Psychiatry 20(8)*;730-7.

[86] Rurup ML et al. (2005). Physicians' experiences with demented patients with advance euthanasia directives in the Netherlands. *J Am Geriatr Soc.;53(7)*:1138-44.

E) Maastricht, The Netherlands: Older nursing home residents with dementia who lacked the ability to complain were rated using the "Pain Assessment Checklist for Seniors with Limited Ability to Communicate" scale, during personal morning care. **Almost half** had some pain.[87]

F) Tel-Hashomer, Israel: Despite traditional medical and nursing care, a large proportion of dying dementia patients experienced increasing suffering as they approached death.[88] Ultimately, **63%** died with a high level of suffering; 29% of patients died with an intermediate level of suffering. Only 7% died with a low level of suffering.

G) Hospice teams have more experience and skill in detecting and treating pain than nursing home teams who are sometimes reluctant or do not know when to refer patients to hospice. The currently used criteria for referral ("FAST")[89] need to be improved. Hurley and Volicer noted that these criteria are not based on actual data; some are vague; and about half the patients could not be rated since their symptoms did not proceed in the expected order.[90] The result: **less than optimum nursing skill and delayed referral to hospice** could leave nursing home patients in a state of suffering—as they wait to be referred to hospice.

H) Special care units for dementia patients, such as the one described by Long[91], can train staff to observe patients' behavior, based on the premise that behavior is the only way demented patients can communicate. Thus, if patients' behavior becomes disturbing, staff uses objective pain scales and aggressive analgesic treatment as they observe patients to assess the results.

I) The problem of detecting and treating pain has four levels: **1)** Is the clinical staff tuned into the patient? **2)** Does the clinical staff consider pain as a possibility? **3)** Is the clinical staff trained to detect behavioral signs of pain? And **4)** Do Advanced Dementia patients show behavioral signs of pain similar to other patients? Unfortunately, the answer to question #4 is probably "No," based on research of Boly, Laureys and others (summarized next).[92]

---

[87] Zwakhalen SM, Koopmans RT, Geels PJ, Berger MP, Hamers JP. (2009). The prevalence of pain in nursing home residents with dementia measured using an observational pain scale. *Eur J Pain;13*:89-93. Zwakhalen and others' previous study [Pain in elderly people with severe dementia: a systematic review of behavioral pain assessment tools. *BMC Geriatr.;6*:3 (2006)] reviewed 12 observational pain assessment scales and concluded two seemed promising, but a group from Norway (Holen and others (2007), *BMC Geriatr.;7*:29) noted significant limitations in one, which left only the PACSLAC.

[88] Aminoff BZ, Adunsky A. (2005). Dying dementia patients: too much suffering, too little palliation. *Am J Hosp Care;* 22: 344–8.

[89] Reisberg, B. (1988). *Psychopharmacol Bull.;24(4)*:653-659. Meeting criteria of level "7c" in the Functional Assessment Staging (FAST) scale is what many clinicians use to determine when to admit a patient to hospice.

[90] Hurley AC, Volicer L. (2002). Alzheimer Disease: "It's Okay, Mama, If You Want to Go, It's Okay." *JAMA. 288*:2324–2331.

[91] Long, CO. (2009). Palliative Care for Advanced Dementia: Approaches that work. *J Gerontol Nurs.;35*:19-24.

[92] Boly M, Laureys S, et al. (2008). Perception of pain in the minimally conscious state with PET activation: an observational study. *Lancet Neurol. Nov;7(11)*:1013-20. (Figure reproduced with permission.)

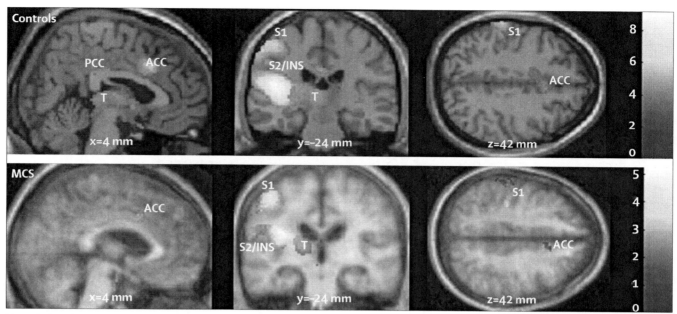

Figure: Brain activation to pain in controls and patients in MCS

While PET activation scans of Minimally Conscious State (MCS) patients show activity similar to those of normal people given electrical shocks, the patients did NOT manifest reliable behavioral signs of pain. This is what Boly, Laureys and colleagues wrote:

> "Patients in MCS are unable to consistently and reliably communicate their experiences, and their behavioral responses to noxious [painful] stimulation are often difficult to interpret. Even... a question such as, 'Are you in pain?' might not elicit a reliable response. The behavioral assessment of motor or autonomic signs (i.e., respiratory frequency, heart rate, blood pressure, papillary diameter, and skin conductance) are not reliable markers of the conscious perception of pain... The evaluation and treatment of pain is therefore an important clinical and ethical problem in patients in MCS."

Many clinicians consider the condition of the brain in MCS patients similar to Advanced Dementia patients. Dr. Laureys (private communication, 2011) revealed his group had not done any PET activation studies on Advanced Dementia patients, although he was interested.

Bottom line: We who are still cognitively intact can *hope* the detection and treatment of suffering in Advanced Dementia will improve in the future. In the meantime, what can we do? Some of us will perform a mental calculus to weigh the significant risk of undetected and untreated pain and suffering versus the possible benefit from continued existence in the state of Advanced Dementia. After deciding what we want, we must inform our future decision-makers about our preferences so they can determine WHEN we would want **Natural Dying**. To make sure others will honor our *Known Wishes,* we can add the **Plan Now, Die Later— Ironclad Strategy**.

What is going on in the minds of Advanced Dementia patients? Is someone home, even though the lights are turned off?

Consider this argument against **Natural Dying**: Since we have so much to learn about what is going on in the minds of Advanced Dementia patients, it is not reasonable to implement irreversible orders for **Natural Dying**. The pros and cons presented below are admittedly hard to understand. Readers can skip the (interesting) details and proceed directly to the questionnaire at the end of this chapter after reading only the next paragraph.

The risks of continuing to exist in the stage of Advanced Dementia, given its irreversible and progressive course, its increased chance of experiencing unrecognized and untreated pain and suffering, and its low possibility of experiencing pleasure or benefit before death—make Natural Dying a reasonable choice. If patients do have some conscious life, loneliness could be an additional reason to justify that it is moral to allow their suffering to finally end. Conclusion: the possibility of conscious experience and therefore suffering makes it compelling to NOT prolong patients' dying.

"Don't give up so easily on life," said my medical colleague, who specializes in aging. He challenged: How can you know for sure that Advanced Dementia patients are not living in a mental state they consider worthwhile—*as long as they show no observable signs of suffering*? Do clinicians understand enough about the minds of Advanced Dementia patients to determine WHEN it is time for **Natural Dying**? What if these patients consider spoonfuls of thickened puree as *sweet nectar*? Is it not possible that they exist in a gentle, quiet kind of bliss? Recent ground-breaking clinical research showed patients were incorrectly given the diagnosis of Permanent Vegetative State based on their *non-responsiveness*. That is because, when asked to do specific mental tasks, an exquisitely sensitive way to observe their responses—fMRI scans—lit up. Example: A "PVS" woman was instructed to *think about tennis* and an area of her brain lit up, like the brains of normal people. Clinicians had to conclude the patient COULD hear and respond. Since she WAS *responsive*, the diagnosis of PVS was wrong. Our problem was our inability to detect her responsiveness using less sensitive observational tools. The researchers concluded: These findings "bring new ethical challenges... [that] will have profound implications for clinical care and medical-legal decision-making."[93] Is it not possible that future research with Advanced Dementia patients will lead to similar conclusions?

Here is my answer: First, the study of Boly, Laureys and colleagues showed PET activation scans of brains of patients in the Minimally Conscious State lit up in response to pain while patients did NOT manifest typical behavioral responses of pain. I am thus skeptical about

[93] Owen AM, Schiff ND, Laureys S. (2009). A new era of coma and consciousness science. *Prog Brain Res.* *177*:399-411.

proposed criteria to postpone **Natural Dying** "as long as [patients] show no observable signs of suffering." While Advanced Dementia patients may not be suffering now, they are at high risk for *unobservable* future pain and suffering. Advance Care Planners can consider this risk as they empower future decision-makers to decide if it is time for **Natural Dying**.

Second, what about *pleasure?* Consider the progressive natural history of dementia: Over the course of years, patients experience a profound loss of memory, intense confusion and frustration, and often, *observable* episodic mental turmoil. In addition, they lose control of bodily functions (incontinence, inability to walk and hold their heads up, trouble swallowing, etc.). After such a long, relentless, progressive, downward course, is it reasonable to postpone **Natural Dying** based on the *possibility* that their taste buds still provide enough pleasure and their minds might be in a state of blissful peace? Okay, some pleasure and bliss are possible. But future decision-makers cannot know for sure. Since Advance Care Planners must guess based on presently available information, they may reasonably decide they do NOT want to continue treatment that will prolong their dying if they reach the stage of Advanced Dementia.

Third, consider the philosophical articles of Drs. Wilkinson, Kahane and Savulescu[94] from the University of Oxford. They focused on the *moral significance* of the fMRI scans that showed a few Permanent Vegetative State patients *could respond*. They admit their explanation is complicated, in part because the concept of *consciousness* is complicated. Their main points are still clear: **A)** *consciousness* is far more complicated than fMRI scans can possibly reveal and **B)** fMRI scans are unlikely to be able to reveal relevant *kinds* of consciousness.[95]

The Oxford philosophers disagreed that fMRI research findings justify the recognition of "neglected personhood" so that clinicians must rethink "one of the most ethically contentious decisions concerning patients with severe disorders of consciousness, [] the withdrawal of life-sustaining treatment." Instead, the Oxford philosophers offered this perspective:

> "Life with minimal consciousness may be *worse* than PVS... If patients are able to feel pain, although they are largely unable to communicate their distress and discomfort... **we may do them significant harm by keeping them alive**: it is doubtful that a

---

[94] Wilkinson D, Kahane G, Savulescu J. (2008). "Neglected Personhood" and Neglected Questions: Remarks on the Moral Significance of Consciousness. *Am J Bioeth.* 8(9);31-3.

[95] This is the authors' explanation: *"Subjective...* phenomenal consciousness or *qualia...* is notoriously difficult to define: a state is phenomenally conscious if *there is something 'it is like' to be in it...* Arguably, the value of phenomenal consciousness is grounded in the **moral significance of interests**... [that include]... *hedonic interests* [that] relate to states of suffering or enjoyment, *desiderative interests* [that] relate to the satisfaction of a person's desires, [and] *objective interests* [that] relate to having a *meaningful existence* by possessing goods such as relations with other people, achievement, or knowledge. It is clear enough why phenomenal consciousness is needed if one is to have hedonic interests. Pleasure and pain matter only because of what it is like to experience them. Arguably, phenomenal consciousness is also needed if one is to have desiderative and objective interests: without subjectivity there is no point of view to which such interests can be ascribed."

life that contains suffering while containing little or no desiderative or objective goods is a meaningful life... If such patients are partly aware and suffering, **we may have a stronger reason to let them die—it may be against their interests to continue life-sustaining treatment**. Beyond considerations of pain and suffering, the compromise of their objective and desiderative interests **may make their lives worse than nonexistence**... Most importantly, **the question of what makes life worth living will need to be addressed** if we are to decide whether we are benefiting or harming this group of patients by keeping them alive." {Bold emphasis added.}

Fourth, **Natural Dying** is more appropriate for Advanced Dementia than for some other devastating brain diseases because, by the time the patient reaches this stage of the disease, its course has definitely proven it is both irreversible and progressive. The future thus holds decreased potential for pleasure and increased potential for pain and suffering and other burdens.

Summary: For Advanced Dementia patients, postponing **Natural Dying** promises little benefit but many burdens. An informed Advance Care Planner has *more right* and (presently) *as good a base of knowledge* to decide *now*, as *other* decision-makers may have in the future.

Is Natural Dying *Morally Wrong*? Does it Always *Hasten Death*?

Consider these four statements that support my answers, which are, "No," and "No":

1. A few patients undergoing **Natural Dying** may live longer. Three examples: Fasting can help prevent aspiration pneumonia. Dehydration can improve heart functioning in patients with cardiac failure. Decreased excretion can reduce skin infections and sepsis.

2. **Natural Dying** is intended only for patients who are *already dying*. Its goal is NOT to hasten dying but to avoid a prolonged dying. It does NOT cause death; it *allows Nature to take its course by NOT continuing treatment that patients explicitly refuse*, or would refuse—had they been asked when they still possessed decisional capacity.

3. Honoring patients' diligently selected criteria for WHEN they would want **Natural Dying** can simultaneously prevent *premature dying*. Drawing a "line in the sand" can help make sure patients DO receive treatment and feeding assistance—right up until the point they meet their criteria. Honoring specific criteria can prevent the all-too-common practice of withholding antibiotics from patients in the middle stages of dementia, who are likely to recover from pneumonia and then be able to enjoy life's simple pleasures.

4. Given the principle of "Substituted Dying" (if you do not die of one cause, you will certainly die of another), people may prefer **Natural Dying** as a way die. Medical dehydration is far more comfortable than the excruciating pain from an obstructed or perforated bowel, for example. **Natural Dying** is more peaceful than suffering from the

toxicity of high fever, persistent weakening cough, and anxiety from air hunger that can be associated with dying from pneumonia. As mentioned before (in Chapter 1), "Pneumonia is NOT the old man's friend." Dr. van der Steen and others concluded, "Death from pneumonia may cause great suffering in dementia patients" and recommended "antibiotics... be used to decrease discomfort *even when death is imminent*." {Emphasis added.} They also warned against "invasive rehydration [because it] was associated with more discomfort"[96]—a finding consistent with Dr. Pasman's studies.[97] They showed that dying by medical dehydration IS peaceful: "Forgoing artificial nutrition and hydration in patients with severe dementia who scarcely or no longer eat or drink is **not associated with high levels of discomfort**." Furthermore, "the **level of discomfort decreased** in the days after the decision was made to forgo artificial nutrition and hydration. In patients who died within two weeks after the decision, the **discomfort level decreased until they died**."

One downside to **Natural Dying** is a possible adverse consequence: delirium can occur during medical dehydration. This typically is seen only in patients who previously received high doses of narcotics. Some clinicians will re-hydrate; others treat with antipsychotics and sedatives.[98]

Questionnaire: What Are Your End-of-Life Preferences?[99]

If someday you meet your specified *Criteria for Advanced Dementia*, what do you want your proxies to do? Write **Yes, No, or Uncertain** next to the words, "***Do you want this?***" (Woman can imagine they have painful, metastatic breast cancer; men, prostate cancer.)

1. I want my proxy to make sure I receive *Manual Assistance with Oral Feeding and Drinking* for as long as it is medically feasible—even if they must put puree at the back of my tongue so I swallow by reflex and even if such treatment prolongs my existence and results in my experiencing more intense and longer suffering from mental anguish and/or physical pain.

Do you want this? Why?

---

96 Van Der Steen JT, Pasman HR, Ribbe MW, Van Der Wal G, Onwuteaka-Philipsen BD. (2009). Discomfort in dementia patients dying from pneumonia and its relief by antibiotics. *Scand J Infect Dis. 41(2)*;143-51.

97 Pasman HR, Onwuteaka-Philipsen BD, Kriegsman DM, Ooms ME, Ribbe MW, van der Wal G. (2005). Discomfort in nursing home patients with severe dementia in whom artificial nutrition and hydration is forgone. *Arch Intern Med 165(15)*; 1729-35.

98 # 060 Pharmacologic Management of Delirium; Update on Newer Agents, 2nd ed. EPERC. 2009. http://www.eperc.mcw.edu/fastFact/ff_60.htm. Retrieved 3-7-11.

99 The questionnaire is also at https://www.surveymonkey.com/s/Treatment-Preferences-Advanced-Dementia; if you answer online, you will contribute to our survey data.

2. I want my proxy to make sure I no longer receive *Manual Assistance with Oral Feeding and Drinking* provided I receive adequate Comfort Care for general pain and discomfort (including hunger and thirst)—UNLESS I clearly indicate I want to be fed (by gestures or by interpretable words)—even though I will NOT be able to understand the alternative of using thirst reducing agents or appreciate the consequence that feeding may prolong my dying and increase my pain and suffering. [Your answer to this *question* must differ from your answer to the next one.]

Do you want this? Why?

3. I want my proxy to IRREVOCABLY make sure I no longer receive *Manual Assistance with Oral Feeding and Drinking* provided I receive adequate Comfort Care. I want my current, competent wishes followed—EVEN IF I clearly indicate I want to be fed by gestures or by interpretable words. I do not want my *Known Wishes* set aside by my "future demented self" or by others who might challenge or remove my proxy based on arguing that fasting is not in my "Best Interest." I specifically reject arguments such as "There is a moral necessity to never seek a person's death as a means of relieving his suffering" (President's Council on Bioethics report of 2005) or "ultimately lose respect for their other rights and freedoms" (U S Catholic Bishops' Conference of 2011). The reason, in part, is because I hold at least one of these beliefs: A) My personhood—the essence of who I was—will cease to exist after my higher brain can no longer function; or B) Continued treatment would then be extraordinary or disproportionate. [Your answer to this *question* must differ from your answer to the previous one.]

Do you want this? Why? [NOTE: Your answers to #2 & #3 should be different.]

4. In addition, for any disease: I want my physician to provide *Palliative Sedation* (sedation to unconsciousness) if all other methods of Comfort Care cannot control my pain and suffering—even if it might end my conscious life or *unintentionally* hasten my death, but see # 5:

Do you want this? Why?

5. After *Palliative Sedation* allows me to rest for a few days, I want my physician to reduce the dose of sedative medications to see if I can tolerate being conscious again—UNLESS I suffer from Advanced Dementia, or if my death is expected very soon. Otherwise, even if my physician believes my pain and suffering may again be unbearable, I still want one trial of reducing the dose of sedative medications. (Such a trial may also allow me to complain that I was not receiving enough sedatives for complete relief.)

Do you want this? Why?

Chapter 5

Sad and Successful Stories of Compassion at the End of Life
Without diligent planning, conflicts and sabotage are possible

"An Unwanted Call to 9-1-1"

Gus held several discussions with his close relatives before he decided to refuse food and fluid as a peaceful way to die. Unfortunately, he was the victim of the *black sheep on a white horse syndrome*. His nephew, who lived and had stayed far away, arrived at his bedside too late to visit while Gus was alert. Feeling guilty, the nephew argued to keep Gus alive, even though Gus had already fasted for seven days and was now in a peaceful sleep. As this issued was argued, Gus had a cardiac arrest. His nephew felt it his duty to leave the room and secretly call 9-1-1. Within minutes, firefighters arrived. They pushed everyone aside, moved a hard board under Gus, pounded on his chest (breaking some ribs), used a huge syringe to inject medication directly into his heart, shocked his chest with electrodes (making his body jerk up sharply), and started an IV in each arm (adjusting the flow to "wide open"—to make sure physicians could administer additional life-sustaining medications, if Gus needed them). Gus still died, but his nephew had sabotaged the peaceful transition that he had wanted.

Strategies to overcome similar pitfalls: Display a form that contains a physician's "Do-Not-Attempt-to-Resuscitate" (DNR) order. This can be a Pre-Hospital (Out-of-Hospital) order, a Physician Orders for Life-Sustaining Treatment (POLST), or a **Natural Dying Physician's Orders** (**NDPO**)—the form the "ironclad strategy" prefers if you want to be sure your transition will be *timely and peaceful*—if your local EMS agency has trained their personnel to honor this form. Most States require 9-1-1 personnel to honor conforming "alert jewelry" as equivalent to a physician's orders. Your **Natural Dying Medallion** can also be engraved with words such as: "No I.V. Hydration" and "No Oral Fluids" (emergency medical personnel should respond to these specific requests even though they may not have been trained to do so).

In addition to a physician's order and alert jewelry, it may be critically important to have your advocate present after you lose consciousness, to make sure others will honor your last wishes. The next story expresses fear of loss of control and anger at possible intrusion. This note was originally published in **The *BEST WAY* to Say Goodbye**. The author insisted that his/her anonymity be respected.

"But they just want to save me."

I am personally and professionally involved with hospice and have read widely on end-of-life issues. I am also passionate about patient autonomy, including my own. Recently I was told that one of my family members, a Catholic priest, learned that my Advance Directive contained certain specific stipulations that he felt compelled to fight because—in his opinion—I have an "unformed conscience" and thus do not have the capacity to make such decisions. The facts that I haven't been a Catholic in 30 years, only see him every 5 years, and that he has zero medical experience, are no barriers to his perceived right to usurp my autonomy and to impose his "perfectly formed conscience" on me.

It gets worse: He alleges that my suffering benefits other souls in Purgatory, and that makes him feel morally obligated to fight my expressed wishes. For nearly fifty years, I have made well-informed decisions. I worked hard to put together a team of doctors whom I trust. They respect my wishes and they will HONOR them—at least as long as I have the ability to express myself. **What if I lapse into a state of unconsciousness?** Then I will suddenly be fair game for a whole host of individuals who want to make a "cottage industry" of my fate.

Others are ready to insert their values into my relationship with my doctors and proxy—in order to save my soul. The priest I mentioned is just one example of why I am so concerned for my fate. I am also deeply concerned about other people. The increasing use of "Will to Live" forms[100] that are touted as better alternatives to Living Wills, and the threat of new "Conscience Laws" that allow health care providers to refuse their patients' requests, may have significant impact on how hospice can serve the dying, as the opponents' quest for aggressive curative treatment pledges it will never stop.

The list of advocacy, religious, and rights organizations that claim they "actually care" about me is growing at an astronomical rate. The fact that they don't know anything about me or my values is no deterrent to their willingness to speak on my behalf. All it takes is an URL, "charity" status, and a handy PayPal button to solicit donations, and they all get to advocate for what *they* believe is in my "Best Interest." But of course, we're not supposed to question their motives or possible conflicts of interest. "Saviors" are as exempt from such accountability as their institutions are from paying taxes.

Strategies to overcome similar pitfalls: A blank line on the **Natural Dying Advance Directive** lets you write the names of specific individuals whom you do not want to make

---

[100] Such documents claim there is a presumption for the right-to-die but advise people of similar persuasion to be explicit so they can receive the treatment they want. They offer a choice of such statements as, "I would like medication to relieve my pain but *only to the extent* the medication would not seriously threaten to shorten my life," OR, "I would like medication to relieve my pain *but only to the extent* it is known, to a reasonable medical certainty, that it will not shorten my life." Other statements are: "Food and water are not medical treatment, but basic necessities. I direct my health care provider(s) and agent(s) to provide me with food and fluids, orally, intravenously, by tube, or by other means *to the full extent necessary* both to preserve my life and to assure me the optimal health possible." See: http://www.nrlc.org/euthanasia/willtolive/docs/california.rev0308.pdf.

medical decisions for you. You can legally designate a proxy (and alternates) to advocate for your preferences about treatment if you no longer can speak for yourself on the companion form. The **Natural Dying Agreement** can enhance the legal standing of your proxy and simultaneously establish your *Known Wishes* for WHEN you would want **Natural Dying** someday, which includes refusing *Manual Assistance with Oral Feeding and Drinking*, Cardio-Pulmonary Resuscitation (CPR), and other potential life-sustaining treatments.

The next story illustrates that a long conflict may ensue if one takes an expedient rather than a comprehensive approach to Advance Care Planning. While fictional, the story bears some resemblance to the cases of Jean Elbaum (NY), Robert Wendland (CA) and Terri Schiavo (FL).

"This short delay won't make any difference to her."

Sara, a former high school principal, found retirement fulfilling. Although childless and widowed for two years, her life was richly rewarding. She lived in a medium-sized California town at Elm Gardens, an independent living community that offered a variety of stimulating activities, which she attended with her best friend, Tammy. She especially enjoyed painting and sharing artistic interests with her friends.

Sara had two chronic medical problems; then she developed a third. In addition to high blood pressure and sugar diabetes, she now had atrial fibrillation (episodic irregular beating of the two smaller chambers of her heart). This increased her risk of a stroke so her doctor prescribed a blood thinner to prevent clotting. After a few months, Sara fell and bled so much her doctor changed her medication to aspirin. For two years, Sara did well. Then at 75, she had a stroke.

The initial damage to her brain caused paralysis of her right arm and leg. She could not speak but she understood what others said. She could not eat and drink since her swallowing muscles were too weak. Time and certain exercises *might* let Sara regain some ability to swallow and speak. Her doctor placed a temporary nasogastric tube (NG) so nutrients could directly enter her stomach. She would receive adequate nutrition while she worked at rehabilitation.

Sara's thinking was unimpaired. She expressed thoughts by writing notes with her left hand and used gestures for emphasis. One day, her face contorted in a fierce grimace as she made a fist. She had written: "I can't stand this darn NG tube any longer." Tammy immediately requested a consultation with her doctor.

The doctor explained minor surgery could insert a "PEG" tube to go through the abdominal wall directly into her stomach, which would be much more comfortable than the NG tube. If her swallowing improved, the tube could be removed. If not, Sara could leave it in. She could decide to discontinue it any time—as long as she was still competent to make her own medical decisions. If she was not competent... well, that's why he was pleased Tammy was present for this discussion. He reviewed Sara's old Proxy Directive. Her proxies had died or were very ill. Sara had no Living Will since she did not want to make detailed medical decisions in advance.

The doctor asked Sara if she would want the PEG tube removed if she had a massive stroke. Sara made a clear gesture to show she DID want the feeding tube removed. Then the doctor said, "Your risk of another stroke is about 12% per year.[101] Let's hope for the best but be prepared for the worst. Plan now, while you can still make your own medical decisions. You have two options. You can choose either one, or both."

The first option was to create a new Advance Directive that could empower Tammy to make all her medical decisions, including withdrawing the feeding tube. This form required two qualified witnesses or a notary for Sara's signature. The second option was easier and faster: Sara's physician could complete a **Physician Orders for Life-Sustaining Treatment** or **POLST** form. He checked the boxes to opt for Full Treatment, except for Cardio-Pulmonary Resuscitation, and explained, "Some professionals feel it is best to have both an Advance Directive and a POLST, but as a practical matter, an Advance Directive just authorizes your proxy to request a physician's orders, which this form already is. Take a few minutes to look over this form. Decide if the choices on it represent your preferences. You can revise the form if your condition changes. If you like, I'll sign it when I return after I see another patient. If you still want an Advance Directive, you can always create one later."

Sara liked the POLST. It seemed simple, comprehensive, and sufficient. They could complete it within minutes without calling a notary or two qualified witnesses. The POLST did not ask her to make detailed decisions about future medical treatments for a variety of unpleasant scenarios. The doctor had already checked the appropriate boxes and would review the orders periodically. Sara saw no reason to obtain, complete, sign, and get witnesses for another form that would only authorize Tammy *to request* a future doctor to write orders. Sara signed the POLST form with her non-dominant hand and felt she had completed Advance Care Planning.

Unfortunately time and exercises did NOT allow Sara to regain the ability to speak or swallow so her PEG tube could not be removed. Sara's spirit and motivation were good, however. She quickly learned a text-to-speech computer program and was soon composing full sentences. She painted with her functional hand and learned a computer-drawing program. She called herself "high-tech Sara" and viewed the movie "My Left Foot" several times. She made peace with her impaired level of functioning and expressed her appreciation for her feeding tube as it allowed her to live, to create art, and to interact meaningfully with people she enjoyed.

A year and a half later however, Sara had a huge stroke. Tammy called 9-1-1 and rode in the ambulance with her. She held Sara's hand and caressed her hair... but did not look up until the ambulance stopped. When she realized where they were, Tammy asked, "Why did you drive to Our Grace Hospital? Sara wanted to go to University Hospital."

---

[101] Based on the *CHADS model*: Gage BF, Waterman AD, Shannon W, Boechler M, Rich MW, Radford MJ (2001). Validation of clinical classification schemes for predicting stroke: results from the National Registry of Atrial Fibrillation. *JAMA. 285 (22)*: 2864–70.

"Not my choice," the driver replied. "The dispatcher said other nearby hospitals were on bypass. That means they're full." The twist of fate that began with the dispatcher's choice of hospital became a long nightmare that Tammy will never forget.

Two days after Sara was admitted to Our Grace Hospital, after a thorough evaluation, her neurologist told Tammy, "A large portion of Sara's brain has been damaged. It's extremely unlikely she will ever regain consciousness from her coma."

Tammy asked, "How long does she have?"

"Actually, with the feeding tube in place, she could live for years."

Shocked, Tammy initially refused to let go of all hope. A week later, however, after several discussions with people she trusted, some Internet research, and recalling her discussion before the PEG tube was implanted, Tammy came to a difficult conclusion: Sara would not want to continue her present existence. She knew "the time had come" to revise the POLST.

Tammy called the neurologist, made an appointment, showed him Sara's POLST, and said, "This is really hard. Sara has been an inspiration to us at Elm Gardens. Always positive and resilient... But now, I must ask—" She sighed. "Can you revise her POLST to remove Sara's feeding tube? Here's the box to check, to stop artificial nutrition and hydration."

The neurologist shook his head. "I'm sorry, but I must refuse. Removing feeding tubes is against my moral and religious conscience."

"But I am sure Sara would want this now."

The doctor shook his head. "Sara's feeding tube is *already in place*. It is *not a burden* and it is serving the purpose for which it was intended: it provides *nourishment to maintain her life*. This type of basic care must be given to every patient, to respect their human dignity."

"But I am absolutely sure Sara would not want to continue tube feeding if she could never regain consciousness. She made this precise point clear, just before she signed that POLST."

After a moment of reflection the physician said, with a final sounding tone, "I'm sorry, but I cannot and will not perform any act if its intention is to directly hasten my patient's death."

Frustrated and angry, Tammy put her head in her hands and cried. She thought, *Sara—the conscious, responsive, human being—was already gone. Why force her body to exist?*

Later, back at Elm Gardens, Tammy called some other physicians at Our Grace Hospital, but none would help. She talked to Sara's other friends... to no avail. Then she called her son. He and her daughter-in-law lived nearby. They called back after a discussion. "Bring Sara to our home. We'll help you. She can die here, privately, in peace. Sara is unconscious so she cannot experience discomfort. That means she does not need to be in the hospital."

The logistics were simple. Tammy's son arranged for a nursing aid to provide bedside help. He and his wife discussed how they would explain the situation to Tammy's grandchildren.

Tammy called the neurologist and asked him to discharge Sara. His answer was alarming.

"For any AMA discharge—'AMA' means *Against Medical Advice*—I must obtain approval from the Chief of Staff. Be patient, Tammy, you'll get an answer, but it might take a few days. In the meantime, don't worry. I can assure you of one thing: because Sara is unconscious, she cannot experience suffering. *This short delay won't make any difference to her.*"

Three days later, Tammy received a letter—not from the Chief of Staff, but from an attorney in the hospital's Department of Risk Management. This "courtesy letter" made Tammy so upset she had to ask her son to finish reading it to her. First, Tammy had no legal standing as Sara's proxy. Second, Our Grace Hospital stood behind its obligation to protect its patients' "Best Interest" if Tammy requested an AMA discharge. They had deep concerns about Tammy's intent, based on her request to remove Sara's feeding tube. Unless Tammy could convince Our Grace she had no intention of starving Sara to death, they would feel obligated to file a report with the State's Department of Social Services that they had *reason to suspect elder abuse.* "Reason to suspect," the letter explained, is definitely NOT an accusation, but almost always prompts an investigation. Third, an AMA discharge would lead the hospital attorneys to petition the Court to appoint a conservator to protect Sara's interest in living and the petition would specifically exclude considering Tammy. Fourth, in carefully worded language that avoided sounding like a direct accusation, the letter brought up a possible conflict of interest by citing lawsuits where the decision-maker was also a beneficiary of the dying person's estate.

Finally, the letter asked Tammy to consider withdrawing her request to discharge Sara AMA. Clearly, the hospital would otherwise attack Tammy.

Feeling defeated Tammy withdrew her request to discharge Sara after she spoke to an attorney. He reviewed the case's strengths and weaknesses. True, Sara never designated Tammy as her proxy, but her conversation with Tammy and the physician who signed her POLST *might* provide *clear and convincing evidence* of what Sara would now want. If so, the physician and hospital were obligated to refer Sara to a non-objecting physician/institution to remove the feeding tube. This is what happened with Jean Elbaum in New York. Also, clear and convincing evidence ultimately prevailed for Terri Schiavo in Florida. The POLST stated the physician's orders were consistent with the patient's known desires, which was good. But this was bad: Our Grace could cite Tammy's conflict of interest and many sources that starving to death was not in a patient's "Best Interest."

Another factor, the attorney advised, was that Our Grace had a huge system behind it so it could afford an expensive and prolonged litigation. The likely result: *To Delay is To Deny*. If they considered the case important to affirm their policy, they could drag it on for years. Meanwhile, Tammy's resources would be drained.

Two weeks later, Sara's neurologist determined that Sara no longer needed hospital care and transferred her to the Our Grace Skilled Nursing Facility.

Five years later, Sara died without ever regaining consciousness. The cost of her residential and medical care exceeded $600,000. Most came from Sara's estate, which surprised Tammy who, like 44% of people surveyed, did not realize Medicare does not pay for long-term care.

As Tammy drove back to Elm Gardens after the funeral, she recalled the neurologist's first words: "Sara is unconscious... so this *short* delay won't make any difference to her."

Comment: This story reveals a weakness of POLST forms: they do not give the "recognized" decision-makers legal standing. While some states call them "**legally** recognized decision-makers," the term "**clinically recognized decision-makers**" is more apt. The bottom line is: if Sara had signed a proxy directive (durable power of attorney for health care), Tammy would have had the power to insist on an AMA discharge. Furthermore, others would have had to assume that Sara, when competent, had already considered Tammy's potential conflict of interest and thus this issue would most likely not have been raised.

Four strategies to overcome similar challenges: **1)** Designate your proxy/agent legally by completing an Advance Directive. These forms typically grant proxies the authority to hire and fire physicians, to change hospitals, and to refuse artificial nutrition and hydration. **2)** On the **Natural Dying Physician's Orders**, write down the names of any institutions to which you do NOT want to be transported. **3)** Create a Living Will to express your specific *Known Wishes* in a *clear and convincing* way. **4)** Sign a **Natural Dying Agreement** to authorize your proxy to specifically request an AMA discharge. Taking these steps make it very likely you will be able to attain your goal of a *timely, peaceful transition*.

These strategies anticipate future challenges. Step 2 facilitates your first choice, to be sent to an institution that *will* honor your wish to withdraw tube feeding rather than object (based on their moral or religious conscience). If you somehow still end up in this kind of institution, your proxy can argue for your reasonably expedient transfer to a non-objecting physician and institution, as required by your State's Advance Directive law. Your third choice, if the process of transferring is taking too long, is for your proxy to demand an AMA discharge based on your *Known Wishes*. One way or another, your proxy should be able to make sure that you can attain your goal of a *timely, peaceful transition*.

A Tale of Two Mothers:
Inadequate forms can lead to premature or prolonged dying

In determining whether or not a patient receives life-sustaining treatment, POLST forms may determine WHEN patients die. If these forms do not reflect patients' wishes, their dying may occur too soon or be delayed as they endure unwanted suffering. The next two "tales" illustrate this risk. The first tale shows how a POLST that reflects the wishes of greedy next-of-kin is easy to complete: in an unwitnessed doctor-patient interview, the physician is in control and as s/he checks off certain boxes. The danger: some physicians are consciously or unconsciously biased and they can be swayed by others.[102] While fictional, the first tale is similar in one way to an Alabama court case: the proxy was the sole heir to her aunt's estate. The second tale is true; it shows how a POLST form can be challenged and summarizes the outcome in a court of law.

"The sooner mother dies, the better."[103]

Twins Annette and Nannette, both 54, are the only offspring of Martha, an 87-year-old widow who suffers from moderate dementia. She resides in a skilled nursing facility. Martha needs manual assistance for feeding, bathing and dressing. She occasionally joins in sing-alongs. Yet most of the time, she just stares, vacantly, into space.

The twins agree: "Mom's quality of life is so low... What a waste of money! Mom can't enjoy life anymore. And this facility *costs us* $60,000 a year, plus another $20,000 for extra care and treatment." (By "*cost us*," they mean, "drains our future inheritance.") They conclude, "The sooner mother dies, the better." The problem: how can they accomplish that?

In strict confidence they explain their concerns to an attorney. He studies Martha's old Advance Directives and then states, "Like most Living Wills, your mother's springs into action only when she is terminally ill, permanently unconscious, or if additional treatment would be futile. Her Proxy Directive is invalid since her husband and best friend have both passed on. I see this quite often. You cannot create a new Living Will based on other criteria since she no longer has decisional capacity for this complex task. If she were not residing in a skilled nursing facility, you might be able to create a new Proxy Directive that designates one of you as her proxy—if a notary acknowledged her signature. One of you cannot serve as a witness to the other since you both are heirs to her estate. The problem is that our State law requires another,

---

[102] Files v. State, 826 So. 2d 906, 908-09 (Ala. Crim. App. 2001). The court found the woman guilty of criminally negligent homicide; in part because of the accused had motivation: She was the heir to her aunt's estate. Also, this "violation" occurred before the law changed to authorize proxies to refuse artificial nutrition and hydration.
[103] Another version of this story with similar comments was published as: Terman, SA. (2009): The Potential Pitfalls of Advance Care Forms. Guest Editorial. *Caring for the Ages. Dec. 2009: 20a-20b.*

independent witness, an Ombudsman, to help make sure your mother was informed about all her options and her signing was voluntary and willful. So this option will not work either. The way I see it, you will just have to wait for her to die."

The sisters almost give until Annette does some Internet research. She discovers her State recently approved a new form called a POLST. The only signatures required are a family member's and a physician's—*no* witnesses and *no* Ombudsman. She remembers Dan, a doctor she dated a few years ago, and their promise: to remain "friends." She calls Dan. "Remember my Mom? She had a little bit of dementia the last time we got together? Well, she is a lot worse. Before she got ill, she told me she would never want to be hooked up to machines... I don't know but this could be worse. She just stares into space. Well... her Proxy Directive is no longer valid since the two named people are no longer alive. And she is not mentally capable of creating a new Living Will. Poor woman. Must she be condemned to linger for years like this? She only has me and my sister whom she can trust. Dan, could you come over and see her? Do you think one of the new POLST forms might work?" Dr. Dan agrees to visit in two days.

In Martha's private room, Dan points to Annette and asks, "Who is this?" Martha replies, "My daughter." Then he asks Martha, "Do you want Annette to make your medical decisions?" She answers, "Yes." He repeats these two questions for Nannette. Dan feels he has diligently chosen a "legally ***recognized*** decision-maker" to discuss and sign the POLST. He proceeds to go through the list of orders, checking the options after discussing them with Annette; Nannette nods every time. Together, they select *Comfort Measures Only*. Dan signs the form under this statement: "My signature below indicates to the best of my knowledge that these orders are consistent with the person's medical condition and preferences." A thought flashes briefly through his mind: *I never asked Martha about her end-of-life wishes, when she could tell me. But there was no need to, as Annette summarized her values, and Martha clearly designated her daughters as her decision-makers.* (Dan had no reason to doubt Annette's motivation.)

Note: Of the four people in the room, none is an independent witness, and no conflict-free Ombudsman is present to oversee the process.

Dan signs the POLST form and passes the form to Annette who signs without reading the statement above her signature: "By signing this form, the legally recognized decision-maker acknowledges that this request regarding resuscitative measures is consistent with the known desires of, and with the best interest of, the individual who is the subject of the form."

Until this moment Nannette had not realized she had been holding her breath. Now, she lets out a sigh. She looks at her mother. As usual, she seems "out of it." She thinks, *The stage is now set: If Mom has a problem with her heart rhythm, gets any kind of infection, or needs tube feeding—then Annette and I can use this POLST to refuse all life-sustaining medical treatment. So she WILL die sooner. Mission accomplished!*

Annette is not worried that her mother's Living Will is likely to remain in her medical chart. Based on her Internet research, this was quite clear: **the most recently dated form would take precedence**. In this case, it would be the POLST that she and Dan had just signed.

Note: When she possessed decisional capacity, Martha possibly had good reasons NOT to designate either daughter as her health care proxy/agent, and now, she might want to receive aggressive treatment to live unless she was terminally ill, permanently unconscious or the treatment would have been futile. But all this has changed: now the POLST will **override** her Living Will making it more likely that she will die "sooner."

POLST forms can serve an important role

Physician/Medical Orders for Life-Sustaining (or Scope of) Treatment (POLST/MOLST/POST) forms cover a wide range of treatment options in various combinations: Full Treatment and Limited Treatment as well as Comfort Measures Only. These forms can serve as the focus of initial discussions and subsequent reviews to update physician's orders so they reflect the changing condition and condition of patients whose "physicians would not be surprised if they died within a year." (This "surprise question" was suggested by geriatrician Joanne Lynn, MD.)

These forms are intended to provide continuity of care by accompanying patients across treatment settings including emergency medical personnel and health care providers in various settings such as skilled nursing facilities, and hospital emergency departments. This goal is not always achieved since physicians at receiving institutions must review and then may rewrite the orders. Thus POLST orders are NOT **durable**. In contrast, *Known Wishes*, as expressed in a Living Will, are durable—if specific and clear and convincing. This is likely what Judge Polito meant by the word "particularized" in the second "Tale," below. "**PNDL**" describes how a Living Will that is **durable** and a physician's order that has **authority** can be strategically combined by printing one on each side of the same piece of paper.

No POLST form mentions *Palliative Sedation* to relieve patients' unending unbearable end-of-life pain and suffering, to my knowledge. No POLST form lets patients choose to stop *Manual Assistance with Oral Feeding and Drinking* if they meet their previously selected *Criteria for Advanced Dementia*. So POLST forms cannot be the solution to people's greatest end-of-life fears. "**PNDL**" describes the **Natural Dying Physician's Orders** (**NDPO**). This form can be thought of as a *last* or *final* POLST. In addition to offering these two choices, it also includes important additional safeguards to overcome the weaknesses described below.

Three potential weaknesses of POLST forms

1. POLST forms do not provide the safeguard to exclude certain next-of-kin whom the patient would not want to have authority to make their end-of-life decisions.

Elderly people are vulnerable to abuse. Their mental, medical, and financial states can limit their ability to stand up for their rights. Most vulnerable are those patients who no longer have decisional capacity and who suffer from a terminal or chronic incurable illness: their continued living depends on what orders their physicians write (that is, what boxes their physicians check on their POLST). In light of this awesome power, consider this statement on the web site of the National POLST Paradigm Initiative Task Force:[104] "Family members may be able to speak on behalf of a loved one. A health care professional can complete the POLST Paradigm form based on family members' **understanding** of their loved one's wishes." {Emphasis added since *dedication* to honoring the patient's *Known Wishes* is required in addition to *understanding*.}

For patients who lack decisional capacity, many POLST forms allow any legally ***recognized*** surrogate decision-maker to discuss the patient's life-and-death decisions with the POLST-signing physician. Typically, *any* next-of-kin who is vocally aggressive with the patient's physician may "qualify," although some States list a specific sequence of related closeness to whom physicians should listen. These lists do not however solve this problem: When still in possession of decisional capacity, the patient may have wished to exclude one or more next-of-kin based on perceived greed, differences in religious values, or another reason. Some States, like California, prompts Advance Care Planners to list specific individuals they wish to disqualify as surrogate decision-makers. For other States, this logic seems reasonable: If you have the legal authority *to designate* certain individuals to make decisions on your behalf, then you also have the legal authority *to disqualify* others. (To my knowledge such disqualifying statements have not been challenged.)

Statutes about Proxy Directives (Durable Powers of Attorney for Health Care or Health Care Agent for Medical Decisions) require strict procedures to legally designate (that is, to authorize/to empower) such individuals. The patient must possess decisional capacity (be of sound mind) and must sign (or otherwise indicate agreement with an independent witness) a written form that meets certain standards. There are also certain signing requirements:

2. Signatures and Witnesses:

Initially, POLST forms did not require signatures of patients or surrogates since physician's orders rarely include anyone else's signature. This is slowly changing. Now the patient's or the surrogate decision-maker's signature is required, in part due to increased emphasis on "POLST conversations"—discussions similar to those that obtain *informed consent*, which always requires signatures. Unfortunately, requiring the signature of a legally ***recognized*** surrogate decision-maker may not solve the *conflict of interest* problem, as indicated in the above story.

---

[104] Posted at www.ohsu.edu/polst/patients-families/faqs.htm#13: "What if the patient's loved one can no longer communicate her/his wishes for care?" (The answer continues with a different issue: "Some state laws have limitations on the power of a patient's chosen decision-maker so check with your health care professional.") Retrieved on March 5, 2011.

For a proxy directive to be legally valid, the patient's signature must be witnessed by a notary or by two individuals that *qualify* by meeting certain factors. For especially vulnerable patients such as residents of skilled nursing facilities, some States require an additional witness who has no conflict of interest and can attest to their willful, voluntary, informed consent: an Ombudsman. Compared to the safeguards built into most Advance Directive statutes, POLST forms thus have inadequate safeguards to prevent abuse by next-of-kin.

Why are the laws that authorize POLSTs less strict than for Advance Directives? Two possible reasons are: **1)** to make it possible to complete end-of-life planning for patients who no longer have capacity; and, **2)** to bypass the bottleneck burden of requiring scarce Ombudsmen to serve as witnesses. POLST laws allow huge numbers of frail and demented patients to complete end-of-life planning. The process is typically made more efficient by having 80% of the initial POLST conversations conducted by nurses or medical social workers. (In some States, admission coordinators and staff who lack clinical degrees can have the POLST conversation, but this may be changing.) The goal: to save physician's time when s/he signs the form.

Bottom line: Eliminating the safeguard of witnessing a competent patient's signed expression of his/her end-of-life wishes may expedite the process of Advance Care Planning, but it does so at the risk of opening the door to possible abuse.

3. POLSTs Can Supersede Patients' Wishes:

POLSTs threaten the durability of Advance Directives. If a patient has both a POLST and an Advance Directive, some State laws require honoring the most recently dated form. A more recently signed POLST could thus override a patient's prior Advance Directive—even if the patient, when competent, previously put much diligent effort into creating her Advance Directive so it truly reflected her enduring wishes. One State, Idaho, passed a statute so their POLST forms always have legal precedence. Yet some State laws proclaim that POLSTs are *not* Advance Directives. This potential challenge to honoring your end-of-life wishes is dealt with by specific forms and the **Plan Now, Die Later—Ironclad Strategy** ("**PNDL**").

"The longer it takes mother to die, the better."

In May 2010, Carol Zornow filed a petition with a New York State court to be appointed her mother's guardian.[105] She wanted authorization to make end-of-life decisions for her Catholic mother. Then 93, she resided in a nursing home where she suffered from advanced Alzheimer's

---

[105] In the Matter of Carole ZORNOW, as, Petitioner pursuant to Article 81 of the Mental Hygiene Law for the Appointment of a Guardian of Joan M. Zornow, an Alleged Incapacitated Person. Supreme Court, Monroe County, New York. http://law.justia.com/cases/new–york/other–courts/2010/2010–20549.html and 2010 WL 5860446 (N.Y.Sup.).

disease. While medically well, she needed manual assistance to ingest food orally. Anticipating the course of Advanced Dementia in order to allow Joan M. Zornow a "natural death," a physician signed a Medical Orders for Life-Sustaining Treatment (**MOLST**) form that directed the withholding of artificial nutrition and hydration if and when she lost the ability to swallow.

The patient's daughter petitioned the court to undo these MOLST orders. The patient's son, Douglas Zornow [defendant] "contended that his mother verbally indicated to him and [to five] other siblings that artificial feeding be denied her if she were unable to take food and water orally." Judge Polito indicated he would not consider their six testimonies since they would fail to meet the required *clear and convincing* standard of evidence. The judge did accept a note that a nurse wrote in a medical chart in 2002 as *clear and convincing* (although the ruling indicates the judge's uncertainty if the patient chart was in a hospital or in a nursing home). The note said a lucid Mrs. Zornow "wished artificial feeding," however nothing was mentioned about any witnesses to the conversation or if the patient was informed that her consent to tube feeding had possible adverse consequences for the specific condition she was in now. No evidence was offered to support these wishes were consistent over time. The judge could have ruled on this legal point alone; interestingly, his ruling went on for another 14,000 words.

Seven months later after initial filing, Judge Polito ruled that the Medical Orders for Life-Sustaining Treatment violated the patient's religious rights since they were protected by this provision in the **Family Health Care Decision Act (FHCDA)**: a "person's religious and moral beliefs take precedence if inconsistent with FHCDA requirements." Had the patient not been religious, **FHCDA** would have allowed family members to refuse artificial nutrition and hydration under any of three conditions; of which this was relevant: "providing food and water causes **inhumane pain, suffering, or other extraordinary burden to a patient who has an irreversible condition**." {Emphasis added.}

Judge Polito provided an extensive summary of Catholic teachings, including the U S Conference of Bishops' *Ethical and Religious Directive # 58*, which he also provided in an Appendix. The judge quoted this Catholic position about administration of food and food: It is **always ordinary care**. Unless the patient is imminently dying, not able to absorb the food, or tube feeding is not available in a remote area—the only *rare* instance that Artificial Nutrition and Hydration (ANH) would not be *obligatory* is if ANH *itself* causes the patient "excessive burden" such as significant physical discomfort. Thus, for Mrs. Zornow, "artificially administered food and water is **obligatory** if she were to become unable to swallow due to the often occurring symptoms of Alzheimer's."

Judge Polito wanted his ruling to apply to all Catholics who did not "particularize" their Advance Directives. He wrote, "Blanket directives are not readily amenable to Catholic end of life determinations as they are for intentional terminations of life based on a '**quality of life**' ethic, which is morally prohibited to Catholics." He also wrote, "The Court would suggest legislative action by reviving [revising] the Family Health Care Decision Act design to set forth the '**sanctity of life**' ethic as the main ethic." The judge ruled, "Any blanket MOLSTs or directives were impermissible unless particularized." However his ruling acknowledged that the law did "allow the limited 'quality of life' ethic to be specifically limited to those who so personally indicate under the level of proof required...." (that is, who expressed their specific *Known Wishes* in a way that meets the *clear and convincing* standard of evidence).

For Mrs. Joan Zornow now, as for so many other patients like her, tube feeding is destined to prolong her dying and increase her risk of unrecognized and untreated pain and suffering so her suffering will likely be longer and greater while she receives no benefit from this treatment.

The best strategy is obviously to express your specific *Known Wishes* in a *clear and convincing* way *before you lose mental capacity*. Religious people can make decisions and generate a Living Will by sorting a deck of *Natural Dying Living Will Cards*. If they want an opinion that this process is moral, they can read the essay by health ethicist, Reverend Kevin McGovern ("**PNDL**," TOPIC 10). He concluded, "The *Natural Dying Living Will Cards*... identify the sorts of circumstances in which hand/spoon feeding or other treatments will become extraordinary or disproportionate [w]ithout conflicting with Catholic teaching."

Making end-of-life decisions for patients without Living Wills

For the millions of patients, like Mrs. Zornow, who never expressed their "particularized" wishes when they had capacity, there is a way to resolve conflicts that may avoid going to court. Using the Zornow family as an example, each sibling could sort a deck of *Natural Dying Living Will Cards* (or **My Way Cards**). As they sort, they imagine what the patient would have decided for each item, WHEN WELL, before the onset of dementia. Note: the process of "trying to make the same decision the patient would have made," is an ethically accepted process called "Substituted Judgment." Each sibling considers how mother would balance Catholic teachings (both old and new) and new clinical information about the increased risk of unrecognized and untreated pain and suffering in Advanced Dementia. As loving children who would not want their mother to suffer, all might agree she would decide to forgo tube feeding.

What if the "vote" was still six in favor to one against **Natural Dying**? If the adult children could not resolve this conflict on their own, they could engage the help of a mediator and a priest. (Perhaps for their mother's sake, they would select one like Reverend Kevin McGovern.) The process of mediation might take less than seven *days*, rather than seven *months*. More important, they could consider all burdens that continued treatment might impose on their mother and then possibly agree. If this process failed, they could still ask a judge to decide—but this time they could ask an expert to testify, to inform the judge that it is *quite common—**not rare**—*for patients in Advanced Dementia to experience unrecognized and untreated pain and suffering. This is an *indirect* consequence of tube feeding that often causes the patient the "excessive burden" of significant physical discomfort.

Comment: This book is not the place to speculate that Catholic leaders and their secular counterparts who argue for the supremacy of the "sanctity of life ethic" may have an additional, unmentioned agenda: their belief in the role of redemptive suffering. Briefly however, the original meaning of the word "compassion" is *to suffer with* (not to act in order to relieve suffering). This book is also not the place to argue that for several Centuries, Catholic theology emphasized the importance of "quality of life ethic" by emphasizing "proportionality" to decide if a treatment's burdens exceed its benefits on a *case-by-case basis*. But it hard to resist discussing recent interpretations of papal teachings, such as the suggestion to take patients home from hospitals or nursing homes to decrease the expense. Often patients just cannot be managed at home and caring for them would further increase the already huge burden on the family. Also, the expense of tube feeding is unrealistically minimized if one considers only the cost of the nutritional supplement rather than the total cost of care. A critical discussion about the global impact of such a ruling must also be elsewhere. Here it must suffice to say it violates the goal of social justice to direct spending enormous sums of money on millions of patients who have irreversible, progressive conditions—when millions of poor people, who could return to good health with relatively inexpensive medical treatment—are denied basic medical care due to lack of funds.

This book is a good place to make two points: First, patients in Advanced Dementia are in fact dying (albeit slowly)—unlike those in the Permanent Vegetative State who may live for many years with artificial nutrition and hydration—and when a patient is dying, view of a treatment's *benefits versus burdens* change. A prospective study showed that there is a "need to improve the quality of palliative care in nursing homes in order to reduce the physical suffering of residents with advanced dementia who are dying." When proxies understand "advanced dementia is a terminal illness" and its "prognosis and expected complications," then patients are less likely to "undergo potentially burdensome interventions of unclear benefit."[106]

The second point refutes Judge Polito's assertion by Catholic authorities that "adequate interventions exist to control pain in 90 to 99% of patients" to infer that continuing artificial nutrition and hydration is NOT a burden to the patient. That assertion ignores an important relevant fact: Many Advanced Dementia patients have unrecognized and untreated pain and suffering simply because they *do not complain* because they *cannot complain*. Several observational scales for pain may help trained caregivers detect suffering in some patients, but not all. A new finding is relevant: *PET activation scans* demonstrated that Minimally Conscious State patients do NOT manifest typical behavioral signs of pain when they receive controlled electrical shocks.[107] Brains of Minimally Conscious State patients are similar to brains of Advanced Dementia patients, which the research team led by Steven Laureys has not yet investigated (personal communication, 2011).

---

[106] Mitchell SL et al. (2009). The Clinical Course of Advanced Dementia. *N Engl J Med.* 361:1529-1538
[107] Boly M. et al. Perception of pain in the minimally conscious state with PET activation: an observational study. *Lancet Neurol* 2008; 7: 1013–20.

These consistent clinical observations leads to a compelling conclusion: continued *Manual Assistance with Oral Feeding and Drinking* prolongs the process of dying, increases the risk of greater suffering and the risk of medical complications without providing much or any benefit. To prolong dying further—by insisting on tube feeding for all Catholic patients who can no longer swallow—violates the First Principle of Medical Ethics, DO NO HARM. The **Natural Dying** strategy is consistent with long-standing Catholic teaching.

Conclusions from "A Tale of Two Mothers": If you want a *timely and peaceful transition*, you must (to use Judge Polito's word) "particularize" your end-of-life wishes. Even if an expert convinced an appeals judge that providing food and fluid is often an extraordinary burden to patients like Mrs. Zornow, and that withholding artificial nutrition and hydration satisfies both Catholic teachings and New York State laws, the process of litigation will have gone on for much longer than seven months while poor Mrs. Zornow will have continued to suffer. For her, this would be an example of *To Delay is To Deny*. To reduce her suffering, others must not only honor her end-of-life wishes, but do so *expediently*.

Completing Physician/Medical Orders for Life-Sustaining Treatment forms is a rapid and convenient way to guide treatment of patients who may die within a year. But these forms: **A)** do not give proxies/agents legal standing, and **B)** do not express in a clear and convincing way, the patient's specific *Known Wishes*. This increases the risk of *premature dying* and of *prolonged suffering*. Safeguards are NOT adequate to protect patients against a next-of-kin's conflict of interest. To the extent that POLSTs do not inform loved ones precisely what the patient would have wanted, surviving family members may experience prolonged litigation, estrangement, and/or long-term guilt. Finally, without an effective strategy in place, POLSTs can override previously created diligent Advance Directives that did reflect the patient's wishes.

Take-home lesson: Create a specific, clear and convincing Living Will; authorize a proxy you trust to advocate your *Known Wishes*; add other components of the "ironclad strategy."

Physician-Proxy Shared Decision-Making can be Prudent

When he was 21 and physically well, "Roland" decided to complete his **Natural Dying Advance Directive/Natural Dying Physician's Orders**. The inspiration came from a friend who had an accident. Both loved to skydive. In addition to the three general conditions specified in the **NDPO**—terminal illness with unbearable pain and suffering, Advanced Dementia, and medical treatment that would be ineffective to restore quality of life independent of a skilled nursing facility or hospital—Roland wrote: "If I am in an accident that will leave me permanently paralyzed in both legs and I am in a coma, I want **Natural Dying**. Do not wait for me to wake up and ask me."

When his physician asked him to explain, Roland responded, "Why wake me up so I can be depressed, if you are certain I will never get out of a wheelchair?" His physician responded, "Because you might change your mind." Roland became extremely anxious at this point so his physician said nothing more, but wondered if it was because his friend's accident was so recent. The physician agreed to sign Roland's forms, given the high risk activities his patient enjoyed, but also clearly pointed to several blank spaces on the form that awaited his initials. The doctor explained, "If the time comes when your proxy considers it time for **Natural Dying**, I must first sign my initials after I contact the appropriate people to discuss your future situation."

Six years later, Roland's motorcycle accident left him with the injuries he had feared: he was comatose and would never walk again. His proxy brought the **Natural Dying Physician's Orders/Natural Dying Advance Directive** to the physician who signed for consent and said it was now time to implement the orders. The physician advised the proxy that he first needed to talk to Roland's two current treating physicians—a neurologist and a rehabilitation specialist. The neurologist stated that according to accepted practice guidelines, it was too soon for **Natural Dying**. "The American Academy of Neurology's guideline is to wait twelve months after a traumatic injury before one can consider a coma to be permanent." The rehabilitation physician stated, "I have extensive experience treating acute spinal cord injuries. *Initially* most patients are depressed; many want their lives to end. But most change their minds. For example, after Christopher Reeve was informed he was quadriplegic; he mouthed these words to his wife, Dana: 'Maybe we should let me go.' Yet he went on to act and direct feature movies, to write a memoir, and to establish an important research foundation."

After these two conversations the physician who signed Roland's **NDPO** explained to the proxy, "Right now, Roland is not conscious so he is not depressed, although he probably will be, if or when he wakes up. When I spoke to him a few years ago, he was too anxious to discuss the possibility that he might change his mind if he had an accident like this. Many patients who sustain similar injuries do change their mind. Actually, there is a good chance he can still have a productive and enjoyable life. Bottom line, it would go against practice guidelines and the community standard of care for me to implement now, the Orders for **Natural Dying**. If Roland recovers his mental capacity to make medical decisions when he wakes up from his coma, and if his psychologist or psychiatrist asserts that his judgment is sound, and he still wants to refuse food and fluid, then, as promised, I will implement these orders. I will also honor his request if his mental recovery is limited; for example, if his consciousness returns to the level of only the Minimally Conscious State so that he does not possess the capacity to make medical decisions." Pointing to the form the proxy was holding, the doctor assured him, "In that case, I *will* honor—actually, I *must* honor—Roland's request for **Natural Dying**."

Roland's proxy was confused. He wondered if the physician had let his friend down. After all, Roland was really clear: he did not want to wake up to this depressing news. The proxy asked another physician for her opinion, but she agreed that it was prudent to wait. The proxy then asked for a consultation from the institution's Ethics Committee. Their consensus opinion was that Roland's physician was acting within ethical guidelines. Although the committee told the proxy he could go to court, they advised him it was unlikely a judge would rule to allow **Natural Dying** until Roland had enough time to wake up and consider, after six more years of adult living and distance from his friend's tragedy, if he would change his mind.

Explanation: Patients can make direct requests to physicians, and their proxies can restate these requests on their behalf, but physicians are not required to respond if the action requires them to break the law, is contrary to their moral or religious conscience, or violates generally accepted health care standards. For example, one cannot expect a physician to honor a request for Physician-Assisted Dying in States where is it illegal. Even where it is legal, a physician can object based on his/her moral/religious beliefs.

In retrospect, the physician who signed Roland's consent for **Natural Dying** might have been clearer by informing Roland he might delay honoring his wish for **Natural Dying**, but he considered Roland too anxious to discuss this possibility. Consulting Roland's treating physicians led to the conclusion that it was prudent to wait before implementing **Natural Dying**. Ethical decisions in clinical medicine often require balancing burdens and benefits. Here, the burden was real and anticipated: depression. However based on the experiences of similar patients, it would likely be temporary. The benefit was potentially huge: a full and productive life. The prudent decision was ethically obvious: to err on the side of life.

Despite the delay, Roland's **Natural Dying Advance Directive** served as his legal, durable form regarding his specific *Known Wishes*. If his recovery from brain injury was so limited that he did not recover the mental capacity to make new medical decisions, that is, "to form and express a fresh autonomous choice" (as ethicist/attorney Ronald Dworkin would say), then his physician would be obliged to implement the orders for **Natural Dying**. In this case, *To Delay* was **not** *To Deny* but to make a prudent decision that balanced relevant burdens and benefits.

Is It Moral to Provide Knowledge About How to Die?

Informing people about a strategy so their future decision-makers know when they would want **Natural Dying** has many potential benefits. It can prevent choosing premature, violent, or criminal dying. Such knowledge can also reduce future pain and suffering and prolonged lingering in total dependency and indignity. This information must be imparted when the person has the mental capability to understand and appreciate it however, which could lead to the following *potential* problem. Since unassisted suicide is no longer illegal, providing this information may lead some individuals to hasten their deaths who would not do so, had they not been provided this information.[108] This is the moral question at stake: Can this knowledge

---

[108] States have the duty to protect their vulnerable citizens. Some people doubt that suicide can ever be rational, but most agree with U S Supreme Court that competent individuals (who are not clinically depressed) have the right to determine what does or does not enter their bodies, even if such refusal will lead to hastened deaths.

be abused? If so, is it reasonable to provide knowledge that is intended to increase a person's options, and then try to restrict the person from using it? This conundrum plays out in the next story—a composite of three of my own patients—about which I must admit: I am the physician who is (still) struggling with *moral angst*.

To Live Long Enough to Warm the Hearts of Others
Reflections on informing my patient about how to die

Her voice was anxious as "Sandra" explained why she called. Yes, her 92-year-old mother "Helen" mother might soon be dying, and she definitely did not want her process of dying to be prolonged or associated with pain and suffering. But the main reason for her urgent call was a serious legal concern for herself. Sandra explained Helen had always been a fiercely determined woman. Yesterday, she announced she no longer wanted to live. She asked Sandra for her help, but stated she would still "do it" even if Sandra refused. Helen was neither terminally ill nor suffering unbearably. Sandra thought her mother could think clearly enough to make sound decisions. She thought her mother was not depressed.

I asked, "How does your mother intend to die?"

"Mom will refuse all food and fluid. She wants me to stand by and make her comfortable. So here is my question: If I help her this way, am I guilty of elder abuse? Could I be prosecuted?"

I was about to mumble that I never give advice to concerned relatives of people whom I dimly know from a two-minute phone conversation, when Sandra said, "Before you answer, consider this. For two years, Mom has not spoken to my brother Richard. He is the only other heir to her estate. Mom told me my share is greater than his. Could a prosecutor use this fact to argue that greed motivated my inaction? Or worse... my cooperating with my mother's death? And..." After a pause, her tone of voice changed. "Doctor, could you try to change my Mom's mind? I... I really don't want her to die."

Intrigued and challenged, perhaps seduced, I agreed to see them both the next day. I spent three hours interviewing Helen and Sandra—together and separately. This is my synopsis:

Two weeks ago, Helen fell and broke her arm. Before that, she had been doing fairly well. Her main problem was weakness in her legs and an unsteady gait. That made her dependent on a four-wheeled walker. Helen complained about using the walker; for example, to stand up she needed to hold onto it with her hands and that made it difficult to cook at the same time. Yet most observers thought she was doing rather well "for someone over ninety." They pointed out that she still dined out at restaurants, insisted on having manicures, and colored her hair. Yet Helen viewed her glass as half empty. Or perhaps she was worried about becoming more disabled. Now, with her arm in a cast, she no longer could use her walker, although she could get around using a wheelchair. She thus chose to remain housebound and arranged for assistance with activities of daily living. An aide came in each Monday through Friday and Sandra assisted her every weekend.

Helen's first orthopedic check-up was yesterday. The surgeon's report was good. Helen could expect her arm to heal completely so she could expect to return to her previous level of functioning. Yet the doctor cautioned her about the risk of falling: her bones were fragile. When they got home, Helen told Sandra she was ready to die, but not sure when. When Sandra asked Helen how, she said she would refuse all food and fluid. That's when Helen asked Sandra for help. Helen was very clear: whether or not Sandra helped would not determine if or when she began her fast. After that conversation, Sandra called me.

Helen trusted Sandra to never insert a tube down her throat to feed her against her will. She knew they'd have to tie her down to prevent her from pulling out a feeding tube. Helen also registered some forms—including a Living Will and Proxy Directive—that specifically authorized Sandra to refuse food and fluid on Helen's behalf under certain conditions, *if Helen could NOT then speak for herself.* But now, Helen *could* speak for herself. In fact, she was making her desire to die exceptionally clear.

Again, Sandra expressed her worry. "What are MY legal consequences if I help my mother? Would it be different *if* Helen's pain and suffering were unbearable, or *if* she were severely demented? Were Helen's present reasons to die compelling? She is worried about falling again. Several friends broke their hips. Surgical pinning let some walk within days. Others had severe complications and endured miserable pain before they finally died. Do you have any advice?"

Based on these interviews, I formed several opinions, which I shared. I ruled out clinical depression for Helen. She enjoyed some aspects of life, could laugh, and had a strong grip on reality. She possessed the ability to make medical decisions about end-of-life preferences. I did not suspect Helen was subject to undue influence by Sandra. On the contrary, the daughter tried hard to convince her mother to remain alive as long as her quality of her life was acceptable. Sandra considered all life precious, especially her mother's, now that they had become closer. In her individual session, Sandra shared that her mother had previously been stubborn, controlling and difficult, and rarely expressed appreciation or affection, let alone love. The more dependent she became, the warmer she was towards Sandra. These bits of shared history seemed consistent with my interviews and observations.

When I interviewed them together, I asked Helen if she trusted Sandra to determine the time when she would want **Natural Dying**. Helen effusively expressed her complete trust and deep appreciation for her daughter's devotion. Upon hearing her mother's words, Sandra's face beamed with a broad smile. "I've been waiting for years to hear something like this."

So far, the interview had been successful. With respect to Sandra's worry, my written clinical opinion could help protect her from being charged with neglect, undue influence, or elder abuse. The interview also confirmed warm, benevolent feelings between mother and daughter.

The ultimate existential question still remained unanswered: Why now? Was it something the orthopedic surgeon said? Had Helen been planning this for a while? Could I, as Sandra requested, change Helen's mind? Was Helen undecided about how long she wanted to live?

I interviewed Helen about her present quality of life. That led her to discuss when she wanted to die. She still enjoyed her daughter and a few still-living friends who were well. Helen admitted deep fears about her own future. Would it bring more disability? More pain? More indignity? I asked, "Are you worried about being... or becoming a burden to your daughter?"

She replied, "Not with respect to finances. I can pay for help. But if I got very sick and dependent, I could become an emotional burden. I know what it is like to take care of someone. I did it for my husband. I don't want to impose this on anyone else. But I'm not there, yet."

I sighed with relief when I heard Helen say, "not there yet." I asked her, "How will you determine WHEN?" She answered, "Not right now; maybe later." This ambivalence sounded better than a determined *now*, but it was still vague. I asked her about her fears. She said, "I'm worried about losing the mental faculties I now possess. That could prevent me from being able to die with dignity in the future." (I made a mental note to address this point, fully.)

Helen discussed these difficult issues in a way that was engaging, open, lucid, and clear. There was only one area about which she refused to talk: her relationship with her son. She shared only this: "We had some problems in the past and I do not want to talk about it now." I asked Helen where he lived and if I could call him. She said, "On the other coast," and, "Not now."

I then explained the **Plan Now, Die Later—Ironclad Strategy**: "Once you complete this paper work, which Sandra and I will also sign, you will have our promise that your fast will not be sabotaged. You no longer will need to worry about having to endure prolonged pain and suffering, or being forced to linger in a state of indignity and total dependency. You will have set the stage to prevent others from sabotaging your plan, whenever you want to begin it."

Helen took my advice to complete all the forms. As I drove home, I felt pleased with myself. I had fulfilled my professional role. My plan potentially extended her life, which still had quality. Her choice was another example of life's greatest irony: *Knowing you can control when you will die, can—and often does—lead to choosing to live longer.* Recalling her ambivalence about when she wanted to die, I did not expect to hear from her for several weeks, perhaps after her arm had healed. When her cast was removed, she might reassess her quality of life.

Three days later, however, in the middle of a Saturday afternoon, just as I was about to take my dogs for an hour's walk, Sandra called. I recalled she assisted her mother on weekends. I hoped her call was just a question or two about the forms Helen had signed. Instead, Sandra said, "Mom refused breakfast this morning. I figured she wasn't hungry. That sometimes happens. But then she also refused lunch. That's not like her. So I asked her, 'What's up?' She said she decided to begin her fast. So, doctor, I have two questions: Can you send over a Thirst Reduction Aid Kit? And, can you come over and try to persuade her to postpone her fast?"

Early that evening, I made a home visit to Helen. I felt confident that my arguments would be convincing. My writing and teaching had prepared me well to step onto my professional soap box and state that she could leave instructions for her future caregivers and health care providers for **Natural Dying** if she reached the conditions she could now specify. Since she had already completed the **Natural Advance Directive** and **Natural Dying Physician's Orders**. Now her daughter and she could complete the **Natural Dying Agreement** and **Affidavit** for an even stronger strategy. Then she could trust the "ironclad strategy" to die when and how *she* wanted, instead of dying *prematurely*. I was prepared, but first I listened to her reasons for starting her fast now; then I made these points:

"Okay, the orthopedic surgeon said your bones are fragile and yes, you might fall again. What's the worst that could happen? You might break your hip, and you might have severe complications that could be the beginning of a slow and painful downward spiral to death. So I promise you—and I know Sandra is also on board: If you need so much pain medication that your mind is not clear enough to make your own medical decisions to start your fast after you break your hip, then these papers will authorize Sandra to ask a physician to implement the Orders for **Natural Dying**. That's a reasonable time to proceed toward your peaceful transition.

"Suppose you don't break your hip but you develop terrible pain from cancer. The same plan will work. If you had a major stroke and fell into a coma from which a neurologist felt you had no potential to recover... here again Sandra and I would make sure your fast would begin.

"If a few years went by and you developed Advanced Dementia, we would make sure that your fast would begin. You can decide on the exact criteria now, by sorting **My Way Cards**.

"We'd also begin your fast instead of allowing any treatment that you would consider futile.

"So you have my commitment. You've done your part by signing all the forms. Your "ironclad strategy" is in place. Why not wait a few weeks? See how your arm heals. If you then discover that you cannot enjoy life as you did previously, you can begin your fast. But if life is good again, then continue to enjoy life. Remember, you can begin your fast any time—"

"Begin my fast any time?" She glared at me as she repeated my last words. "What if I lose my mental faculties? What if they change the law?"

I asked her to explain and she replied, "Politicians change laws. That's their job. A few years ago, my advisors told me that the only way I could give my daughter my home without paying taxes was to put my home in her name. But then... they changed the law! How do I know they won't change the laws that you base your 'ironclad strategy' on?"

I just nodded in silence as I thought of Governor Jeb Bush. In October, 2003, Bush changed Florida's law for *one patient*: Terri Schiavo. The law he pushed through the legislative branch of government was obviously unconstitutional when it was drafted, passed, and signed... but it still took the Florida Supreme Court almost a year to rule it violated the separation of powers doctrine. During that time for Terri Schiavo, *To Delay was To Deny*: it prolonged her process of dying. I did not reveal these thoughts to Helen. Later, I considered why: If I had revealed them, she might have interpreted my doing so as agreeing with her argument to die now. I wanted to maintain my position as clearly trying to convince her to remain alive.

If she had mentioned Jeb Bush herself, however, I would have had this counter-argument: Given the subsequent apologies of the politicians involved in the Schiavo saga, and how some of them fell into further ethical disgrace, it now seems extremely unlikely that similar political grandstanding will be repeated. All I said was: "Anything is possible, but let me ask you: does changing the law seem so likely to you that you are willing to die right now, rather than risk the possibility of change?"

Helen blinked and smiled, perhaps to acknowledge that I had put my finger on a flaw in her argument. Then her face turned sad. "There's another reason, doctor. Can I assume you are in favor of 'Dying with Dignity'?" I nodded, waiting for her to define what she meant. She continued, "It's really important to me, too. So let me tell you a story.

"When I fell at home, I pushed the MedicAlert button and the Emergency Medical Technicians arrived within minutes. They were wonderful. They made a call and promptly gave me medications for anxiety and pain. They carefully transported me to the Emergency Department at the hospital. That's where I had problems. After a nurse took my blood pressure and asked me some questions, she wheeled my gurney into the hallway. For the next five hours, nobody paid any attention to me. I yelled out when my bladder got so full it caused me pain... but it didn't do any good. Eventually, I had no choice but to wet myself all over. After that, I laid there in smelly urine for over two hours, staring at the ceiling. I felt abandoned and neglected. Sure, the orthopedic surgeon eventually arrived. And yes, he did take good care of me. But until then, it was a nightmare. I was absolutely humiliated." She stared hard at me again. "Doctor, listen to me: I never, never want to go through that kind of indignity, again. Now, can your 'ironclad strategy' make sure that won't happen?"

I shook my head. Then I said, "Okay, the 'ironclad strategy' can't prevent every possible humiliating experience. It cannot guarantee you will die without spending several hours of indignity. But let me ask you: Are those *several* hours so horrible that you are willing to forgo *several* months of living at your previous level of functioning? Are you not willing to trade some unpleasant *hours* for some mostly pleasant *months*?"

I did not reveal that her life expectancy was almost four years.[109] Perhaps I am guilty of some paternalism, here. When people feel burdened by their present or potential future disability, and when they detest being dependent, sometimes the longer they expect to be in such a state, the worse. So my approach was to take it "*months* at a time." Still, she argued right back.

"Doctor, if and when you reach the age of 92, perhaps you'll understand. You get to the point in life where another dinner, another movie, another sunset... none of it makes any difference. It's

---

[109] www.ssa.gov/OACT/STATS/table4c6.html (2004)

enough. I just want to have a dignified, peaceful transition." She looked at me and sighed. "I'm tired of pain, of worry, of wondering how much physical and mental functioning I'll lose tomorrow. I'm tired of wondering when another friend will die. I miss my husband and my old friends. I have a good relationship with my daughter. We have a wonderfully warm relationship now. And I made peace with myself and I've made peace with my God. So I'm ready to go."

She never mentioned her son. I wondered why, but decided not to ask. The interview was already one long argument and I did not want to threaten her trust in me. Previously, she indicated she would let me know when she wanted to talk about him. I was also sensitive about her privacy and did not think it wise to intrude about a problem relationship while I insisted she convince me it was time for her to die. If I had asked her for permission, that would have put the issue of her son on the table: there would be no way for her not to talk about... at least *why* she did not want to talk about him. I concluded: an important topic, but the wrong time.

Other issues weighed on my mind as I drove home. Why had I lost the argument? Because I had only one card I could play: the "ironclad strategy." She however had three trump cards: One, politicians can change the laws. Two, her transition might be preceded by intolerable indignity. Three, she had accomplished what she wanted to do in life: she had made peace with her daughter, herself, and her God.

Although I lost the argument, I felt I had done my professional best. I had balanced two positions: I honored her *autonomy* by acknowledging her right to determine what happened to her body... and when. This included her right to refuse food and fluid even if it led to her death. But I also valued the *sanctity of life*, which requires my diligent attempt to preserve precious life, if at all possible. I had argued as best I could to dispel Helen's fears.

Of course, I disagreed with her timing... but I had to ask myself: Did *my opinion* have any significance? What is the moral significance of my "disagreeing"? Sure, I would make a different decision if I were in her situation. But would I make it because I am a *different person*, or because—as she challenged me—I don't know what it is like to be 92? Or since I am not as afraid as she, of suffering from more disability and dependency? These were questions I could not answer. While not comfortable with leaving things as they were, I took solace in knowing that Helen could change her mind and stop her fasting within the next few days. I resolved to go back in two days to try again to change her mind. Meanwhile, what she was doing was considered legal, ethical, and moral according to my colleagues in medicine, law, ethics, and philosophy. (I reaffirmed this by posting a detailed question on a bioethics listserv.)

On Sunday, I called Sandra. Helen was still fasting. I suggested Sandra call Helen's physician to ask him for a referral to hospice. The professionals from hospice would either help convince her to change her mind, or offer their expertise in end-of-life care.

The hospice team visited Helen on Monday morning. By then, she had gone two full days without food or fluid. They determined that Helen could be placed into a diagnostic category to allow her admission as a terminally ill patient. There were three possibilities: "Adult failure to thrive" (ICD-9 Code 783.7), "Debility, Unspecified" (Code 799.3), and "Inanition," aptly defined as "exhaustion, as from lack of nourishment or vitality" (Code E904.1/E904.2). The precise diagnosis was not as important as the willingness of hospice personnel to provide Helen with their expert Palliative Care. By Helen enrolling in hospice, Sandra could qualify for free bereavement counseling, as an included benefit.

On Monday evening, I visited Helen. Again I tried to change her mind. Again, I failed. I found no consolation in the fact that hospice admitted her, implying they also decided to go along with her plan. There was no getting around three facts: **1)** The woman I saw six days ago was NOT terminally ill; **2)** her broken arm could have healed; and, **3)** she might have returned to her previous level of reasonably good functioning.

These thoughts made me wonder: Did my actions lead Helen to a *tipping point* to decide to die?

> I had explained the "ironclad strategy" to many other patients. It provided needed solace to relieve their time urgency to die. No longer did they fear losing sufficient mental and physical ability to determine when living would become unbearable. It thus prevented premature dying. Helen stated her skepticism about current laws, which politicians can change. Was this the reason she was dying now? *Perhaps.* Yet she did not suffer from a progressive debilitating disease.

> I offered Helen assurance that her dying would be comfortable. I explained how to use the components of the Thirst Reduction Aid Kit that I delivered. Was Helen dying now because she was convinced her dying would be peaceful? *Probably.* She previously told her daughter she was determined to die by fasting—with or without her daughter's help.

> Referring Helen to hospice was my idea. I timed my request so Helen would have fasted a few days. Had I referred her too early for hospice to accept her, would Helen be dying now? *Maybe.* Again, she said she was determined to die, with or without help.

> Was there any action I omitted that could have influenced Helen to postpone her decision to die now? Not that I could think of, and I tried.

Perhaps... Probably... Maybe... Words of ambiguity. In my mind, they hung in stark contrast to the absolute irreversibility of death.

My only solace was it still was not too late. Helen could still change her mind. I would visit again.

Helen had fasted for five days.[110] I was surprised at how well she looked, thought, and talked. Yet she seemed agitated. Most patients undergoing medical dehydration do not suffer from an agitated delirium. The few who do, had been taking narcotics. Helen's thinking was clear, although I guessed she was holding something back when I asked if anything was bothering her. Sandra motioned me into the next room, to talk in private. She told me what happened.

Her son Richard had called. His intention was to deliver a sweet goodbye. Instead, old wounds reopened. Sandra filled me in about a huge family fight that had occurred two years ago. It

---

[110] Readers should not assume all patients have five days to change their minds; some have irreversible changes in fewer than five days while others can change their minds and reverse their organ damage after more days.

ended with Helen and Richard each accusing the other of walking out. They had not spoken since. The phone call earlier today resembled their previous shouting matches except that Helen did not have enough energy to raise her voice. Sadly, rather than forgiveness, each argued that the other should be the one offering an apology. Who hung up on whom? What difference did it make? The point is, their conversation ended without reconciliation.

Richard was not my patient so I felt it was more appropriate to first tell Sandra that he could call me anytime, than to call him myself. Since he just had a terrible argument with his mother, it might be best if he picked the time. If he did not call in a couple of days, depending on Helen's condition, I would call him. Meanwhile, I told Helen she was approaching the point of no return. Soon, she could no longer change her mind to resume eating and drinking and expect to return to normal functioning: damage to her organs would become irreversible.

Driving home, I felt sad about Helen and Richard. One reason I entered the end-of-life field was because much healing can take place in family therapy sessions when all know this might their last chance to say, "I love you," "I'm sorry," "I forgive you," or resolve a conflict. After such sessions, survivors' lives often change dramatically… and forever. Too bad Richard was still a thousand miles away. I hoped he would call, even though I was not sure if I could help.

It took a long time to fall asleep that night. I questioned myself again regarding how active my role had been to facilitate Helen's choice to die now. The words *perhaps, probably* and *maybe* were quickly being replaced by certainties: She *would* pass the point of no return. Then she *would* lose consciousness. In several days, she *would certainly die*. Was this morally right or morally wrong? The question remained unanswered as I finally fell asleep.

The next morning, I woke up with a logical argument already formulated in my mind:

Knowledge empowers. It sets people free. If you give people knowledge, they must be free to use it the way they see fit, and when. You cannot control how or when they use the knowledge you give them. In the specific case of strategic end-of-life planning, knowledge must be given when the person is still mentally competent. In many cases, this means the patient will not (yet) be terminally ill. It is not reasonable to withhold the knowledge until the patient is terminally ill because by then, many patients will no longer be mentally competent. Thus, imparting knowledge to a non-terminally ill person such as, "It is legal and peaceful to die by medical dehydration," must inevitably allow the non-terminally ill person the freedom to die even though s/he is not (yet) terminally ill. Thus, what I did to facilitate the impending death of Helen was morally neutral. I am responsible only for imparting the knowledge at a time when she could understand it. Once I had given this knowledge, I had neither the power nor the right to restrict her freedom from using it.

This logical conclusion did not assuage my feelings even though it seemed better than my three previous rationalizations. The first was clinical: emotional or psychiatric suicides are usually impulsive; people almost never commit suicide by fasting. The second was one of universal knowledge: is there anyone who doesn't know that you will die if you stop eating and drinking? The third was a utilitarian calculus about which I *felt* sure even though there is no data to prove it. Education about the option, Voluntary Refusal of Food and Fluid has two effects: **A)** It can *prevent premature*, violent, and criminal (mercy killing) deaths; and **B)** It can provide a tipping point so that previously ambivalent non-terminally ill patients will use this "legal peaceful option" to *hasten death*. I believe the number of patients in (**A**) exceeds the number in (**B**). —A small consolation for me, as one who deeply believes *every life* is precious and sacred.

I still felt unsettled about this moral conundrum. Like two people who argue, dig their heels in, and ultimately agree to disagree, I felt I had to resign myself to accept this final thought: I must be humble enough to accept that Helen's decision about timing is up to her, not to me. I cannot judge her actions and I do not know what is best for her. Later, I called this view, the *agnostic approach*, but I still wondered if it was just my *cop out*. My mind kept on returning to alternatives... I wondered: should I rethink the criteria for helping patients complete these forms? If I did require patients be terminally ill, then many would not be competent. Around and around I went. I was trying to let my mind settle on accepting the irresolvable...

And then Richard called. He blamed me for my lack of professionalism. He blamed me for not calling him sooner. And he blamed me for not insisting that his mother talk to me about their problematic relationship during my initial interview. He was loud and harsh. It went on for a full hour. The phone burned my ear. During it all, I remained non-defensive. I just let him rant.

Near the end of the hour, Richard softened. He thanked me for listening and asked me for my advice. I recommended he write a letter to his mother from his heart. I suggested he share only his best feelings for her and leave out his hurts. He asked, "What do I do with my anger?" I encouraged him to discharge his anger with his therapist so he could leave it out of his letter. He said this would be hard. I noted how angry he was at me at the beginning of our call, an hour ago, but now he was thinking quite constructively. I suggested he ask someone who could be objective to read his letter before he sent it, just to be sure that no unrecognized vestiges of anger remained. He said he would try. I invited him to call me again.

The next day, when I arrived at Helen's home, Sandra shared the good news. Richard had e-mailed her a wonderful letter to read to their mother. Then Sandra called Richard and held the phone near Helen. As weak as she was, she could say some loving words of forgiveness. Sandra was delighted; she never imagined her mother and brother would resolve their conflict. (For reasons of confidentiality, I did not tell Sandra that I had spoken with Richard by phone.)

The next day, Sandra told me Richard had called his mother again. By then, Helen was too weak to talk, but she could still gesture. As Richard talked on the phone, Sandra told him when Helen smiled and when she raised her thumb. Both were sure Helen heard Richard's final, loving goodbye.

Helen died later that afternoon. Her transition was peaceful. Sandra and Richard were at peace, too, with the way their mother died, with her timing for when to die, and with the satisfaction that a difficult relationship had reconciled—just in time.

As I mulled over Helen's dying, I came to this conclusion: As processes, dying and healing do not have clear points of beginning. For the transition to be peaceful for the patient and for her loved ones, patients must make peace with themselves and their loved ones. For Helen, the processes may have begun with her confronting her mortality and her awareness of her increasing dependency. She was thus able to heal her relationship with Sandra and to relate to her in a loving and appreciative way for the first time in their lives.

Because of the deep rift between Helen and her son, however, the peacefulness afforded by five days of fasting was not sufficient to quell Helen's anger. At that point, reconciliation was still not possible. By the ninth day of fasting, however, Helen was peaceful enough. By then, she was able to listen and to receive her son's love and forgiveness. Similarly, Richard knew it would not be long before his mother died. He was highly motivated to attempt to be more loving. Richard had also done his work, included his phone call with me and writing the letter.

While it is unusual for reconciliation to be possible only after so many days of fasting, this insight gave me the moral solace I had been searching for: it allowed me to feel at peace. I could conclude that Helen's choice for a "timely" transition was right. Let me explain.

If Helen had an opportunity to die more quickly, say by ingesting a lethal dose of pills prescribed by a physician (which is legal in the States of Oregon, Washington and Montana), then Richard and she would not have had the opportunity to reconcile: she would have died *too soon*. On the other hand, if my arguments successfully persuaded Helen to wait until she had major complications from breaking a hip, or a major stroke, or severe dementia, then her lack of mental clarity would have prevented her from reconciling with Richard. In these or other scenarios, she would have died *too late*. Helen's peaceful fasting made reconciliation possible. For her personality and situation, her own choice of what was "timely" turned out "just right."

I recalled Helen's third reason to explain why she wanted to die now. She felt her life was finished and she was at peace. Perhaps even she did not anticipate what was most important: Beyond dying with dignity, not trusting politicians, and wanting relief from worrying about future suffering and loss of functioning—I believe Helen discovered and thus taught me, that...

When it comes to putting a value on the length versus the quality of one's life,

> *It matters less how long your own heart can stay warm...*
> *Than how long it takes you to warm the hearts of others.*

More Success Stories: Our Fathers. . . Ourselves

Dying people can teach us about living as well as about dying. But we have to be willing to be with them and be open to learn. Between April 2007 and April 2008, three important figures in my life died: my step-father Harry, my father-in-law Guy, and my Uncle Murray. I shared my experiences with my step-mother, my wife's family, and my cousin. First, to honor my father, here is a brief account of his death: Irving Terman died in 1981 after he suffered through three brain operations for a tumor of the lining of the brain (meningioma). Although benign, this tumor recurred twice and continued to grow. My father and I never talked about dying, although he did share his concept of death with me. His illness was characterized by a long and gradual decline and intermittent, mild suffering. When he died, we were all relieved that he was at peace, but I was 3000 miles away. Perhaps one reason that I am so drawn to help people attain *timely, peaceful transitions* is because I was not with him when he died.

H arry, **my step-father**, outlived one after another of the several physicians who provided his medical care. He increasingly wanted to talk to me about the process of dying. He stated few others were willing so he appreciated the opportunity I gave him.

Some of Harry's inquiries were philosophical; others were practical. He wanted to know what options were possible when "his time" came. I shared that if he chose to refuse all food and fluid, dying by dehydration is a peaceful way to die. Harry and I developed a clear understanding. It is summed up by how he could answer two carefully posed, future questions:

A) Do you want treatment for your dry mouth?, or
B) Do you want something to drink?

Asking both questions increases reliability. Harry's answers had to be consistent. He understood "something to drink" would prolong the process of his dying and might increase his suffering. In contrast, agents from a Thirst Reduction Aid Kit would decrease his symptoms of dry mouth during **Natural Dying** but not prolong his dying. I explained the variety of available agents: swabs, drops, sprays, gels, and mouth washes and why they were effective. Some were refreshing; others, soothing. He could try as many as he liked and use them as often as he liked. If he wished, he could change his mind and drink something to postpone his dying.

In April, 2007, the time had come for me to ask these questions, but first I asked him if he wanted one more shot at curative therapy. This is how I put it: "Shall we drive down to Sloan Kettering to see if their experts have anything new to treat your cancer?"

Harry replied, "No. I'm writing the last chapter of my life." After WWII, Harry became a fine printer. His profession made this metaphor apt.

Next I asked, "Is your mouth dry?" He replied, "Yes."

When I asked the two questions that we had previously discussed, his answers were clear. Both times, he said: "Just reduce the dryness."

This conversation took place on Wednesday morning. On Saturday morning, his last breath was not unlike any other breath, except it was not followed by another. The hospice nurse said that his dying process was among the most peaceful she had ever seen.

During his life, Harry taught me many things. As he died, he taught me this: it is possible to stick to the ultimate existential decision based on a discussion held months before.

Parkinson's disease had plagued **my wife's father Guy** for almost thirty years. By 2006, his neurologist considered his disease "end-stage" so he referred him to hospice. By then, Guy had already agreed to a DNAR order (do not attempt resuscitation) and to forgo antibiotics, should a pneumonia recur. I was not present when Guy made those decisions. I chose to remain professionally distant for two reasons. First, I did not want to influence Guy's end-of-life decisions. Second, I considered myself a member of the family rather than another medical consultant; I realized trying to be both could be problematic.

For years, Guy's physical limitations made it necessary for another person to manually assist his oral feeding and drinking. In May, 2007, he did two things he never did before: Instead of sucking in liquid, he bit down on the straw. Instead of swallowing, he left partially chewed food in his mouth. Members of the family asked me: Was Guy trying to tell us something? What would I advise? At this point, it seemed reasonable—for Guy's benefit—to share my experience.

While Guy and I never had a detailed conversation similar to those I had with Harry, he did share his general values about living: If his quality of life deteriorated to such an extent that he was left with no pleasure or meaning, he would not want to endure further burdens to prolong his existence. By May, 2007, Guy's hospice care had been extended two times. His mind was no longer clear enough to appreciate the consequence of asking his caregivers to aggressively encourage him to eat and drink. He could not appreciate that it would prolong the process of his dying and risk an increase of his suffering. It was too late to obtain his informed consent to refuse *Manual Assistance with Oral Feeding and Drinking*. Instead I talked to Guy's primary and first alternate proxies, whom he had authorized to make his medical decisions. They knew his values and preferences so they could exercise "Substituted Judgment." They agreed with the decision to direct Guy's caregivers to stop *Manual Assistance with Oral Feeding and Drinking*. Although "Substituted Judgment" sufficed for decision-making, we all took additional solace that this course of action was also consistent with Guy's "Best Interest," given his vastly deteriorated physical and mental condition, and chronic back pain.

Two days after the fast began, Guy mumbled, "I want something to drink." Several of Guy's grandchildren were at his bedside and one said, "If he wants something to drink, why not give him some? It's cruel not to." She did not realize that the consequences of drinking could be to increase and prolong his suffering. But this time of stress was not appropriate for education.

Reaching a compromise turned out to be easy, however. I suggested that Guy's proxy instruct his caregivers to offer Guy a *little* fluid using a teaspoon; *wait*, and then ask if he wanted more. Guy wanted so little fluid that it did not significantly prolong his dying. As things calmed down, I explained why a *timely, peaceful transition* depended not giving him too much fluid.

The suggestion to offer Guy a little and then wait sprang from an experiment my colleague, Ronald B. Miller, MD, told me about. Sheep had surgery to temporarily divert the contents of their esophagus to outside the body. The sheep could not absorb what they ate or drank. When the sheep were offered water, they drank only moderate quantities before they stopped. Evidently, the amount drunk was determined by their eyes and brains, not metabolic feedback from their bodies as their intake was insufficient to restore a normal state. Perhaps something similar occurs in dying patients who may urgently ask to eat or drink, but imbibe little.

Several days passed—more than expected for his transition. I realized that Guy's dying was being prolonged by his cardiac pacemaker. His proxy asked the hospice nurse if she could turn it down, or off. She deferred to the hospice medical director, but this doctor never called back—after several requests through the nurse. The family was not only impatient; they were distressed since Guy's moaning increased unless he received higher and higher doses of opioids. Ultimately I called the cardiologist who initially referred Guy for the intra-cardiac device to be surgically implanted. He was initially resistant and argued that the device would ultimately not prevent his death. I then presented my theory: the pacemaker was prolonging the process of dying by artificially providing sufficient cardiac output to oxygenate his brain. Meanwhile, his discomfort was increasing as judged by his need for higher doses of narcotics. These remarks convinced the cardiologist as he then wrote an order for a technician to make a home visit to deactivate the pacemaker. After this visit, Guy's heart rate dropped from 70 to less than 40. Two days later, Guy finally had a peaceful transition.

Perspectives on Intra-Cardiac Devices

Three million people currently have surgically implanted intra-cardiac devices. A recent survey asked members of the Heart Rhythm Society if they would "Turn off [a device] because of patient's right to refuse therapy" if the patient asking was terminally ill and suffering from pain due to cancer. Of the medical professionals who responded, 98% would comply IF the device was a *defibrillator*; 87% would comply if the device was a *pacemaker* that the patient was NOT currently dependent upon, but only 58% would comply if the patient's heart DID depend on the *pacemaker currently functioning* (so that death was expected soon after complying).[111]

Strategies: The principle embraced by the 1990 U S Supreme Court *in Cruzan*—"Any competent adult can refuse any medical treatment"—did NOT specify any "conditions" to honor this patient's right. Refusing treatment did NOT depend on its physiological functioning, if the treatment could be considered "inside" the body, or if current functioning was needed to preserve the patient's life. In fact, every time this right was stated, it included the possibility it *might* lead to the patient's earlier death. It is understandable why clinicians might hesitate,

---

[111] Kapa S, Mueller PS, Hayes DL, Asirvatham SJ. Perspectives on withdrawing pacemaker and implantable cardioverter-defibrillator therapies at end of life: results of a survey of medical and legal professionals and patients. *Mayo Clin Proc.* 2010 Nov;85(11):981-90. Epub 2010 Sep 15. doi:10.4065/mcp.2010.0431.

however. They are being asked to act on a device that seems totally within the body after which act the patient's death soon occurs. Yet the act is only to withdraw a treatment for which the patient initially had to give his/her informed consent. It does NOT make ethical sense to deny the patient the right to withdraw consent for continuing treatment. The patient did not lose his/her right because the device "seems" totally within the body. Actually, the patient MUST consent to replace batteries from outside the body, which is necessary from time to time—and then, physicians do honor their refusals. Why? Because even the minor procedure to replace an electric battery would be considered legal battery without obtaining consent. Also, bioethicists make NO distinction between refusing to start, and asking to stop life-sustaining treatment.

The above considerations are included in the **Natural Dying Physician's Orders**, in the second line of Order #1 (under "Do Not Attempt to Resuscitate"): "Discontinue and do not restart cardiac pacemakers, defibrillators, or Left Ventricular Assist Devices." (This wording was suggested by Cardiologist, Lofty Basta, MD.) The **Natural Dying Agreement** adds these *patient* clarifications in anticipation of commonly expressed concerns: "I want my physician to disregard the fact that the device currently functions totally within my body. I want my physician also to disregard the clinical impression that its functioning currently seems necessary to prolong my existence—even if it seems likely that deactivating the device may lead to **Natural Dying** in a matter of minutes because of my underlying diseased heart."

Uncle **Murray**: I was not present at his bedside in April 2008, but I kept in close telephone contact with him through my cousin, Bonnie, his daughter. Uncle Murray always tried to see life in a positive way. Although legally blind, he was aware of the movement of figures dancing to music he could hear. He remarked to his caregiver during a recent activity, "This is such a lively place. There's always something exciting going on here." But after he fell off the couch and broke his hip, he had so much pain that he had to be transferred to a hospital. In contrast to the upbeat ambience at the assisting living facility, the hospital must have seemed socially sterile. Murray's pain and frustration finally drained his lifelong positive energy. The physical therapists could not get him out of bed to cooperate with his physical therapy exercises. Then one day, he refused all food and fluid.

Several days later, Uncle Murray died in the arms of my cousin.

Here is how my cousin described the experience: "He just stopped breathing. It was so peaceful. I cannot imagine how it could have been more peaceful. I can only wish that when it's my time to go, it will be as peaceful for me as it was for my father. And... previously... I must admit... I had a deep fear of dying. Now after being with my father as he died, I no longer have that fear. I know I can die this way too. So I am no longer afraid."

My Father's Death

By Susan M. Wolf [112]

"**M**y father's death forced me to rethink all I had written over a period of two decades opposing legalization of physician-assisted suicide and euthanasia....

"My father was diagnosed with a metastatic head and neck cancer in 2002.... For five years he did well. Things changed in June of 2007. The last CyberKnife treatment was billed as the worst, with significant pain likely to follow. Sure enough, ten days later, my father's pain on swallowing became severe. He began losing weight—a lot of it. He weakened. He fell twice in his apartment.... The head and neck surgeon who had found the primary tumor in 2002 [took] one look at my father and order[ed] a gastrostomy tube to deliver nutrition.... The medical picture was becoming worse. A surgical procedure revealed cancer in the liver. Pulmonology added pneumonia to the roster of lung ailments.... But **no physician was putting the whole picture together**....

"Then one morning he said he wanted to stop. No more tube feeding. No one was prepared for this switch from [his] lifetime of 'spare no effort.' He told me he feared he was now a terrible burden. I protested, knowing that I would willingly bear the 'burden' of his illness. I suspect that what others said was more powerful, though. I was later told that **the doctor urged him not to stop, warning that he would suffer a painful death, that morphine would be required to control the discomfort, and that my father would lose consciousness before the day was out**. Instead of assuring my father that health professionals know how to maintain comfort after termination of artificial nutrition and hydration, **my father was scared away from this option. Weeks later, my father would wish aloud that he had carried through with this decision**....

"Hospital personnel announced that it was time for my father... to transfer to a rehabilitation facility.... I alerted a member of the palliative care team that **my father had evidently been misinformed** at the prior hospital about the consequences of stopping artificial nutrition and hydration. I urged [the Palliative Care physician] to find a time to reassure him that he indeed had choices, could refuse treatments if he wanted to, and could be confident that his comfort would be maintained.... His values and his subjective experience—whether he wanted more interventions or had reached his limit—were key.

---

[112] Wolf, SM. (2008). Confronting Physician-Assisted Suicide and Euthanasia: My Father's Death. *Hastings Center Report 38(5)*: 23-26. Professor Susan M. Wolf is a leader in the field of end-of-life philosophy and law at the University of Minnesota. Excerpted with permission from the author and publisher. Bold font was added to emphasize the points on which I subsequently comment.

"Soon my father was back in the ICU.... Tube feeding was so uncomfortable that it was administered slowly through the night. Pain medication was a constant.... He was briefly transferred to the pulmonary care unit... [for] lung mucus and secretions, as well as pneumonia.... His nurse was not answering his calls, and his immobility left him at her mercy.... I saw this tough-as-nails litigator reduced to fearful dependence.

"A new problem. My father had developed a massive bleed. Nursing had found him in a pool of his own blood, lying among the clots. The gastroenterologists took him in for a procedure, spending hours trying to find the source of the bleed. They never found it....

"He waited until we gathered at his bedside. His speech was halting now, but his determination obvious. 'Tell me my choices.'... 'That's what I want. To terminate.' He made it clear he wanted to stop tube feeding and IV hydration.... It was then that he uttered three words that shook me. '**Can we accelerate?**' It seemed he was asking for more—a fast death, by assisted suicide or euthanasia.... **My father was beyond assisted suicide by swallowing prescribed lethal medication, as he couldn't swallow anything**.

"In some ways, it would have been psychologically easier, or at least faster, to bring the ordeal we all were experiencing to a quick end.... But instead I stayed, redoubling my attention to him. I stroked his thick white hair. **He and I reminisced.** He was always a great raconteur. We talked and talked over the next days. **The decision to stop tube feeding actually seemed to lighten his load**. A decision. In a way, it was a relief.

"He was out of the ICU now, in a hospital room awaiting transfer to hospice. As he began to doze more and talk less, we watched carefully for the slightest sign of discomfort. We had promised we would assure his comfort....

"The last time I saw my father, he was motionless. His eyes were closed. He had stopped speaking. He appeared unresponsive. **His breathing was quieter, rasps gone with dehydration**. I struggled, remembering the rabbi's caution that the ones we love most may need permission to leave us, to die. 'I know you may have to leave'....

"He died not long after.

"I would not want to bear the burden of having 'accelerated,' of causing his death by euthanasia or assisted suicide; this is hard enough. My father's death made me rethink my objections to legalizing assisted suicide and euthanasia, but in the end it left me at ease with what I've written. Staying, keeping vigil, fighting to secure a comfortable death, stroking his hair, standing guard as death approached was my duty. It was the final ripening of my love. We both changed, even closer at the end."

Comments

Professor Susan Wolf's memoir exemplifies some best and some worst experiences in dying.

I was disheartened that Susan's father received misinformation that scared him from making an earlier decision to refuse food and fluid. The doctor was wrong: fasting is not so painful that he would need narcotics to make him unconscious within a day. For many patients, fasting increases their level of comfort. But he might have lost consciousness within a few days. Receiving correct and timely information could have saved him intense suffering as he endured the burdens of additional medical complications, pain, and surgery. Certainly, it can feel devastating to accept any form of treatment that will effectively end a person's conscious life. For a daughter, it means the end of intense sharing by communicating. On behalf of her father, since most of us believe *we are our thoughts*, when our thoughts are gone... then what has made us unique persons no longer exists. Prolonging the dying process for Susan's father did have a significant and not to be underestimated positive result: the two were able to enjoy a few more days of talking and reminiscing. Still, we do not know if Susan's father would have consented to this process if he had known how much additional suffering he would have had to endure. Perhaps whatever they shared could have been done earlier, without additional suffering. Another option could also have been considered: *Respite Sedation*. First the patient receives anesthesia for total relief of suffering; after a few days, the dose of sedatives is lowered or discontinued, to see if the patient's suffering is no longer unbearable so that conscious life can again resume. (See "**PNDL**," TOPIC 5 on how to ask for and consent to *Respite Sedation*.)

Timely and correct information could have had another benefit in addition to allowing Susan's father to experience a peaceful transition. Timely medical dehydration would have probably prevented increased suffering and his becoming so desperate that he felt compelled to pose the three-word question that shook Susan at such a deep moral level. By the time he asked, "**Can we accelerate?**" From a clinical perspective, he no longer was a candidate for Physician-Assisted Dying since by then, he could no longer swallow. Euthanasia (administration of lethal medication by the hand of another) is absolutely illegal. Thus, his only option for relief of pain was *Palliative Sedation*. Question: Why was this option not offered earlier?

"**PNDL**" includes some *questions* for patients to ponder and discuss with their physician as they discuss and give informed consent for *Palliative Sedation*. The trade-off, loss of consciousness and ability to interact socially, is something one can think about in advance.

Fortunately, Susan's father finally found relief after he refused all food and fluid, and his physicians controlled his suffering after he had the opportunity for a final loving interaction and heartfelt goodbye.

Myself: We all must die someday, but few people like to think about it all of the time.[113] Still, it is worthwhile to spend a bit of time contemplating how we would like to die. Many think the best way is the quickest, as often happens from a heart attack or stroke or accident. They could be right, but consider this: Dying suddenly allows us no opportunity to exchange healing goodbyes. At the other extreme is the slow deterioration of the brain as one's ability to think declines from Alzheimer's or another disease that causes dementia. About this slow way to die I quote Thomas DeBaggio from his first book, **Losing My Mind: An Intimate Look at Life with Alzheimer's** (cited in footnote 62, page 47):

> **"I** see the signs of verbal atrophy every day. Cut my legs off but don't take away my ability to think, dream, and write. It is too late to reconstruct the dreams of my youth or create a new life." Thomas also wrote, "Getting used to the idea of dying is difficult, emotionally and physically, but what awaits me is losing the idea of dying and that is incomprehensible and at the same time, it may be liberating."

Thomas DeBaggio thus shared his greatest fears: fear of losing his life, and fear of losing his ability to comprehend this loss. At some level, I believe Thomas felt that, when he did lose "the idea of dying," he will have also lost his ability to say goodbye. The consequence is the loss of ability to complete the most important area of our lives—our relationships.

For me personally, the best way to die includes having the ability and time to share treasured memories and to exchange healing goodbyes with the people I love—when I still know who they are... when I still know who I am.

I also hope to have the good fortune to have time to finish my last creative projects. In this respect, I can relate to the artist in O. Henry's story who painted the "last leaf" on the wall. While not an artistic masterpiece, his painting made a big impact on Johnsy's attitude, extended her life, and made it possible for her to dream again about painting the Bay of Naples.

We need dreams to realize we are alive
As much as we live to realize our dreams.

We are lucky if we have time to accomplish our dreams.
We are wise to seize opportunities to say our goodbyes.

---

[113] A personal note: I rarely contemplate my own death as I write about the process of dying. Instead, I concentrate on solving a puzzle. In general, I ask the question, How can people control what happens to them after they no longer can speak for themselves? I thus use a common psychological defense mechanism—compartmentalization—to keep my emotions at bay and go on with my writing. Yet there are times (like the present moment), when I must reflect inwardly and that does lead to deep feelings.

Among life's greatest experiences is the rewarding feeling that comes from completing a life's ambition. Painting and writing are two ways; there are countless others. One is the feeling of completion when we have said what we need to say to those we love, when we have spoken from our hearts, when we have given and received forgiveness. That is what it means to exchange healing goodbyes. So perhaps the best way to die is when we have used the gifts of thinking and feeling to communicate what most needs to be said.

We don't even need words to communicate. "Listen" to how Susan and her father said goodbye:

I took his hand. I told him I loved him. I stroked his hair, still full and silvered. I spoke to him from the heart, words that remain between him and me. Then I heard myself say, 'If I am a good mother, it's because you were a great father.' And to my surprise, he moved his jaw. Not his lips or his mouth. But he opened his jaw three times. It was our signal, the one we'd worked out in the ICU. Three means 'I-love-you.'"

Of Life and Leaves

Leaves are sweet green in their prime.
As their lives close, they become brittle.
Yet brilliant Auburns delight before they fall.

We too become brittle beyond our prime.
Yet our paths can strive for inner peace
And to heal... by exchanging goodbyes.

By appreciating the meaning of our lives, and
By sharing with those who will remember us,
We too can delight before our fall.

The "Plan Now, Die Later—Ironclad Strategy"

Introduction

When it eventually comes, everyone prefers death not to be preceded by prior suffering. Ideally it should happen suddenly, while sleeping comfortably at home. Until then, everyone spends great effort trying to control their lives to maximize pleasure and to minimize pain. Frankly, this book's goal is similar: to control dying or at least to minimize how long and how intense we will suffer. The challenge is greater than for any other chapter of our lives. We must PLAN now since then almost two-thirds of us may not be able to speak for ourselves. What we may want can be difficult to get since others may challenge our desires. (See **Stories of Success and Compassion**, called "**Stories**" for short—the previous section of this book.) We need an *effective strategy* to attain this goal for our last chapter of life: a *timely, peaceful transition*. "Timely" means neither *premature* (too soon) nor *prolonged* (too long); *peaceful* strives to minimize physical discomfort for patients and emotional discomfort for patients and loved ones.

The top two fears about dying are unbearable pain and suffering, and lingering for years in Advanced Dementia. Unfortunately, there is reason to fear the two will be combined. This book explains why. Also, our loved ones may find themselves in conflict, suffering stress and anxiety as we die and long-term guilt after—if they are not sure what we wanted. Expressing our *Known Wishes* in a Living Will can reduce or eliminate our suffering and be a gift for others.

Advance Care Planning is the process of planning ahead. To prevent both fears, our plan must be *effective*. Most people are not informed that there are vast differences among Advance Directives/Living Wills. Many, even popular ones, are NOT likely to be effective; but patients and families often will not realize this sad fact until it is too late. Why not effective? Some reasons are historical. Living Wills rarely cover dementia because when State legislators began passing laws to establish Living Wills in the 1970s, only one-tenth as many patients suffered from dementia as do today. Today, those planning in their fifties can expect to see another three-fold increase in dementia. That's a 30-fold increase over the span of one lifetime! By 2050, some "joke" that there will be only two kinds of people: those who suffer from dementia and those who help to care for someone who suffers from dementia. Another reason: as designed, the forms tread lightly on the *perceived (not real) conflict* with religious beliefs. Of course, unless people are informed, they are naturally attracted to "short and simple" forms.

Now for the good news: You have two basic rights. They provide the basis for attaining the goal of a *timely, peaceful transition*. Following this book's recommendations makes creating an effective set of Advance Care Planning forms relatively easy. In fact, the key decision-making tool is illustrated and readable at the third grade level. This book can guide you through the more legalistic steps; help is also available. Following the recommended steps, including how to select an individual to be your designated proxy/agent, can make you feel confident *now* that for the final chapter of your life, others *will* honor your end-of-life *Known Wishes*.

1: Your Two "Rights"[1]

Only you can decide what happens to your body. No one has the right to intrude on your body without your permission. Almost a hundred years ago, Justice Benjamin Cardozo ruled, "Every human being of adult years and sound mind has a right to determine what shall be done with his own body."[2] When doctors offer you medical tests and treatments to try to improve your health, they must inform you about the potential risks of causing harm as well as benefits, and let you choose. They must ask for your permission before they "touch" your body. This is called **informed consent**. Your first right provided the basis for a famous 1990 U S Supreme Court case, about Nancy Beth Cruzan. In this case, the Court ruled that **any competent adult can refuse any medical treatment**, even if your continued living depended on that treatment.

Your second right was established by federal and state laws. You can decide NOW what happens to your body **years in advance**. This right is embodied in a 1990 federal law, the *Patient Self-Determination Act*. In turn, this stimulated all States to enact laws for this right.

To put these rights together: If your mind has decisional capacity to make end-of-life decisions, you have the right to refuse or consent to future treatment; that is to do Advance Care Planning. How do you do that? You imagine a future condition and express what treatment you DO, or do NOT want. You write down your wishes in a form called a **Living Will**. You sign this form in front of two *qualified* witnesses or a notary so it is legally valid. You can also authorize another person to make medical decisions for you if you are not able to speak for yourself. Your **proxy** (**agent**) can also make sure others honor your prior wishes. The form to name a proxy/agent is called a **Proxy Directive** or **Durable Power of Attorney for Health Care**.

To be effective, details are all-important. For some kinds of choices, expressing a clear choice is relatively easy. Example: "If my doctors say I will never again be conscious, then I would not want treatment via a breathing machine or tube feeding." To express your wishes about NOT lingering for years in Advanced Dementia—when you may suffer from *unrecognized* and untreated pain and suffering—is, however, far more challenging. Here are some reasons:

1. The course of the disease varies too much among patients for professionals to reach a consensus of where to draw the "sharp line" between the middle and advanced stages.

2. People have different feelings about what specific *symptoms, losses of function, unwanted behaviors,* and *conflicts with lifelong values* they would have to endure for them to then say, "I no longer want any treatment that would prolong my dying."

3. To avoid prolonged dying, the only "solution" I know is controversial. (It should not be.) To overcome common challenges, you must plan in advance. To strive to this goal, the book explains exactly how to set up the **Plan Now, Die Later—Ironclad Strategy**.

---

[1] This print version of the combined book has page numbers that are 100 greater than in the separate book.
[2] Schloendorff v. Society of New York Hospital, 1914, at 93

The tools in this book make this otherwise formidable task relatively easy. Sorting **My Way Cards** (or *Natural Dying Living Will Cards*, for religious observers) is an interactive way to learn about your future condition and to express your wishes in a personalized form: your **Natural Dying—Living Will**. This form *comprehensively* expresses your *specific wishes* in a *clear and convincing way* so your future physicians and decision-makers will know WHAT you DO or do NOT want... and WHEN. Recommended: Combine this Living Will with other forms that employ strategies based on the way medicine is practiced in the context of health law.[3]

Early Living Wills were not very helpful. In hindsight we can now appreciate there were two extremes. One was too general. It said, "**IF** my condition is hopeless, **THEN** I want no heroics." These Living Wills had the correct "If _____ , **Then**_____ ." format, but physicians often could not interpret such vague statements. The other extreme was too specific. One "Medical Directive" presented six specific conditions ("situations") for Advance Care Planners to choose or to forgo twelve interventions (treatments). In theory, this form might be "too specific" if in the future, your specific diagnosis and specific treatment options are not included among the seventy-two "boxed" choices. In practice, the form was rarely completed because this task was so formidable. Jack Freer, MD, internist and bioethicist, wrote: "I tried to use Emanuels' Medical Directive[4] for two years, right after it came out. In those days, New York was a dark and dangerous place. Its highest court had recently ruled *in O'Connor* that, in order to forgo life-sustaining treatment, one must provide *clear and convincing* evidence the patient had explicitly refused the precise treatment for the precise condition in question. This Medical Directive seemed to fit the bill perfectly. I gave the form to a number of patients. Almost all got *decision-fatigue*. The only patient I know who completed the entire form was a retired philosophy professor. He also happened to suffer from Obsessive Compulsive Disease."

More than twenty years later, these two problems—too vague or too specific—still plague many widely used forms. You can download almost any State form for free.[5] Realize however: "State forms are not very specific, and you may increase the chance of a physician following your wishes if you provide more detailed instructions."[6]

Most other Advance Care Planning forms leave out two essential Advance Care Planning components for which this book emphatically recommends specific strategic forms:

---

[3] See "Acknowledgments" where I thank three health care attorneys, and the General Disclaimer (prior to Ch.1.). This book does not offer individuals legal or medical advice. For additional help and more information about the forms, contact the non-profit organization, **Caring Advocates** at www.CaringAdvocates.org or 1 800 647 3223.

[4] Emanuel LL, Emanuel EJ. The Medical Directive: A new Comprehensive Advance Care Document. *JAMA* 1989;261(22), 3288-93.

[5] For free forms: **Caring Connections** at www.caringinfo.org/i4a/pages/index.cfm?pageid=3289. **Compassion and Choices**: www.community.compassionandchoices.org/page.aspx?pid=378&nccsm=15&__nccscid= 14&__nccsct=Advance+Directives. State forms list the requirements for "qualifying witnesses" and for "proxies."

[6] Wellness Worksheet 108. Advance Medical Directives. Insel/Roth, *Core Concepts in Health,* Tenth Edition © 2006 The McGraw-Hill Companies, Inc.

1. To prevent **unbearable pain and suffering that cannot otherwise be relieved**: a consent form for relief by sedation to unconsciousness (*Palliative Sedation*); and,

2. To avoid **lingering in Advanced Dementia** based on meeting one's selected criteria: forms that clearly express this choice: to refuse help by hand or spoon feeding (that is, to cease *Manual Assistance with Oral Feeding and Drinking*).

Perspective: Advance Care Planning is more important today than ever. The improved science of medicine helps people survive acute infections, heart disease and cancer. The result: people live long enough to die of chronic diseases such as Alzheimer's and related dementias. Many die for *years* instead of for *days*. For much of this time they cannot make medical decisions. Less well-known: their personal suffering may be great. Why? Because dementia patients cannot tell others they hurt. Hence their doctors may not recognize they have pain. The result: their pain and suffering go untreated or under-treated. Recently published evidence revealed that for patients in similar conditions, demented patients may receive only about one-third as much pain medication as do non-demented patients; for example, a broken hip. Worse: some patients are treated with psychiatric drugs for their "odd" behavior that may make them feel worse. An additional motivation for effective Advance Care Planning comes from this worry: a demented patient may become a huge burden to the very people s/he loves most—by draining their emotional, financial, and physical resources. Sadly, the patient may not be able to recognize his/her loved ones, let alone appreciate the huge sacrifices they are making.

An important but often overlooked point: If you know that you have an *effective* plan in place, it can lead you to change your view of yourself—from an "involuntary, desperate sufferer" to a "willing survivor in search of more meaning to exist." This is one of life's greatest ironies:

Knowing you can control when you will die, can —and often does—lead to choosing to live longer.

Suppose someone is worried about being forced to endure treatment that will likely lead to a prolonged, painful, and burdensome dying in Advanced Dementia. Suppose s/he is NOT aware there is legal, peaceful, effective future solution. Then s/he might conclude the only reasonable choice is to take steps *NOW* to end his/her life—while s/he still *can*. Whatever the means—be it legal (such as Voluntary Refusal of Food and Fluid); quasi-legal (such as contacting a non-physician self-help organization for information about how to "self-deliver"); or illegal (such as asking another person to commit a "mercy killing")—his/her dying will be *premature*. Even liberal Holland does not provide a solution for Advanced Dementia. For Physician-Assisted Dying or Euthanasia to be a legal act, Dutch law requires the patient to discuss his/her options with a physician; both must agree there is NOW no other way to avoid unbearable suffering. What is the problem with this requirement? Any patient whose dementia has reached the stage where it causes unbearable suffering has already experienced so much brain deterioration that s/he can no longer discuss anything, let alone make this awesome medical decision. Mentally, s/he is not able to have the required conversation. While some patients do discuss the option of ending their lives while in the early stage of dementia and claim their extreme anxiety about their future state is now unbearable, almost no Dutch physician considers this unbearable enough to help them die. Good call. Otherwise, these patients would give up a few years of living with reasonable quality. The following is based on a true story:

2: "An Educated Choice, but Still Premature Dying"

About fifteen years ago, as the president of one of the country's finest universities, "Thomas Duke, PhD," was a recognized leader in education. He was well aware of the general horrors of Advanced Dementia and had witnessed its devastating progression by observing his grandmother's disease. So when he no longer could deny his recent problem with short-term memory, he called a colleague, a top neurologist. Before he would submit to a thorough work-up, Dr. Duke asked the neurologist to promise to maintain complete confidentiality. He was to tell no one, including his family, if he had the dreaded diagnosis.

When the results came back, "Dementia, probable Alzheimer's type," Thomas became sad, but not clinically depressed. He went into a problem-solving mode while he hid his feelings from his loved ones. As he mulled over his options, his family sensed something was wrong. Thomas put them off by saying his back was hurting. After about two weeks of deep thinking, he came to this resolve: he would fast from all food and fluid. One morning he remained in bed, announced that he did not feel well, and asked his wife to serve him meals in bed. He pretended to eat by moving the food around his plate. He poured out liquids and food in the toilet when no one was looking. It took three days of total fasting for Thomas to convince himself that he could continue this plan until he died. He waited another day before he revealed his plan to his wife—which he did only after she promised to keep his secret. They cried together as he explained his limited options. She understood his reasoning and reluctantly accepted his decision. Thomas then designated her as his health care proxy. He signed the necessary papers. He asked his wife to promise *in writing* that she would make sure no one gave him tube feeding after he fell asleep. After that, Thomas openly refused all food and fluid. He contacted his closest family members and friends. They visited to exchange meaningful goodbyes. Five days later, he fell asleep. Two days after that, he died peacefully.

When others asked the cause of Dr. Duke's death, his wife offered the partial truth that Thomas had suggested: "He had a neurological disease. It made it *impossible* for him to eat and drink."

About a dozen years later, when his wife told me this story, I did *not* share my dismay at what would have been *possible*: Had Thomas known about the **Plan Now, Die Later—Ironclad Strategy** (even though it did not exist then), he most likely would have found in it, the confidence he required to live a few more "good" years and still achieve his goals: not to become a burden on his family and not to have others remember him as a demented person. If the **Plan Now, Die Later** option had then been available, it could have offered him another "educated choice"—one that would have avoided *premature dying*. He might have enjoyed two to four years of living with reasonable quality and meaningful interaction with his family. I felt sad that this choice was not available for Thomas, when he needed it.

The death of Thomas was the opposite of the saying above: He firmly believed that someday, he would no longer have control over when he died. He was convinced he would become trapped in a condition he considered "worse than death." Thus he decided to end his life sooner, while he still had the ability to exercise control. He died when he *could* instead of when he *wanted*. Now there is an alternative: PLAN while you *can*; then die when you *want*. Attain your goal *and* avoid *premature dying* by creating your **Plan Now, Die Later—Ironclad Strategy**.

Lingering in Advanced Dementia is one of the two greatest end-of-life fears. The other is being forced to endure unbearable pain and suffering. The American Medical Association's Code of Ethics says, "The social commitment of the physician is to sustain life and relieve suffering. Where the performance of one duty conflicts with the other, the preferences of the patient should prevail."[7] The term "suffering" is used in two ways: One is for extremely unpleasant and burdensome experiences other than pain; the other refers to patients' physical, emotional, and spiritual responses to any of these unpleasant experiences, including pain. While *Palliative Sedation* (which is similar to anesthesia) can **always** provide relief for any type of suffering, unfortunately some professionals will not provide it to some dying patients. For example:

3: "Abandoned by Hospice"[8]

After he was admitted to hospice, a terminally ill lung cancer patient did fairly well for a while. When he experienced "intractable nausea, vomiting, weakness, and fear—despite their skillful treatment—he asked for 'total sedation.' The hospice team felt uncomfortable about such sedation and refused to provide it. No alternatives other than the status quo were presented." The patient felt that he had to discharge himself from hospice. He then contacted an independent Palliative Care Physician who arranged for him to receive *Palliative Sedation*. Over a few hours of step-wise increasing doses, the patient lost consciousness. Four days later, he died peacefully. But patient and family "felt abandoned by the local hospice program at their time of greatest need, and the hospice staff caring for the patient felt demoralized and guilty." For patient, family, and hospice staff, this final challenge of life was far from peaceful. Comments: Hospices are in general wonderful, but sometimes "people" lose perspective. Was this patient denied a *Palliative Sedation* because physical pain was not one of his target symptoms? Fortunately, he was alert and found alternate treatment.

---

[7] *Document E-2.20*, American Medical Association's Council on Ethical and Judicial Affairs [2005]. *AMA Code of Medical Ethics*. Chicago, IL; 2006. http://www.ama-assn.org/ama/pub/category/8457.html.

[8] This is a true account. The story, including the quotes are from: Quill TE, Lo B, Brock DW, Meisel A. Last-Resort Options for Palliative Sedation. *Ann Intern Med*. 2009.151:421-424.

4: How Living Wills Deal with Unbearable Pain and Suffering

The AMA Code of Ethics also states, "[a] competent adult patient may, in advance, formulate and provide a valid consent to the withholding or withdrawal of life-support systems in the event that injury or illness renders that individual incompetent to make such a decision," and the **obligation of a physician** includes **"providing effective palliative treatment even though it may foreseeably hasten death**." {Emphasis added.} Note: U S physicians are legally protected from being forced to act in ways that conflict with their moral convictions or religious beliefs. *Conflicts* between patient's wishes and physician's willingness to comply thus *can and do occur*. The reality is that preferences of the patient do NOT always prevail. This is why you need an "ironclad strategy" to have confidence that *some* future physician will honor your end-of-life preferences. The place to start is to **express your specific wishes in a clear and convincing way**. How well do other Advance Directive forms fulfill this requirement? Do they request *Palliative Sedation* to relieve **otherwise untreatable, endless, unbearable pain**? Below are some representative Advance Directive forms:

Example 1. Legalzoom.com's entire instructional directive (Living Will) is below.[9] Note that pain and suffering are not mentioned:

> If you have a terminal condition where there is no hope of recovery, which health care instruction would you like to leave?
>
> |___| I do not want to be kept on artificial life support.
>
> |___| I want my life to be prolonged as much as reasonably possible.
>
> If you have **any further health care instructions**, please **write them** in the space below.

Comment: While the form provides space, it offers no further guidance.

Example 2. The **California Medical Association** form has these two paragraphs:[10]

> If I am suffering from a terminal condition from which death is expected in a matter of months, or if I am suffering from an irreversible condition that renders me unable to make decisions for myself, and life-support or life-sustaining treatments are needed to keep me alive, then:
>
> A. I request all treatments other than those needed to keep me **comfortable** be discontinued or withheld and my physician(s) allows me to die **as gently as possible**.

Comment: The words, "comfortable" and "gentle" are unfortunately vague.

---

9 http://www.legalzoom.com/living-wills/living-wills-overview.html
10 http://www.cmanet.org/upload/AdvDir2003Finalwatermarked.pdf

Example 3. The **California Hospital Association**[11] reflects the optional form illustrated in the statute, **California Probate Code 4701**,[12] and the similar **Uniform Health-Care Decisions Act**, which many States have adopted (some, with minor modifications):[13]

> I do not want my life to be prolonged if (1) I have an incurable and irreversible condition that will result in my death within a relatively short time, (2) I become unconscious and, to a reasonable degree of medical certainty, I will not regain consciousness, or (3) the likely risks and burdens of treatment would outweigh the expected benefits,
>
> [Under the section, "RELIEF FROM PAIN":]
>
> Except as I state in the following space, I direct that treatment for alleviation of pain or discomfort be provided at all times, **even if it hastens my death**: _____.

Comment: This form clearly prioritizes relief from pain over the extension of life.

Example 4. The **Five Wishes** form[14] provides this statement:

> I do not want to be in pain. I want my doctor to give me enough medicine to relieve my pain, even if that means that I will be **drowsy or sleep more** than I would otherwise.

Comment: If the only acceptable symptoms that guide the amount of medication for pain are the minimal "drowsy" or "sleep more," then physicians who understand these symptoms as limiting may grossly undertreat your unbearable suffering. For **pain**, the **Five Wishes** form presents no other choices and provides no space to write in (as it does for other areas of concern)—to encourage further thought and discussion.

Example 5. The **My Way Cards** tool generates a **Natural Dying—Living Will**.[15] This is *Card 6.6*:

> **I do not want to endure endless, severe pain. Give me enough medication so I don't suffer.**
>
> **I understand that even the lowest amount I need for relief might put me to sleep until I die.**

---

[11] www.calhospital.org/sites/chadocuments.org/ files/file-attachments/Forms_3.pdf

[12] www.law.onecle.com/california/probate/4701.html

[13] Uniform Health-Care Decisions Act: National Conference of Commissioners on Uniform State Laws. *Issues in Law & Medicine:* Summer, 2006. www.findarticles.com/p/articles/mi_m6875/is_1_22/ai_n24992417/

[14] Form available from Aging with Dignity: http://www.agingwithdignity.org/five-wishes.php

[15] For religious observers, Caring Advocates offers ***Natural Dying Living Will Cards***.

The *instructions* to sort **My Way Cards** are basically, "If a **card/item** describes your future condition, how would you want your future decision-makers to respond?" Sorters have three choices: "**Treat & Feed**," to live as long as possible; "Consider **Natural Dying** along with other card/items"; and "This symptom is **Enough**—*by itself*—for Natural Dying."

The **Natural Dying—Living Will** has this *note* for Item 6.6: "If 6.6 is 'Natural Dying' or 'Enough,' I will discuss *Palliative Sedation* with my physician and decide if I want to consent. If I do sign to give my consent, I will ask my physician to sign the **Natural Dying Physician's Orders**, a form that turns my Living Will REQUESTS into doctor's actionable ORDERS."

The **Natural Dying Physician's Orders** has these words after "Comfort Care": "<u>Attached</u>: **Consent Form to Relieve Unbearable Suffering by *PALLIATIVE SEDATION*.**"[16] Patients can complete this consent form prior to an office visit with their current physician.

5: About *Palliative Sedation* (Sedation to Unconsciousness)

1) *Palliative Sedation* (sedation to unconsciousness) is similar to anesthesia and can always alleviate pain and suffering—even if other Comfort Care methods have failed. **2)** The American Medical Association's Council on Ethical and Judicial Affairs recommended guidelines include this statement: "Physicians should ensure that the patient and/or the patient's surrogate has given **informed consent** for *Palliative Sedation* to unconsciousness."[17] **3)** To my knowledge, no other Advance Directive and no POLST-type form asks patients to consider, discuss, and consent to *Palliative Sedation* (sedation to unconsciousness) other than the **My Way Cards/ Natural Dying—Living Will/Natural Dying Physician's Orders**. **4)** While it takes three steps (sorting, discussing, and consenting) including a visit to your current physician, the effort can help you **avoid days to weeks of unbearable pain and suffering**. **5)** A discussion with your physician might reveal **your physician is NOT willing to comply** with your requests. If so, you may wish to find another physician. **6.** Your consent to *Palliative Sedation* with your current physician can provide convincing evidence of your end-of-life wishes. If your last physician is another, this new physician must review your previous physician's order and your signed consent and then either honor your wishes or refer you to a physician who will.

Using the **Consent Form to Relieve Unbearable Suffering by *PALLIATIVE SEDATION*** provides you opportunities to express your ***personal preferences regarding Palliative Sedation***; for example: **1)** Would you prefer to endure moderate discomfort if you can still relate to family members? *Or* do you have a low tolerance for suffering from which you want relief? **2)** Do you prefer **gradual** titration and using the **minimum** dose to be certain your dying is not hastened? *Or* do you want **rapid and complete** relief from suffering? **3)** Do

---

[16] This consent form can be obtained from Caring Advocates at www.CaringAdvocates.org or 1 800 647 3223.
[17] Levine MA. Sedation to Unconsciousness in End-of-Life Care. CEJA Report 5-A-08. www.ama-assn.org/ama1/pub/upload/mm/369/ceja_5a08.pdf

you want to be awakened after a few days of rest (***Respite Sedation***) to see if you can resume conscious living *or* just continue sedation until you die?[18] **4)** Do you want relief for any kind of unbearable suffering *or* do you want relief only for some kinds of suffering? Some people distinguish among THREE kinds of suffering: **Physical discomfort** includes extreme symptoms of pain, extreme shortness of breath, delirium (agitation, confusion, disorganized thinking, and hallucinations), convulsions, bleeding, nausea and vomiting; **Mental anguish** includes anxiety, depression, fear, anger, and frightening hallucinations; and **Existential suffering** includes fear of dying; uncertainty about what is on the other side of death; anguish over anticipating total loss from not being part of this world; and for people of religious faith, concern about making peace with God, including deep concern over redemption and/or absolution—forgiveness for sins committed.

Why do you need an "ironclad strategy"? Dr. Farr Curlin and colleagues published a survey that revealed about one out of six U S physicians has a moral or religious objection to "sedation to unconsciousness" (their study used the older term, "Terminal Sedation").[19] About half of objecting physicians would not refer their patients to physicians willing to provide this treatment.

Advance Care Planners also need to know about the following potential obstacle:

Some physicians will agree to treat unbearable **physical discomfort** but not **mental anguish** or **existential suffering**. The American Medical Association Council on Ethical and Judicial Affairs[15] "concur[red] with those who argue that **existential suffering... is not an appropriate indication for treatment with *Palliative Sedation* to unconsciousness**, because the causes of this type of suffering are better addressed by other interventions..." AMA's recommendation: "Enlist the support of the patient's broader social and spiritual network in order to address issues, which are **beyond the scope of clinical care**." Bottom line: According to the AMA's committee, your future physician can diagnose your suffering as "existential" but should not treat you—since it is "beyond the scope of clinical care"—even if psycho-social and pastoral-spiritual counseling have failed to relieve your endless, unbearable suffering. **Many professionals disagree.** Some favor the "whole person" view of suffering and/or consider it clinically impossible to distinguish one type of suffering from another.[20]

By far, the greatest fear about *Palliative Sedation*, among physicians and the general public—especially the devoutly religious and people with disabilities—is that *Palliative Sedation* might hasten death. (See "Stories," Chapter 2.) Dr. Marco Maltoni and his colleagues begin their

---

[18] Rousseau PC. (2002). Existential suffering and *Palliative Sedation* in terminal illness. *Prog. Pall. Care 10*: 222-224; (2003). *Palliative Sedation* and Sleeping Before Death: A Need for Clinical Guidelines? *J Pall. Med. 6*: 425-427. (2004). *Palliative Sedation* in the management of refractory symptoms. *J. Supportive Oncology 2*: 181-186.

[19] Curlin, FA, Lawrence, RE, Chin, MH, Lantos, JD. Religion, conscience, and controversial clinical practices. *N Engl J Med.* 2007. *356*: 593-600.

[20] Cassell J, Rich BA. Intractable End-of-Life Suffering and the Ethics of *Palliative Sedation*. *Pain Medicine.* 2010; 11: 435–438.

article by citing nine articles that "attest, directly or indirectly, to the absence of an impact of *Palliative Sedation* on survival duration." Maltoni's own research[21] was the first prospective study to directly examine overall survival. Their study presented data that combined the data of mild and intermittent sedation with *deep, continuous sedation* so I asked Dr. Maltoni for further details and then received his permission to quote this previously unpublished data:

> "The median survival of the 63 patients who received continuous deep sedation was 8 days (95% CI 5-11, range 0-62). The median survival of the 251 patients who received no sedation was 9 days (95% CI 8-11, range 0-331), p=0.169, which indicated that there was no difference in survival due to deep continuous sedation."

If Dr. Maltoni's result is replicated, the long-held fear that *Palliative Sedation* hastens death will someday be classified as a *formerly held myth*. In the meantime, patients can teach their physicians that **Respite Sedation** can be **distinguished from euthanasia** using the **Consent Form to Relieve Unbearable Suffering by *PALLIATIVE SEDATION***. This form also requests relief from *any kind of unbearable suffering*. If a physician refuses to sign the consent, whether based on moral or religious conscience or the AMA's position on "existential suffering," patients can ask another physician who is willing to sign. Patients should instruct their proxies that their job description includes finding a future physician who *will* honor this consent form, if the original physician who signed is not available.

6: How Living Wills and other forms deal with refusing spoon feeding to avoid lingering in Advanced Dementia

Recall your rights: You determine **what** treatment your body will accept, years **in advance**.

Some kinds of treatment are in a gray area or beginning to change. One relevant area is **feeding**. As dementia progresses, most patients develop two problems:

A) They **forget how,** or **lose the physical ability to eat by themselves**; and,

B) They have **trouble swallowing**.

Note: "**Being fed by another**" is very different from "**eating independently**." If your mind is well now, you have the **right** to decide what you will want—if you ever have such problems.

While all POLSTs and most Advance Directive forms ask Advance Care Planners about their preferences about tube feeding (artificial nutrition and hydration), worldwide very few forms ask patients if they wish to consent to receive, or would instead refuse in advance *Manual Assistance with Oral Feeding and Drinking*—once they reach the stage of Advanced Dementia.

---

[21] Maltoni M, et al. *Palliative Sedation* therapy does not hasten death: results from a prospective multicenter study. *Ann Oncol.* 2009;*20 (7)*:1163-9.

Only **My Way Cards** use patient's own criteria to decide WHEN to refuse oral feeding and drinking. The following fact is important but rarely emphasized during Advance Care Planning:

➜ **Continued oral feeding** in Advanced Dementia **A) can prolong the process of your dying**, and **B) can increase the risk of unrecognized and untreated pain and suffering.**[22] Here are several examples of Advance Care Planning forms: {Emphasis added.}

Example A. The **Physician's Order for Life-Sustaining Treatment** (**POLST**) forms of several States followed the wording originally used by the leaders who created the program in Oregon. All POLST forms display these statements *without a check box*; hence the non-physician professionals who conduct "POLST conversations" are likely **to assume** patients have NO choice on this issue and that there is NO need to discuss the legal choice of refusing *Manual Assistance with Oral Feeding and Drinking*. Here is a sample of several forms:

Oregon: "**Always** offer food by mouth if feasible."
Pennsylvania: "**Always** offer food and liquids by mouth if feasible."
New York: "…food and fluids are offered as tolerated using careful hand feeding."
Washington State: "**Always** offer food and liquids by mouth if feasible."
West Virginia: "Oral fluids and nutrition **must** be offered if medically feasible."

Hawaii: "**Always** offer food and liquid by mouth if feasible and **desired**."
California: "Offer food by mouth if feasible and **desired**."
La Croix, Wisconsin: "**Comfort measures are always provided**."

Note the passion reflected by the words "**always**" and "**must**" that most forms use. Hawaii keeps "always" but adds "desired." California deleted "always"—however the phrase "if desired" is vague. La Croix, Wisconsin has the most enlightened wording (as of May, 2011). While any physician can (and *should*) cross out any item on any pre-formatted order form **if it is contrary to the patient's wishes**—to my knowledge, this rarely if ever happens using a **POLST**. To do so requires a well-informed, assertive patient or proxy/agent, and a courageous physician. The following statement regarding oral feeding honors the principle of informed consent and does not violate the First Principle of Medical Ethics, DO NO HARM:

"Offer patient oral food and drink ONLY if it is medically feasible (that is, NOT likely to cause aspiration pneumonia and NOT likely to lead to a prolonged dying by slow starvation) **AND** has some potential to improve the patient's functional status; **OR** if the patient previously expressed the **desire** for this treatment *clearly and convincingly*, and *consistently* over time."

---

[22] An example is this book's first story (in "Stories"): For several years a Minnesota woman suffered from untreated pain discovered only after the nursing home began a new experimental program (the *Awakenings Program*). See also Chapter 4 in "Stories," about unrecognized and untreated pain and suffering.

Example B. Oregon's statutory Advance Directive includes the following instruction:[23]

> "Advanced Progressive Illness. If I have a progressive illness that will be fatal and is **in an advanced stage**, and I am consistently and permanently unable to communicate by any means, swallow food and water safely, care for myself and recognize my family and other people, **and** it is very unlikely that my condition will substantially improve:"

Comment: This form offers **no choice about being fed orally**; it offers a choice only about *tube feeding*. The term "**in an advanced stage**" is vague. Using the word "**and**" includes **all** symptoms and losses of function. The consequence, which may or may not be inadvertent, is to require a stage of dementia that may be more advanced than a person would want.

Example C. State of Vermont (long form)[24]:

> "If I am conscious but become **unable to think or act for myself** and will likely not improve, I do not want the following life-extending treatment: (breathing machines, feeding tubes, antibiotics, other medications whose purpose is to extend life, **any other treatment to extend my life**, other: _____)."

Comment: Advance Care Planners who are satisfied that the words emphasized above refer to Advanced Dementia must write in specific instructions to add hand/spoon feeding.

Example D. The organization, Compassion & Choices, offers "The Dementia Provision."[25]

> "If I remain conscious but have a progressive illness that will be fatal and the illness is in an advanced stage, and I am consistently and permanently unable to communicate, swallow food and water safely, care for myself and recognize my family and other people, **and** it is very unlikely that my condition will substantially improve, I would like my wishes regarding specific life-sustaining treatments, as indicated on the attached document entitled *My Particular Wishes* to be followed."
>
> "**If I am unable to feed myself while in this condition I do / do not (*circle one*) want to be fed**." (This choice is added since it is NOT in *My Particular Wishes*.)

Comment: "The Dementia Provision" form adds an important option, but it omits refusal of **assistance to drink**. Taking fluids without food can lead to the slow process of dying from **starvation** that can last for months because at bed rest, the body goes into conservation/ "survival" mode. Starvation is not likely to be comfortable. In contrast, refusing both food and

---

[23] http://www.oregon.gov/DCBS/SHIBA/docs/advance_directive_form.pdf?ga=t

[24] http://healthvermont.gov/regs/ad/AD_attachmentA.pdf

[25] http://community.compassionandchoices.org/document.doc?id=235

fluid typically leads to dying within two weeks from medical **dehydration**, which can be peaceful. Since the form uses the word "**and**," it includes **all** symptoms and losses of function that may require a stage more advanced than the person would want.

Example E. Alzheimer's Society, United Kingdom.

"I declare that if at any time, I am unable to participate effectively in decisions about my medical care, and [if] two independent doctors (one a consultant) are of the opinion that I am unlikely to recover from illness or impairment, and the gravity of my condition/ suffering is such that treatment seems to be **causing distress beyond any possible benefit**, then in those circumstances my directions are as follows:

"That I am not subjected to **any medical intervention or treatment aimed at prolonging or sustaining my life** such as those in 'Detailed instruction' below, even if this means my life is at risk. This does not necessarily mean withdrawal of life enhancing medication as I would not want the withdrawal of any treatment which may reduce distress or provide pain relief or may adversely affect my quality of life [and] that **any distressing symptoms**, including any **caused by inability to eat, drink or simply receive nutrition**, are to be fully controlled by **appropriate analgesic** or other treatment, even though that treatment may shorten my life."[26] {Emphasis added.}

Comment: *For me, this form was difficult to understand.* After several re-readings, I concluded I could decide NOT to receive assistance with feeding and drinking—if written in the blank box and that if my refusal causes discomfort, I would receive only Comfort Care. (Good.)

For many, this form will be difficult to complete: Advance Care Planners must complete the "Detailed instruction" in the BLANK BOX without further guidance. The form does NOT list the option to refuse assistance with oral feeding/drinking. Advance Care Planners must already know about Advanced Dementia and their legal end-of-life options to complete the blank box. Note: U K physicians are legally obligated to honor valid Living Wills.

Example F. Natural Dying—Living Will generated by sorting **My Way Cards** or *Natural Dying Living Will Cards*. Of the 48 cards/items, five are relevant. Two cards have these words, but are not illustrated here. Card **8.1** is: "To get me to eat & drink by myself, skilled helpers must encourage me a lot and show me how." Card **8.4** is: "Others try to feed me but I turn my head away. Or I close my teeth tightly. Or I spit out the food. These actions show that I do NOT want others to force-feed me." Cards **8.2**, **8.3**, and **8.5** are illustrated below:

---

[26] Form "463_Advance_Decision_form1-3.pdf" as a download from http://alzheimers.org.uk/site/scripts/download_info.php?fileID=412.

Helpers try hard to feed me and use many skills. But they cannot get enough food in me.

I am very thin. I will starve to death—slowly. [8.2]

I cannot eat in the usual way. I forget to swallow so food stays in my mouth. Helpers place very soft food at the back of my tongue—so that I SWALLOW by REFLEX. This is forced-feeding. [8.3]

Food could go down the "wrong way." If it enters my lungs I could get very sick (pneumonia).

Feeding me through a tube will NOT lower the risk of this happening. TUBE-FEEDING is one way to force-feed me.

[8.5]

Instructions: Sorters will have already viewed illustrated cards informing them about the choice, **Natural Dying**. Advance Care Planners "sort," that is, "decide about" each card/item twice, so that their future decision-makers will know their specific selected criteria. (See also the details in the "*Instructions*" in Example 5, above.)

7: Your "Three Choices"—if you have a feeding problem as you suffer from Advanced Dementia

Choice #1 is to consent to tube feeding. You may consent in advance to permit a surgeon to place a small tube into your stomach through which you can be fed. Or, you can refuse this treatment in advance. Your future decision-makers and you should be informed about the problems of tube feeding.[27] Here are some:

A) You may need leather or cloth straps to restrain both of your hands, or high doses of medication to calm you down—to prevent you from yanking out your feeding tube (which some patients do many times);

---

[27] Teno, J. et al. Decision-making and outcomes of feeding tube insertion: a five-state study. (2011.) *J Am Geriatr Soc. 59(5)*:881-6. One in 7 family members said physicians inserted feeding tubes without asking for permission; 1 in 9 family members felt pressured by the doctor. To prevent pulling the tubes out, nearly 40% of tube-fed patients were restrained physically or by medications.

B) Tube feeding does NOT reduce risk of pneumonia;

C) Tube feeding may not help you live longer; and,

D) Tube feeding removes human touch from the act of nurturing, and can have adverse effects. While some doctors and institutions recommend tube feeding for Advanced Dementia patients, it is NOT the standard of care.[28] You do have two other choices. Unfortunately, not all doctors will tell you about them—at least in the United States.

Choice #2 is *Comfort Feeding Only* or *Aggressive Manual Feeding*—as *others decide*. Unless you proactively refuse assistance with oral feeding, your physician and others will decide whether or not you will receive either of these feeding options. *Comfort Feeding Only*[29] sounds... yes: *comforting*. But the comfort may benefit *only* your caregivers—NOT you. Most likely, you will continue to lose weight and suffer from hunger while you cannot tell others you are suffering. Inadequate calorie intake can lead to more intense feelings of hunger than a complete fast of calories, which stimulates ketosis that provides a mild euphoria.

Question: If while competent, you were informed that *Comfort Feeding Only* leads to dying slowly from starvation (unless you die sooner from another cause), would you consent to it? If not, state your preferences about *Comfort Feeding Only* while you still can.[30]

Aggressive Manual Feeding sounds like others will try hard to feed you, to maintain your precious life. That's fine if it is what you want. But aggressive manual feeding can cause both direct and indirect harm. Direct harm occurs if food does NOT go into your stomach but instead goes down your windpipe where it may lead to pneumonia and a possible sooner death. Indirect harm can occur from prolonging the process of your dying while your risk of greater pain and suffering increases. You cannot complain so your physician may not recognize your suffering. Perhaps someday, *Aggressive Manual Feeding* will not be provided without

---

[28] The rates of inserting feeding tubes in U S nursing home patients with advanced cognitive impairment when hospitalized decreased slightly between 2000 to 2007, from: 7.9 to 6.2 per 100 admissions; the range was 0 to 39 per 100. Teno JM, Mitchell SL et al. Hospital Characteristics Associated With Feeding Tube Placement in Nursing Home Residents with Advanced Cognitive Impairment. *JAMA. 2010;303(6):544-550*. http://jama.ama-assn.org/content/303/6/544.full. An earlier study revealed that 34% of nursing home residents who had advanced cognitive impairment had a tube feeding inserted. Mitchell SL, Teno JM et al. Clinical and Organizational Factors Associated With Feeding Tube Use Among Nursing Home Residents with Advanced Cognitive Impairment. *JAMA. 2003;290:73-80.* http://jama.ama-assn.org/content/290/1/73.full.pdf+html

[29] Palecek EJ, Teno JM et al. Comfort Feeding Only: A proposal to bring clarity to decision-making regarding difficulty with eating for persons with Advanced Dementia. 2010. *J Am Geriatr Soc 58:580–584.*

[30] Speculation: Some leading professionals may view *Comfort Feeding Only* as an intermediate step in policy change toward **Natural Dying** because the latter choice is more difficult to explain and is more controversial. Since *Comfort Feeding Only* may *increase* rather than *decrease* the suffering of individual patients, recommending it raises two ethical questions: Is it morally right to suggest a method to further a political process—if it may harm individual patients? Is it morally right to suggest a method likely to cause an individual patients' suffering to reduce the suffering of caregivers? (Immanuel Kant's most likely answer is, NO!)

obtaining informed consent; in the meantime providing it violates the First Principle of Medical Ethics, DO NO HARM.

Question: If you were informed that *Aggressive Manual Feeding* can cause both direct and indirect harm leading to dying sooner or years of pain and suffering, would you consent to it? If not, state your preferences about *Aggressive Manual Feeding* while you can.

One way to express your preference is to indicate that you prefer the following choice:

Choice #3 is Natural Dying. This choice refuses both tube feeding and being fed orally by the assistance of another person's hand. The choice refuses all potentially life-sustaining, burdensome treatments that might prolong your dying. But you will still receive all the Comfort Care you need, including extra attention to your mouth so you do not feel thirsty. Hunger usually subsides quickly. Death from **Natural Dying** usually occurs after one to two weeks, and is often quite peaceful. The choice of **Natural Dying** can prevent lingering for one to three years or more with unrecognized and untreated pain and suffering.

There are two ways you can let your future decision-makers know WHEN you would want **Natural Dying**: You can mark the items in Chapter 4 (pages 50-51) in "Stories" that contain the *Criteria of Advanced Dementia for Natural Dying*, or sort **My Way Cards/***Natural Dying Living Will Cards*. Sorting leads to a **Natural Dying—Living Will** that expresses your *Known Wishes*, which others *should* honor. There still can be challenges, however. State laws allow physicians to refuse to comply if *your* wishes conflict with *their* moral or religious beliefs. Also, others may challenge your wish for **Natural Dying** by claiming it is NOT in your "Best Interest." Even your "future demented self" may express the desire for assistance with feeding or drinking—in direct conflict with your diligently created *Known Wishes*. The "ironclad strategy" provides ways to overcome these obstacles, which this book will explain.

8: Arguments Against Natural Dying & Counter-Arguments: Is Assisted Oral Feeding *Basic Care* or *Medical Treatment*?

First: some arguments *against* **Natural Dying** and some *counter*-arguments. Then: a guest author explains why **Natural Dying** does not conflict with Catholic teachings. Finally: a strategy that can resolve a conflict between your *Known Wishes* and the desires your "future demented self" may express, which strategy can also overcome challenges from others.

Arguments that assisted oral feeding is **always basic care** are usually based on common experience and belief. The belief, "All humans deserve the preservation of their dignity and that includes preservation of their lives," resonates with our experience with newborns (but not the dying, however.) Logically, if assisted oral feeding is **always basic care**, then **informed consent is not required**—even if feeding is intrusive or may lead to harm. Only these additional points of argument are required: life is precious and living sometimes has adverse consequences, including suffering. (This last statement may minimize your actual burden.)

Reasons why assisted oral feeding *IS* medical treatment: To develop and implement a treatment plan to feed you, physicians often coordinate the skills of several professional disciplines. Physicians typically meet with dieticians, nurses, and if appropriate, dentists. Speech pathologists importantly evaluate patients' ability to swallow with radiologists (also physicians) who provide videos of swallowing flow studies. Your primary physician may conduct a team meeting so several disciplines can consider these data and determine how best to provide you nutrition. Finally, your physician writes medical orders such as "thickened puree" with specified nutritional characteristics, and detailed directions for trained staff to use certain feeding skills. One technique is to carefully place each spoonful of puree at the very back part of the tongue to induce swallowing—by REFLEX. In the opinion of many professionals, the contribution of several medical disciplines coordinated by a physician who writes medical orders *obviously* qualifies **assisted oral feeding** as **medical treatment**.

Not all medical treatments require **informed consent**. Those that do are **intrusive** or have **potential to cause harm**. Assisted oral feeding IS intrusive: After hearing arguments about not letting prisoners die from hunger strikes, U S Supreme Court Chief Justice William Rehnquist replied, "It seems odd that your bodily integrity is violated by sticking a needle in your arm, but not by sticking a spoon in your mouth. I mean... how would you force-feed these people in a way that would not violate their bodily integrity?" (Vacco v. Quill, 1997.) *Comfort Feeding Only* can lead to harm by slow starvation; *Aggressive Manual Feeding* can cause harm by lethal aspiration pneumonia. Both can lead to indirect harm by prolonging dying that increases the risk of unrecognized and untreated pain and suffering. Thus, **assisted oral feeding is not only medical treatment, it requires INFORMED CONSENT**.

9: Catholic Views: Con and Pro

Religious arguments *against* and *for* the morality of refusing the treatment of food and fluid to prolong dying are not only important to religious observers but also to non-observant patients who happen to find themselves as patients in faith-based health institutions. These arguments are also important to patients in many States whose laws give precedence to the following of religious beliefs, such as *In the Matter of Carole ZORNOW*. (See "Stories," Chapter 5.)

The Westchester Institute for Ethics and the Human Person briefly summarized the conservative Catholic view. This organization's mission is "anchored in the classic perennial and Catholic view of the human person." Its 2010 "White Paper," **"Catholic Teaching on Assisted Nutrition and Hydration,"**[31] explained the consequences of the November, 2009,

---

[31] http://www.westchesterinstitute.net/resources/white-papers/491. Retrieved on April 10, 2011.

vote by the U S Conference of Bishops to revise their *Ethical and Religious Directives for Catholic Health Care* # 58 for the Fifth Edition: Unless the patient is imminently dying, not able to absorb the food, or no tube feeding is available in a remote area, the only **rare** instance that Artificial Nutrition and Hydration would not be considered **obligatory** is if Artificial Nutrition and Hydration *itself* caused the patient "excessive burden" such as significant physical discomfort—as contemporaneously determined by proxies, loved ones, attending physicians and a priest or ethicist trained in the Church's moral teaching on these matters. The White Paper concluded: "It would be **immoral** for [Catholics] to indicate in their **living wills or advance medical directives** an across-the-board desire to **forgo or have withdrawn—without any further consideration**—the provision of **food and water** if they should suffer some **severe cognitive impairment**." In other words, the **durable** Advance Directive that this book helps people create would NOT be morally allowed.

Next is an invited guest essay from Kevin McGovern, a health ethicist and Catholic priest. What makes his contribution particularly impressive is that his father personally experienced great **benefits** from tube feeding. A survivor of throat cancer, his life was extended enjoyably for several years. Yet Reverend McGovern's essay explains the important difference: Providing tube feeding and assisted oral feeding for patients who suffer from Advanced Dementia may become "disproportionate and extraordinary." (A few footnotes were added to his essay.)

10: A Catholic View on the
Natural Dying Living Will Cards

by Reverend Kevin McGovern
Director, Caroline Chisholm Centre for Health Ethics

Some Catholics might feel hesitant about using the ***Natural Dying Living Will Cards***. For example, a conscientious Catholic might ask if the cards accord with Catholic teaching about planning future health care. This short article seeks to address these concerns:

Catholic teaching holds that each person has a moral responsibility to use those means of sustaining our lives that are effective, not overly burdensome and reasonably available. These are called ordinary or proportionate means of preserving life. On the other hand, each person also has the moral right to refuse any treatment that is futile, overly burdensome or morally unacceptable. These are called extraordinary or disproportionate means of preserving life.

When treatment is offered, how do we discern if this is an ordinary or proportionate means of preserving life, or an extraordinary or disproportionate means? When we try to put this into words, it's actually quite complex. In the Catholic tradition, one of the best explanations is found in the Congregation for the Doctrine of the Faith's 1980 *Declaration on Euthanasia*. In a section headed 'Due Proportion in the Use of Remedies,' it states that this discernment involves "studying the type of treatment to be used, its degree of complexity or risk, its cost and the possibilities of using it, and comparing these elements with the result that can be expected, taking into account the state of the sick person and his or her physical and moral resources." Note that there are actually a lot of factors that have to be considered.

Who should make this discernment? The Declaration adds that "in the final analysis, it pertains to the conscience of the sick person, or of the doctors, to decide…" Often, too, when the patient is no longer able to speak for themselves, it is their family or health care proxy who must decide or speak for them.

Some cases are fairly simple. One example is treatments that offer few if any benefits. If a treatment does not cure, nor slow down the progress of disease, nor relieve pain, discomfort or distress, nor help to maintain a patient's lucidity or consciousness, it is a disproportionate means which may be refused.

Other examples that are fairly easy to discern are treatments which impose significant burdens. If a treatment is physically too painful, or psychologically too distressing, or socially too isolating, or financially too expensive, or morally repugnant, or spiritually too distressing— again it is a disproportionate means which may be refused.

In real life, cases are often more complex. This is particularly so in cases which involve dementia. The ***Natural Dying Living Will Cards*** are designed to help this discernment of ordinary and extraordinary means in these difficult cases which involve dementia.

Dementia is caused by progressive degeneration in the brain. It is manifest in such signs and symptoms as memory and communication problems, changes in mood and behavior, and a gradual loss of control of physical functions. As dementia progresses, the capacity to feed oneself is often lost. One possible treatment is *Manual Assistance with Oral Feeding and Drinking*—or hand feeding or spoon feeding, as it is commonly called. This is often tried, at least for some time. Another possible treatment is Clinically Assisted Nutrition and Hydration (CANH)—whose usual form is commonly called tube feeding. Nowadays, this is rarely provided for patients with dementia.[32]

Both hand feeding and tube feeding impose some burdens. To discern whether these treatments would be ordinary or extraordinary means for a particular patient, these burdens must be compared with the benefits that are provided. At the same time, as the Congregation for the Doctrine of the Faith noted in 1980, we must also consider "the state of the sick person and his or her physical and moral [or psychological] resources."

---

[32] Possibly true for Australians, but certainly not true for Americans. See footnote in TOPIC 7 that cites a survey that revealed 34% of nursing home residents with advanced cognitive impairment had tube feeding.

All this is what the **Natural Dying Living Will Cards** allow us to do. The cards detail various circumstances which may occur as the dementia progresses. Many of these circumstances bring with them some extra burdens. At the same time, they render the patient more frail, and diminish their physical and moral resources. They also reduce the patient's capacity to strive for the spiritual purpose of life by knowing, loving and serving God, self and neighbor, and even their capacity just to enjoy life. These diminishments arguably reduce the benefits of ongoing, life-preserving treatment.

Are there some circumstances in which benefits and burdens are such that ongoing treatment even by hand/spoon feeding becomes extraordinary or disproportionate? Or are there some circumstances in which the burdens of ongoing treatment even by hand/spoon feeding are just too much for an already very frail patient? The **Natural Dying Living Will Cards** enable patients or their health care proxies to discern if even hand/spoon feeding becomes for them in some circumstances an extraordinary or disproportionate means of preserving life.

It should be stressed that this discernment does not involve any judgment that this patient's life is not worth living. It is a discernment not about the patient's life, but about their treatment. It is precisely a discernment that in the patient's changing circumstances, this treatment which was once ordinary and proportionate has now become disproportionate and extraordinary.

In 2004, Pope John Paul II gave an important speech about tube-feeding and patients in what is variously called either a vegetative state or post-coma unresponsiveness. In 2007, the Congregation for the Doctrine of the Faith answered some questions about this teaching, and offered more explanation about what the pope had said. To reflect this teaching more accurately, in 2009 the U S bishops revised Directive 58 in their *Ethical and Religious Directives for Catholic Health Care Services*.

Does this teaching require that an elderly Catholic with dementia should have a feeding tube inserted? Because this question has made many Catholics anxious and worried, it is important that we consider it here:

Someone in a vegetative state has suffered profound brain damage. This damage may have been caused by a brain injury, or by a period in which the brain was deprived of oxygen. Someone in a vegetative state has normal cycles of sleep and wakefulness. However, they do not seem to respond in any way to the world around them. Thus, they do not recognize nor even look at people, nor talk, nor respond in any purposeful way to the world. Terry Schiavo was arguably in a vegetative state.

Pope John Paul said that for a person in a vegetative state tube-feeding "always represents a natural means of preserving life" and its use "should be considered, in principle, ordinary and proportionate, and as such morally obligatory." The U S bishops added that "medically assisted nutrition and hydration become morally optional when they cannot reasonably be expected to prolong life or when they could be excessively burdensome for the patient or would cause significant physical discomfort, for example resulting from complications in the use of the means employed."

Thus, Catholic teaching does not require that everyone in a vegetative state must be tube-fed. It certainly does impose an obligation to tube feed many people in a vegetative state. However, there is no such obligation if tube feeding will not preserve life, or if its administration would be excessively burdensome. Thus, for example, in 2005 an Australian Catholic named Maria Korp was in a vegetative state after being locked in the trunk of her car for four days. However, she also had significant wounds that would not heal, and despite the best medical care her condition continued to deteriorate. Ultimately, she was not absorbing food from tube feeding, and the presence of the tube had become unduly burdensome for her. In this case, two Catholic ethicists agreed that "within the principles or policy of the Catholic Church, this was a situation in which it was appropriate to stop feeding." Ms. Korp died ten days after the feeding tube was removed.

The same principle and the same exceptions apply to tube feeding for Catholics with dementia. Here however, the medical facts are different. Dementia is a terminal condition: its progressive deterioration leads inevitably to death. By the time a person has lost the capacity to feed themselves, experience has taught us that as a general rule even tube feeding does not slow this inevitable deterioration towards death. Careful studies have shown that at this stage of dementia, tube feeding does not generally prolong life, nor improve nutritional status and weight, nor reduce life-threatening complications such as aspiration pneumonia. At the same time, inserting a tube into someone's stomach does impose significant burdens, especially if a person with dementia must be restrained so they do not try to pull this tube out of their stomach.

There may be exceptions when tube feeding might offer some benefit to a person with dementia without imposing significant burdens. However, as a general rule, tube feeding should not be attempted when a person with dementia loses their capacity to feed themselves.

In 2010, one of the departments of the Catholic Bishops' Conference of England and Wales, the Department for Christian Responsibility and Citizenship, produced a booklet titled *A Practical Guide to the Spiritual Care of the Dying Person*.[33] On page 27, they noted that the Catholic

---

[33] Go to www.catholic-ew.org.uk/Catholic-Church/Publications, then click guide-to-spiritual-care-of-dying.pdf. (Also in print, published by Catholic Truth Society, 2010.) Commissioned by the Catholic Bishops' Conference of England and Wales. Contributors were: Dr. C. Gleeson, Consultant in Palliative Medicine; Dr. D. Jones, Professor of Bioethics; Fr. P. Mason, Chaplain; and Rev. Dr. J. Hanvey SJ. The Guide states (p 28): "Decisions concerning the provision or withdrawal of Clinical Artificial Nutrition and Hydration (CANH)... should take into account the patient's needs and his or her wishes and values... In the United Kingdom, **a competent patient has the legal right to refuse medical treatment** and **CANH is counted as medical treatment for this purpose.**"

obligation to provide tube feeding may cease "in the last days of life when nutrition will have little or no effect in sustaining life or earlier in some conditions, such as dementia, where steady weight loss despite Clinically Assisted Nutrition and Hydration is recognized as part of the late stages of the illness." This statement confirms that Catholic teaching does not simply demand the insertion of a feeding tube into Catholics with dementia who have lost the capacity to feed themselves.

The ***Natural Dying Living Will Cards*** do go beyond official Catholic teaching at one point. (This is not to say that they disagree with Catholic teaching, but rather that they offer an opinion about a matter which has not yet even been considered by official Catholic teaching.) Official Catholic teaching recognizes that tube feeding can legitimately be refused in certain circumstances. The ***Natural Dying Living Will Cards*** hold that it is also legitimate in certain circumstances to refuse *Manual Assistance with Oral Feeding and Drinking* or hand/spoon feeding. When a person with dementia seems to have lost the capacity to feed themselves, food and drink should still always be placed before them so that they have the opportunity to eat and drink. But if they do not eat and drink, the cards hold that it is legitimate in certain circumstances not to try to hand feed them. In many cases, this procedure is more than just trying to help someone to eat. It can involve placing soft food at the back of the patient's tongue so that they swallow simply by REFLEX. If this is not force-feeding, it is very close to it. Its burdens include coughing and spluttering as food goes down the wrong way; its risks include aspiration pneumonia.

If you accept this opinion about hand/spoon feeding, the ***Natural Dying Living Will Cards*** will allow you or your loved one to identify the sorts of circumstances in which hand/spoon feeding or other treatments will become extraordinary or disproportionate. Without conflicting with Catholic teaching, they will permit you or your loved one to identify the sorts of circumstances in which hand feeding or other treatments could and legitimately should be refused, withheld or withdrawn.

11: What if a dementia patient's request for life-sustaining treatment conflicts with a previous Advance Directive?

Imagine you have reached the stage of Advanced Dementia. You must be hand/spoon-fed and given fluid by another person's help. If food and fluid are placed right in front of you, you just stare at them. Your brain has deteriorated to such a devastating extent that it no longer knows how to use a spoon or a straw, even when food and fluid are offered.

Still, there are times that you can express some desires. Suppose your fast began a few days ago after your proxy and physician agreed (by *shared decision-making*) that it was time for **Natural Dying** (based on your previously expressed competent wishes). Also suppose you previously signed a Proxy Directive that designated a proxy who promised to do his/her best **to** make sure others honor your *Known Wishes*. BUT now, *you point to the bowl of offered puree and/or a bottle of water. You open your mouth. You grunt.* Observers are convinced you are asking for help to eat or to drink. Yet it is quite *unlikely* you want your dying to be prolonged. You may simply want to reduce your temporary symptom of dry mouth and do not understand or remember the alternative: thirst control agents can provide relief without prolonging dying/increasing suffering. Or, you may want a taste out of curiosity. Or your request may stem from habit. Whatever your reason, NOW there is a **conflict**:

In the *past*, when your mind was well, you said you would want NO food and NO fluid. *Presently*, your brain is not well and you DO clearly ask for food and fluid.

Who should others listen to? Should they follow your ***prior*** written Living Will and the faithful oral instructions of your proxy? *Or* should they listen to what you are asking for ***now***?

Reasonable, honest people can argue both ways. As long as they argue, you will be fed—even if they eventually listen to your proxy and your Living Will. The consequence is *To Delay is To Deny* and possible continued suffering. Example: Terri Schiavo's feeding tube was removed in October 15, 2003. Under a new law that was later determined unconstitutional, the tube was reinserted six days later. The case was fiercely debated. She died over seventeen months later. To avoid a prolonged conflict, state **in advance** how you want this potential conflict resolved.

Your two choices are: You DO want help with feeding and drinking *OR* you do NOT want help with feeding and drinking—**EVEN IF** you clearly ask. Your Living Will can make the "EVEN IF" decision **irrevocable in advance**. [The First Edition of **Peaceful Transitions** explains why this choice is a "Ulysses Contract."] For some people, this is not an easy decision...

You may not want to deny yourself the last bit of pleasure of life—of eating puree—even if the time it takes to die is longer and you risk greater pain and suffering. Or you may decide to stick with your past plan for **Natural Dying**.

If you choose **Natural Dying**, you can still have food and fluid placed in front of you. You will still get all the Comfort Care you need. **Natural Dying** can be more peaceful than dying from a lung infection (pneumonia), which is a risk if you ask others to continue to feed you.

Your decision can help your loved ones who may feel less anxious, confused, and guilty if they know what you wanted. Your Living Will can be a "gift" to them. So, decide now, if you can.

Can you decide now what you will want, if there is a conflict? If so, indicate below:

|___| *I DO want another person to assist my oral feeding and drinking.   OR:*

|___| *I do NOT want another person to assist my oral feeding and drinking.*

This illustrates **one of four choices** in the set of **My Way Cards** (**My Choice Card "D"**):

I want NO medical treatment that might keep me alive. I want to stop all help from others with feeding or drinking—<u>EVEN IF</u> I show I want this help in the future.

➜ Do <u>NOT</u> help me with feeding or drinking. If my mouth is dry, just provide Comfort Care. This is why: I do not want my dying to take a long time, and I do not want more pain before I die.   (XX)

Write down your answer, if you are sure. Otherwise, continue reading.

There is an additional reason why you might want to make this decision—to refuse *Manual Assistance with Oral Feeding and Drinking*—**irrevocable**: it gives your **proxy more power** to make sure also that **others** will honor **your** *Known Wishes*; it enhances your "*ironclad strategy.*" Here is why:

Suppose you decided to tell others to listen to your "future demented self" instead of your Living Will and your proxy. This instruction leaves the door wide open for others to voice their opinion about what they think is "best" for you. They can paternalistically claim that *they know* what is in *your* "Best Interest." You may consider *life sacred* but still not want to endure only suffering for a long time. Now suppose you have a very religious relative who wants to assume control... OR, your clinical care was assigned to a very religious nurse. Either person's belief about the *sanctity of life* may be so strong that s/he loses sight of your end-of-life wishes and the burdens of *your* suffering. To him/her, *living for as long as possible* is the *only* consideration. S/he might actively try to prevent your *timely, peaceful transition...*

    —Even if your Living Will clearly said you would want **Natural Dying**.
    —Even if feeding you will make your dying take much longer.
    —Even if you are likely to experience more severe pain and suffering before you die.

—Even if you require burdensome medical treatments that you said you would not want.

—Even if your proxy argued you clearly did not want to suffer more and longer.

Your proxy could argue: **A)** Your goal was **never to intentionally hasten your dying; B)** You want certain treatments to cease because these **treatments no longer can benefit you** or because these treatments have become **burdensome by causing you harm**; or, if your family is religious, **C)** spoon feeding that was once ordinary care has now become extraordinary and disproportionate due to your current condition. . . .

But your proxy would likely **lose this argument**—if your Living Will states your "future demented self" can receive another's hand to assist feeding and drinking upon your request. Why will your proxy then lose this argument? —Simply because this is *how the law is written.*

The law does NOT require patients to have decisional capacity to receive life-sustaining treatment if they request. In contrast, the law DOES require persons to be mentally competent to **refuse** treatment. This *asymmetry* or difference in the law is intentional; it protects sick patients by preserving their lives. The law says: "Listen to the patient's present wishes for life-sustaining treatment. Honor them since if they err, it will be on the side of life." However, if your goal is a *timely, peaceful transition,* the consequence will be to sabotage your plan. For your plan to succeed, you must have an *effective strategy* in place to resolve this conflict.

If you want to make sure *others* will allow your **Natural Dying** if you reach the stage of Advanced Dementia, you must DO MORE than to *tell others* to follow the wishes in your Living Will; you MUST ALSO tell them to disregard the desires your "future demented self" may someday express. Here's how: *You **give your proxy extra power** to override requests by your "future demented self."* Then your proxy can effectively do his/her job: to facilitate your end-of-life *Known Wishes*—even if **others** challenge them. This is the "ironclad strategy."[34]

Think again about making this choice **irrevocable**, now that you know this additional fact: Your proxy will have more power **to make sure others will honor your *Known Wishes***—if the instructions in your Living Will tell *others* to listen to your Living Will and to your proxy, instead of your "future demented self."

Can you decide now what you will want, if there is a conflict? If so, indicate below:

---

[34] For more information about making this **irrevocable choice**, you can listen to audio messages. You can either listen to the MP3s online at www.MyWayCards.org, or call to listen to recordings at the phone numbers listed, which are local numbers in the US, UK, AU, as well as worldwide by SKYPE.

*|__| **I DO want another person to assist my oral feeding and drinking.**   OR:*

*|__| **I do NOT want another person to assist my oral feeding and drinking.***

If you have decided that you do NOT want *others* to listen to your "future demented self" but want instead for others to honor your Living Will and your proxy—so NO other person will assist with oral feeding and drinking—then consider the **Natural Dying Agreement**, below.

12: For a Stronger Strategy: the "Natural Dying Agreement"

The **Natural Dying Agreement** works at two levels: The first is at the level of *content*: The form lets you make specific, detailed requests in three important but contentious clinical areas: **A)** to deactivate intra-cardiac devices—if you ever have one; **B)** to receive sedation to unconsciousness (*Palliative Sedation*)—if ever needed; and **C)** to refuse consent for continuing *Manual Assistance with Oral Feeding and Drinking* if you meet your own criteria. The form has space for you to write, in your own words and handwriting... *WHY* you want *WHAT* you want. (The form also lists common reasons for you to consider.) **D)** The form suggests arguments to overcome some laws that otherwise may present obstacles to attaining your goal.

Second, the "**Natural Dying Agreement**" works at the level of *process*: This begins with your agreeing to an *irrevocable, bilateral contract*[35] with your proxy. This demonstrates your conviction and obtains your proxy's signed commitment. Most important, the form also authorizes your proxy to override decisions made by your "future demented self." This part of the form is modeled on the Advance Directive from the State of Vermont. This State calls the form a "waiver"—a term that acknowledges signing the form gives up certain future rights.[36] It is ironic: transferring power to make life-determining decisions to your proxy gives you a stronger strategy so others will honor your end-of-life wishes. Why? Because this granted authority empowers your proxy to overcome similar challenges by others who may oppose your wish for **Natural Dying**. (See the sample argument in TOPIC 13.)

Signing a "**Natural Dying Agreement**" gives up your *future* right to request another's help with oral feeding and drinking—but ONLY AFTER you have **lost the ability to make medical decisions** as determined by two independent clinicians. To make sure you really want this, the **Natural Dying Agreement** form has additional instructions and safeguards: **A)** Your physician *must* witness your consent to this waiver. **B)** An independent person with no conflict of interest *may* also attest that you understood its consequences and signed voluntarily. (This person is required for residents of skilled nursing facilities in some States.) Note: "You can always change your mind after you sign a **Natural Dying Agreement _IF_** you still possess the mental ability to make decisions (that is, if you have **capacity**)."

---

[35] "Bilateral" is explained in the footnote in TOPIC 17.
[36] http://healthvermont.gov/regs/ad/AD_attachmentA.pdf, Part 6 (pages 13-16).

How does the "waiver" work? Consider this slightly modified excerpt from the Vermont form:

Vermont form [modified]: "There may be situations in which you might be objecting to or requesting treatment but would **then** want your objections or requests to be disregarded. If you have had treatment in the past that scares you or is uncomfortable or painful, you may likely say, 'No,' when offered in a future health crisis. **Now** you know that this is the only way for you to come through a bad time or even survive **later**. You understand it is necessary [so] you would want it again if you had to have it. [Signing] this [agreement with your proxy] will help you let your proxy and others know what you really want for yourself."

Three common examples: **A)** You need dental work to prevent a tooth abscess—a serious infection—so it does not spread to your brain. **B)** Physicians routinely deny some requests of demented patients. Suppose a patient was placed in a locked facility because there is a high risk that the patient would cause a car accident and set his home on fire. Then, the patient demands his doctor unlock the door of the locked facility and return his car and home keys. He clearly explains why: "I want to drive home. I prefer to live there." For the safety of the patient and others, his physician will NOT unlock the door or return the keys. *No prior waiver* is needed in this case because society widely accepts this decision. **C)** Some psychiatric patients sign a "waiver agreement" to remain in a hospital and to take medications—EVEN IF (because of their future paranoid thinking) they then request their freedom and refuse to take medication.

Note: Vermont's example is for *accepting* treatment over your apparent objection, but the Vermont form explains that waivers can also be used to *refuse* specific treatment over your apparent objection. The **Natural Dying Agreement** form does both.

13: An Argument Based on the "Natural Dying Agreement"

How does the **Natural Dying Agreement** empower your proxy to overcome others' challenges? Here is an example argument based on the powers the form grants:

As explained above, the law's *asymmetry* allows patients who lack capacity **to receive** life-sustaining treatment, if requested, which gives your "future demented self" the power to sabotage your plan for a *timely, peaceful transition*. The **Natural Dying Agreement's** strategy overcomes this challenge by empowering your proxy to override requests by your "future demented self." This strategy can also overcome potential arguments by others:

Argument: "Caring wholeheartedly for a frail patient or a disabled loved one is **incompatible** with thinking that **engineering their death is an acceptable** therapeutic option."[37]

Counter-argument: "I am Mrs. _____'s proxy/agent. She now suffers from Advanced Dementia and lacks capacity. When competent, she signed an *irrevocable* Agreement that gave me the power me to override her future requests if fulfilling them would sabotage her goal for a *timely, peaceful transition* after she met her criteria of Advanced Dementia.

Since she gave me the power to disqualify even her future self, it is obvious that she would also want me to disqualify *anyone else* who might disagree with her *Known Wishes* or her *firm belief* of what she has considered as in her 'best interest.'

"Regarding how the patient would respond to your argument that includes the inflammatory phrase, 'engineering their death,' here is my understanding of the patient's values: She would say that death is NOT an *option* for any mortal. She accepted the principle of "Substituted Dying": *If one does not die of one cause, one must die of another.* She wanted all to honor her expressed desire NOT to be subjected to treatment that would prolong her dying—especially if it such treatment increased the burden of unrecognized and untreated pain and suffering.

Important caveat: Giving this much power to your proxy/agent requires your **trusting** this individual and alternates you name—if your first choice proxy is not willing, able, or reasonably available to serve in this role. Having well-designed forms is necessary but not sufficient; you also need a strong advocate to use these forms. See TOPIC 17, "How to Choose a Health Care Proxy/Agent."

14: Your Strategic "Trump Card": the "Natural Dying Affidavit"

The **Natural Dying Affidavit** is a one-page declaration that you can swear is "true and correct" before a notary. It has legal force because courts usually accept Affidavits as evidence. Your proxy/agent may keep this form in a safe place and use it only if necessary—like a "trump card"—to motivate your future physician or institution to honor your *Known Wishes*. The form **A)** States your rights; **B)** Summarizes your *Known Wishes*; **C)** Directs your proxy "to seek declaratory or injunctive relief to effectuate [your] originally expressed, competent wishes…"; and **D)** Directs your proxy to sue any entity who fails to honor your *Known Wishes*, or who accedes to requests by your "future incompetent self" that delays your **Natural Dying**.

---

[37] From **President's Council on Bioethics Taking Care**: *Ethical Caregiving In Our Aging Society*. Washington: US Executive Office of the President. (2005). www.bioethics.gov/reports/taking_care/index.html. {Emphasis added.}

This Affidavit may help motivate an institution or physician who would otherwise be reluctant to comply with your end-of-life treatment preferences. If this sworn declaration by itself does not suffice, your proxy/agent can then quote the following sources and examples of lawsuits:

Watson and Daguro[38] provided a list of possible legal causes of action: Breach of Contract; Medical Battery; Negligence; Lack of Informed Consent; Intentional Infliction of Emotional, Physical and/or Financial Distress; and Wrongful Life/Prolongation of Life. These authors listed several Advance Directive lawsuits: Anderson v. St. Francis-St. George Hospital, Inc. (1996); Wendland v. Sparks (1998); Duarte v. Chino Community Hospital (1999); Haymes v. Brookdale Hospital Medical Center (2001); Osgood v. Genesys Regional Medical Center (2002); Livadas v. Strong Memorial Hospital (2005); Howe v. Massachusetts General Hospital (2005); and Neumann v. Morse Geriatric Center (2007).

Example 1: *In Osgood v. Genesys*,[39] a physician misled the patient's mother (also her designated durable power of attorney) to consent to a ventilator: he misrepresented the ventilator as Comfort Care. He knew the patient previously had clearly stated she wanted *no artificial life support if she could not have a meaningful life.* Subsequently, the patient went into a coma from which she emerged with serious brain damage. She screamed almost constantly, which likely reflected her experiencing pain. The initial jury award was for **$16 million**. This figure was reduced. During the appeal, the case settled; amount not disclosed.

Example 2: A case was filed in California's Alameda Superior Court on November 18, 2010. Plaintiffs in *Hargett v. Vitas* claim that the hospice physicians failed both to inform the patient and surrogate decision-makers about the option, *Palliative Sedation*, and also failed to provide adequate treatment for the patient's unbearable end-of-life pain. As of publication time, the outcome of this case has not been decided.[40]

Summary: Adding the **Natural Dying Agreement** and **Natural Dying Affidavit** to your **Natural Dying Advance Directive/Natural Dying Physician's Orders** can give you peace of mind that you have completed all the necessary forms to create an "ironclad strategy" so that others will honor your end-of-life *Known Wishes*. When this task is finished and you have designated your proxy, ordered your medallion, and sent your forms to a national registry (which the following pages describe), you deserve to take a deep breath, stop thinking about

---

[38] Dr. Eileen Watson, EdD, MSN, RN, ANP, GNP, LNC-C and Attorney Pamela Daguro presented Session Code #302 at the American Association of Legal Nurses Conference on April 24, 2009. Retrieved from www.dcprovidersonline.com/ then search for Advance Directives: Self-Determination, Legislation and Litigation (or Session AALNC9302A)

[39] No. 94-26731-NH, (Mich. Cir.Ct. Genesee Co. March 7, 1997)

[40] Case No. BG 10547255 (1-10-PR167981): Intentional and negligent affliction of emotional distress—a violation of Welfare & Institutions Code Section 15600 et seq. Michelle Hargett Beebee died at age 43 of pancreatic cancer. See complaint at: http://community.compassionandchoices.org/document.doc?id=716. Further information is at: http://compassionandchoices.org/page.aspx?pid=474

your plan for dying, and enjoy living the rest of your life knowing you need not worry about being trapped in a condition you feel is "worse than death."

Now you know your rights, your goals, and the forms that you can use to attain your goals. One way to understand how all the forms work individually and together to overcome common potential challenges is to read the following *fictional* story. This story had to be fictional for two reasons: First, it recounts the last half of one person's life—a total of 45 years—while the "ironclad strategy" is less than five years old (as of 2011). Second, it is unlikely that a single person would encounter *all* of the professional obstacles and challenges and have *all* the clinical problems this single story illustrates. In these two dimensions, this is a "composite" story. Still, the story portrays experiences based on several real patients. Reading this story will show both the common challenges one may experience and how the **Plan Now, Die Later— Ironclad Strategy** is designed to overcome them.

15: If Your Goal is Natural Dying: Where do you start? How do you revise your strategy over the years?

When he was **45**, "Fred" wanted to let others know what kind of treatment he would, or would not want, if he became severely ill and was too ill then to speak for himself. At his relatively young age, he had both short-term and long-term concerns. Although unlikely, anyone could have a car accident, but Fred also played horse polo. So for him, a head injury was a real possibility. Fred was sure that he would NOT want to exist for years if he was unconscious. That would be devastating to his family. He was also worried about Advanced Dementia, having seen his aunt deteriorate slowly from this devastating disease. He wanted a clear and effective Living Will that would avoid a state of merely existing for years. Of course, he also did not want to suffer from unbearable pain at the end of his life.

Fred was brought up in the Catholic tradition so for his family, he chose to sort the **Natural Dying Living Will Cards**, an alternate to **My Way Cards** that also generates the **Natural Dying—Living Will**. He wrote down his choices on the included wallet card and faxed the card to **Caring Advocates**, a non-profit organization. The letter they sent back with the Living Will asked him to consider completing the **Natural Dying Advance Directive** and to give them permission to send his physician a blank copy of the **Natural Dying Physician's Orders**. Fred promptly provided his physician's name and address so the form would arrive prior to his office appointment to discuss end-of-life Advance Care Planning.

Unfortunately, Fred's physician was not happy with the forms. He refused to sign the **Natural Dying Physician's Orders**. He explained that two orders conflicted with his religious/moral conscience: **A)** the attached consent form that requested *Palliative Sedation*, and **B)** the order

NOT to Assist Feeding and Drinking. Later, Fred's Internet research led him to a 2007 survey published in the New England Journal of Medicine that showed one out of six physicians objected to providing "*Palliative* (Terminal) *Sedation*"—even though for many terminally ill patients, it is only way to get relief from unbearable pain and suffering.

Fred did not want to linger in Advanced Dementia. He had seen skilled staff "mildly" force-feed his aunt for two and a half years. Nursing home staff spooned puree onto the very back of her tongue to make her swallow by reflex. For the entire time, she had absolutely no ability to enjoy life. Worse and for the first time in her life, she became violent. After she died, Fred learned her behavior could have resulted from pain. She could not complain so her doctors may not have recognized or adequately treated her pain. Demented patients receive about one-third as much medication for pain relief as non-demented patients who have similar conditions, like a broken hip. Sometimes they get anti-psychotic medications when pain medications are needed.

For himself, Fred would not want spoon feeding to prolong his dying if it increased the risk of unrecognized and untreated pain and suffering when in the stage of Advanced Dementia. Instead he would want **Natural Dying**, including refusing *Manual Assistance with Oral Feeding and Drinking*. To make his strategy strong, he had selected the *irrevocable choice* of **My Choice Card D** so his "future demented self" could not override his current instructions. That card said, "I want to stop all help from others with oral feeding & drinking—EVEN IF I show I want help with oral feeding & drinking."

Before he left the office of his physician, Fred asked for the name of another doctor who would sign the **Natural Dying Physician's Orders**. An office nurse handed him a list of names and phone numbers. Fred called several more physicians. All said, "No." Fred began to ask why. Eventually, one physician was kind enough to explain: "The doctors at our faith-based hospital are required to follow institutional policy. This policy requires us always to provide nutrition and hydration. There are only two exceptions: if the patient is about to die, or if the act of providing food and fluid itself causes the patient great physical discomfort. This policy even applies to patients whose medical prognosis is that they will never regain conscious life."

Eventually, Fred found a physician affiliated with University Hospital who was willing to sign his **Natural Dying Physician's Orders**. In the space provided under Order # 2 of this form, Fred wrote the name of the faith-based hospital and its affiliated skilled nursing facility as institutions to which he would never want to be transferred or transported. That way, he would not have to leave that hospital in order to have his **Natural Dying—Living Will** honored.

Fred was glad that he did not wait until he was sick or terminally ill to engage in Advance Care Planning. By that time, he may not have had enough energy to find a willing physician.

Fred also completed another form. It was on the other side of the same sheet of yellow heavy stock paper as the **Natural Dying Physician's Orders**. Called the **Natural Dying Advance Directive**, it referred to and incorporated Fred's **Natural Dying—Living Will**.

On it, he named his brother as his proxy. One section of the **Natural Dying Advance Directive** form gave Fred the option of disqualifying any individual from having future authority to make medical decisions on his behalf. In the space provided, Fred wrote down his sister's name because he knew her religious beliefs were much stronger than his.

At this point Fred had a good plan to fulfill his end-of-life wishes. He had created a comprehensive, specific, clear and convincing expression of his *Known Wishes*. Fred had learned that Advance Directives are legally **durable**—unless someone later challenges the patient would have changed his mind. So Fred re-sorted the *Natural Dying Living Will Cards* in a month to prove his wishes were consistent over time. A year later, he reviewed his **Natural Dying—Living Will** and wrote, "This document still accurately reflects my wishes."

Despite the initial challenges to get a physician to sign his forms, Fred felt at peace. He knew that his State had a law that obligated other physicians to honor patients' *Known Wishes* for end-of-life treatment; otherwise they risked losing their immunity from being sued.

At 55, Fred had more motivation to review his Advance Care Planning documents: He now had a surgically implanted intra-cardiac device. His pacemaker would turn on intermittently, to keep his heart beating at a normal rate. Fred asked his cardiac surgeon if he would agree to deactivate the device, if the time ever came when Fred or his legally authorized proxy requested. The surgeon refused to answer his question. Instead he replied, "You haven't even changed batteries once. Why ask that now?" That led Fred to do more Internet research. He discovered a survey that revealed four out of ten members of the Heart Rhythm Society would refuse to comply with a request to deactivate a pacemaker—if the patient's heart function currently depended on the device. Fred felt this was wrong: He had to sign a consent form to put the device in... so professionals should similarly honor his request to deactivate the device.

Fred wondered what he should do next. Instead of looking for another cardiologist who might or might not be around in the future, he took steps to strengthen his strategy to fulfill his end-of-life treatment preferences. He downloaded a **Natural Dying Agreement** and **Natural Dying Affidavit** from the Caring Advocates website. He discussed the **Agreement** with his proxy/brother. Both of them and Fred's his new physician signed it. Fred also added his son as a proxy, who also signed it. Fred read the **Affidavit** and then swore that it was "true and correct" before a notary. Then Fred sent all his Advance Care Planning forms to a **national registry**. There, the forms could be stored and made available to authorized people. They could request an immediate FAX or Internet PDF download of all the forms. Fred also ordered a **Natural Dying Medallion** that he had engraved with his most important wishes. He did not want to wear it now, of course, so he gave it to his son, to store in a safe place.

At 65, Fred reviewed all his documents. He wrote yet another statement that he had not changed his mind about his end-of-life *Known Wishes*. He changed his son from proxy number two to proxy number one. He moved his daughter into fourth position after naming a friend as number three, based on his feeling that his daughter might be too emotionally attached to him to make objective end-of-life decisions.

At 75, Fred's heart was much weaker. He made a difficult decision. If his heart stopped beating, he would want a "Do NOT Attempt Resuscitation" (DNR) order. Fred and his physician completed a state-approved Out-Of-Hospital DNR form. Fred ordered and wore a **DNR-Registry Medallion**. Emergency medical personnel were legally obligated to honor this metal pendant—just like the paper form his physician had signed. Fred had his medallion engraved with these instructions: **A)** "DNR"; **B)** "Do treat me otherwise"; **C)** "Pacemaker"; and **D)** his "Unique Identifying Number"; **E)** the phone number needed to request a FAX and Internet address to download forms from the national registry was already engraved.

At 80, Fred's physician and Fred, with the help of his son whose authority as proxy began when Fred signed the original forms, completed a **Physician Orders for Life-Sustaining Treatment (POLST)**. Unlike the **Natural Dying Physician's Orders**, the POLST form included options for "Limited Treatment" and "Full Treatment, as well as for "Comfort Measures Only." In addition to the DNR order, Fred's physician added the order: "Do NOT Hospitalize unless needed for Comfort Care." Fred was afraid of hospital-acquired infections, but still wanted short-term artificial nutrition and hydration and antibiotics, if such treatments could sustain his life. The plan was to review and if necessary, revise the Physician Orders for Life-Sustaining Treatment, every few months or if Fred's medical condition changed. Fred's son told the physician that his father had noticed mild problems with his short-term memory and that he never wanted his dying prolonged if he reached the stage of Advanced Dementia.

Fred's son read aloud, the directions from the POLST's back page: "POLST does not replace the Advance Directive. When available, **review the Advance Directive and POLST form to ensure consistency, and update forms appropriately to resolve any conflicts**." Fred's son was worried. These directions were vague. What would happen after his father lost decisional capacity? Then, *a physician could update only one form*: the POLST. As the last dated form, it would then take legal precedence. Fred's son asked the physician to write these words in the "Medical Interventions" part of Fred's POLST form: "If the patient's condition ever meets the criteria described in the attached **Natural Dying Advance Directive**, the attached **Natural Dying Physician's Orders** will override the POLST." Now Fred's son felt confident that his father's diligent Advance Care Planning efforts would take precedence in the event of a conflict—even if the last revision of his POLST was the most recently signed form.

By **age 85**, Fred was in the middle stage of Alzheimer's dementia. He no longer could make his own medical decisions. While he could not recall his past values or remember what gave his life deep meaning, he still could enjoy life's simple pleasures. His daughter was having a tough time dealing with the changes in "this man who just looks like my Dad." One day, Fred's physician called his daughter. "Your brother did not answer his phone so I'm calling you. I'm sorry to tell you this, but your father has pneumonia. Will you consent to full treatment with antibiotics and hydration?" Fred's daughter hesitated as she thought about how horrible it would be to see her father continue his slow, relentless decline until he eventually lost the rest of his personality. Her visits to the "Memory Unit" gave her glimpses of this process in other residents. After thinking a moment, she answered, "No."

Later that same day, when she called her brother, she cried as she explained her decision. "It seemed time to let him go. He'll only get worse." But Fred's son pointed out that it was he, as the number one legally designated proxy, not his sister, who had the current authority to make decisions about medical treatment. The son called the nursing home, gave his consent for full treatment, and insisted the nurse contact the doctor right away. Fortunately, it was not too late for Fred to make a full recovery. After two weeks of treatment, Fred returned to his previous state of functioning. Once again he was able to enjoy some of life's simple pleasures.

After Fred recovered, his son showed his daughter a copy of Fred's **Natural Dying—Living Will**. Fred had clearly chosen **Treat & Feed** for card/item **8.6**, which said: "First I can enjoy things like sing-alongs, finger painting, eating, and being touched. But then I get very sick. Ask my doctor if I might get better. If 'Yes,' then TREAT me (full treatment for a reasonable time)." Fred's son apologized to his sister, for not showing her this form, before.

At 90, Fred was approaching the stage of Advanced Dementia. He also had prostate cancer that had begun to spread to his bones so he likely would suffer increasing pain. Fred had clearly stated he did not want endure pain. At the son's request, Fred's physician and he reviewed Fred's **Natural Dying—Living Will**. In a process called "shared decision-making" they agreed: Fred now met his previously selected criteria for **Natural Dying**. "That time" had come. Each knew what to do: Fred's son downloaded and printed all of Fred's forms from the **national registry**. He retrieved the **Natural Dying Medallion** from storage. He placed this medallion on Fred after removing the **DNR-Registry Medallion**. Now, the **Natural Dying Medallion** would alert emergency medical first responders NOT to send him to a hospital unless needed for Comfort Care. Another instruction stated NOT to start an IV for re-hydration to avoid inadvertently sabotaging Fred's lifelong plan to attain a peaceful transition. This medallion also had engraved: "I gave consent for *Palliative Sedation*" and "Do not restart my cardiac device." While emergency medical first responders were not legally bound to honor all these orders, it was likely that they would honor them—especially if someone showed them a copy of the physician-signed **Natural Dying Physician's Orders** that would be prominently kept on the refrigerator door. In the box at the very bottom of the form, Fred's physician had signed after the words, "TO IMPLEMENT Orders 1 – 4," but only after he had made certain phone calls, as the form prompted him to do, as they are part of the form's "safeguards."

Fred's physician contacted Fred's family, friends, other clinicians, clergy, and other significant people Fred previously listed in his Advance Directive. To keep track of his calls, the physician initialed each blank line on the form. Among the people he called was Fred's sister who lived 900 miles away. She was particularly appreciative to learn what was happening and said she would visit soon. Fred's physician had already referred Fred to hospice; now he alerted this expert professional team to provide extra Comfort Care to the mouth to reduce Fred's symptoms of thirst. There was no need to treat hunger, as it generally subsides quickly.

There was no problem for the first three days. Food and fluid were placed in front of Fred but no one provided Fred with *Manual Assistance with Oral Feeding and Drinking*. Fred's son encouraged this attitude: If Fred's brain does not know how to use a spoon or a straw, it will be his disease of dementia that will cause his **Natural Dying**. The Memory Unit insisted on offering—that is, on placing a tray of food and drink near Fred—but they removed it after an hour as its contents were untouched. Fred did not seem disturbed by the sight or smell of food, but it was hard to tell. So... all was going as Fred had long planned...

...Until the morning of the fourth day. As the nurse was turning him, Fred opened his mouth, pointed to the glass, and grunted. Clearly, his gestures were asking for help to drink. No one moved, but the nurse was obviously upset. As she reached over to pick up the glass of water, Fred's son firmly said, "No." She blurted out, "It's inhumane not to help him drink, given how clear his request was." For a long moment, they just glared at each other. Then she left.

When Fred's son came in the following morning, two women were standing by his father's bed. The nurse was holding a clipboard with an official looking form on it. Next to her was Fred's sister, looking grim. The nurse announced she had just completed a form to report suspected elder abuse. She threatened to file it unless others were allowed to help Fred drink. Fred's sister nodded and said, "How could you? It's against the religion he was brought up in."

Fred's son asked the nurse and his aunt to join him in a private conference room so they could discuss his father's options. On the way, he got Fred's medical chart from the nurses' station. It contained all his Advance Care Planning forms. He showed them Fred's **Natural Dying—Living Will** and explained, "This form has accurately reflected Fred's *Known Wishes* since he was 45." He showed them Fred's selection of the "irrevocable choice," **My Choice Card D**. This card had this statement, "I INSIST my future decision-makers stop all life-sustaining treatments and Manual Assistance with Oral Feeding and Drinking—EVEN IF I clearly indicate I want to eat or drink." On the **Natural Dying Agreement** form, Fred had written these words in his own handwriting: "I do not want my 'future demented self' to sabotage my goal for a *timely, peaceful transition*. I DO want to avoid a prolonged dying. I do NOT want to risk more pain and suffering. Therefore listen to the competent instructions I am writing now, NOT to what I may say in the future—if I then suffer from dementia or I lack decisional capacity."

Fred's son showed them his father's five-year updates. None had changed his *Known Wishes*. Then he showed them the **Natural Dying Physician's Orders**. On this form, Fred had explicitly consented to this physician order, "Do Not Assist Feeding & Drinking." Fred had crossed out the words, "Always place food and fluid near the patient, if awake." Fred had also crossed out other words that made it clear NOT to "fulfill patient's request for food and fluid if mentally unable to make medical decisions." Both Fred and his physician signed this form and a notary had acknowledged both Fred's signature and that he had crossed out some words. Finally, Fred's son showed them where, on the **Natural Dying Agreement**, his father, he, his prior physician, and an independent person all had signed. This Agreement gave Fred's proxy (his son) legal authority to override Fred's future request to receive food and fluid.

Finally, Fred's son asked them to read an essay by Catholic health ethicist, Reverend Kevin McGovern. He only had one copy with him, in the book **Peaceful Transitions**, but he found another online, on his wireless laptop. "It will take only ten minutes to read this." He turned to his aunt. "This is something I have thought about for a long time. I hope this essay will alleviate your qualms that in Fred's present circumstances—suffering both from Advanced Dementia and from prostate cancer—treatment to assist him with feeding and drinking would be *extraordinary and disproportionate*; forgoing this treatment does NOT conflict with Catholic teaching."

After they finished reading the essay, Fred's son asked, "Do you have any questions?" (This was his polite way of asking the nurse and his aunt if now, they were convinced.) The nurse replied, "I still need some time to think about all this." His aunt just nodded. That was the moment Fred's son decided to use the "trump card."

He placed the **Natural Dying Affidavit** so that both could read it at the same time. "Let me explain that, under the penalty of perjury, my father swore before a notary that this declaration was 'true and correct.' My father authorized me to use this form if necessary." Then Fred's son pointed to two items on the Affidavit, which he read aloud: "My father instructed me, his proxy, 'to seek declaratory or injunctive relief to effectuate [his] originally expressed, competent wishes, including [his] wish to receive NO nutrition and hydration, and to use funds from his estate to sue anyone who ...accedes to requests by my *future incompetent self* to delay my **Natural Dying**.'" Fred's son looked for clues in the two woman's facial expressions. No definite clue. Again, trying to be diplomatic, he said, "Why don't you take a few minutes to look over all these forms? I realize it's a lot to consider all at once."

As the nurse gathered the papers, Fred's son asked in a gentle tone of voice, "Have you ever taken care of a patient who chose **Natural Dying**?" Sheepishly, she admitted, "No." Fred's son then explained: "The immediate cause of death is usually 'medical dehydration.' Patients often die of their underlying disease, but rarely of starvation. Usually death comes in less than two weeks, and for some of this time—especially toward the end, patients sleep comfortably. Providing fluid only prolongs their dying and often increases their suffering. For many patients, **Natural Dying** is a very peaceful way to die. My father IS dying now... from dementia. That's a better way to die than suffering pain from cancer for a much longer time."

The nurse shuffled through the stack of papers as his aunt "waited." Fred's son guessed the nurse was not really reading but only mulling over what he said. After a few minutes of silence, she quietly said she had changed her mind about filing the report of suspected elder abuse. That is when his aunt began to sob quietly into her handkerchief.

Fred died several days later. To all—except perhaps this nurse—his dying seemed timely, but even she admitted Fred's dying was very peaceful. Fred's sister remained quiet the whole time.

Perspective: Fred achieved all his goals. First, he lived as long as he wanted. He received treatment for pneumonia when he was in the middle stage of dementia. After treatment, he was again able to enjoy some of life's simple pleasures. He avoided *premature dying* because his *Known Wishes* were specific: he DID want to be fed and to be treated if he did NOT meet his chosen criteria for Advanced Dementia. Also, he had selected one specific **My Way Card** that requested treatment to stay alive in this very situation. (This card is included in the **My Way Cards** because this situation is so common.)

About five years later, Fred attained a *timely, peaceful transition* by **Natural Dying**. After he met the criteria he had previously chosen, his son effectively used the **Plan Now, Die Later— Ironclad Strategy** to overcome a threatening challenge from a nurse and Fred's sister. Without this strategy, Fred's **Natural Dying** might have been delayed.

Without the **Natural Dying Agreement** and **Natural Dying Affidavit**, the institution's conservative risk management attorneys might have supported the nurse and Fred's sister by insisting that Fred receive *Manual Assistance with Oral Feeding and Drinking* while the elder abuse allegation was being investigated and while they obtained an ethics committee consultation. Various consultants may have taken much time to discuss "this interesting case" from several points of view. If the conflict did not resolve quickly, Fred's son might have felt it necessary to go to court, which would have been costly as well as time-consuming. While all these additional authorities may have been designed to protect Fred's life, their effect may have been merely *To Delay is To Deny*. Fred was in pain from prostate cancer and was not benefiting from continued life-sustaining treatment. His previous Advance Care Planning forms made it clear he would not want treatment to extend his highly burdensome existence.

Fred's success in attaining his goal of a *timely, peaceful transition* resulted from implementing several strategies. **A)** Despite some initial obstacles, he diligently completed a set of Advance Care Planning forms that clearly and convincingly expressed his specific *Known Wishes*. **B)** He reviewed his choices periodically, to prove that his treatment preferences were consistent over time; **C)** He anticipated potential challenges from specific physicians, institutions, and relatives; **D)** He strengthened his strategy by choosing the irrevocable option to refuse *Manual Assistance with Oral Feeding and Drinking* (**My Choice Card D**); **E)** He further strengthened his proxy's power to override his future decisions by signing a **Natural Dying Agreement**; **F)** He added the "trump card" to his strategy by swearing the **Natural Dying Affidavit** before a notary; and **G)** he provided two ways to inform others about his end-of-life wishes: he stored his forms in an accessible **national registry** and, at the very end of his life, he wore a **Natural Dying Medallion**.

"Fred's" composite case history shows why it is so important to develop an *effective* Advance Care Plan. If we cannot speak for ourselves, this plan can prevent others from causing our lives to end prematurely. It can also avoid our being forced to endure a prolonged process of dying with suffering if we consider being trapped in that state as "worse than death."

For many people, it initially seems counter-cultural to not eat and drink. Yet this is normal as our lives come to their natural end. In fact, this is the way people have been dying for millennia—before the introduction of modern medical technology. To overcome possible challenges from certain people and some institutions, we must invoke effective strategies so we can feel certain that others will honor our end-of-life wishes. Note: While Caring Advocates offers the "Natural Dying" series of forms for an "ironclad strategy," this non-profit organization can also combine its offerings with other forms that people may wish to include. Some examples are: State-approved forms, a "Five Wishes" form, and medallions made by other providers—to mention a few. Also, some U S States offer their own registry to store documents. Caring Advocates respects each person's choice to set up an individualized plan using their preferred choice of components.

16: Summary: Advance Care Planning for half a lifetime

At age **45**, "Fred" completed these forms:

1. **Natural Dying—Living Will** by sorting *Natural Dying—Living Will Cards*;
2. **Natural Dying Advance Directive**;
5. **Natural Dying Physician's Orders**; and,
6. **Consent Form to Relieve Unbearable Suffering** by *Palliative Sedation*.
Note: Form 3 (Designation of Proxies/Agents; Specifying Their Authorities) and
Form 4 (Natural Dying Organ Donation Consent Form) would also be completed
even though they are not mentioned in Fred's story.

At age **55**, Fred completed these forms:

7. **Natural Dying Agreement**; and,
8. **Natural Dying Affidavit**. Fred sent all 8 forms to a **national registry**.
He also purchased a **Natural Dying Medallion** for his son to keep safe.
Note: Most people complete all eight forms at one time, but Fred was only 45
when he began Advance Care Planning.

At age **65**, Fred changed the sequence of proxies and re-confirmed his *Known Wishes*.

At age **75**, Fred ordered and wore a **DNR-Registry Medallion**.
Some of the engraved words stated: "DNR, but DO Treat Otherwise."

At age **80**, he used a Physician Orders for Life-Sustaining Treatment to be revised periodically.

At age **85**, his proxy used the **Natural Dying Advance Directive** and the **Natural Dying—Living Will**, *to insist on life-sustaining treatment* while in the middle stage of dementia.

At age **90**, his proxy replaced the POLST with a **Natural Dying Physician's Orders** whose orders were signed and implemented by his current physician.
Replaced **DNR-Registry Medallion** with **Natural Dying Medallion**.
His proxy used the **Natural Dying Agreement** and **Natural Dying Affidavit** and referred to a key essay by a priest/health ethicist to avoid a threatening conflict so his end-of-life *Known Wishes* would be expeditiously fulfilled.

Fred's son was an excellent proxy, but not perfect. He fulfilled the job description; that is: **Make sure others will honor my *Known Wishes*.** His one failing was not communicating well with alternate proxies (for example, his own sister) in the event he was not available. As mentioned previously, to be effective your "ironclad strategy" must have a capable advocate. Next we discuss what to look for—as you select individuals to serve as your proxy.

17: How to Select Your Health Care Proxy/Agent

Selecting a health care proxy/agent (durable power of attorney for health care) is NOT like advertising on Craig's List. Candidates rarely present résumés that summarize their previous job experience. Former, satisfied customers are in no position to provide letters of reference. Candidates may never have applied for, or held a similar position. They may offer no relevant educational or apprenticeship experience. Yet you will still assign a "first-time novice" this awesome responsibility: to make critical, life-determining decisions on your behalf.

To develop a job description that is useful for both selection and expectations, first consider the following brief historical perspective of Advance Directives.

Pendulums have swung back and forth in terms of the preferred "style" for Living Wills and Proxy Directives. Initially too vague, Living Wills swung toward too specific and then back. If someday your condition was not defined by your *Known Wishes*, your proxy would need to rely on more general guidelines to make the same decision you would have made. (This is called the "Substituted Judgment" method of decision-making.) While *values histories* seemed promising, another innovative approach is to use "Go Wish" cards that Dr. Elizabeth Menkin developed. This "game" presents Advance Care Planners 35 items; they eventually rank order the top ten.[41] A study of 33 subjects[42] showed two items in the top five were "To be free of pain" and "To be mentally aware." Providing proxies with only this information is inadequate to guide future decisions, however. These two wishes can be in direct conflict; for example, if a patient's pain is still unending and unbearable after other treatment modalities have failed to provide relief, then the patient's only alternative is "sedation to unconsciousness" (*Palliative Sedation*). Someone who took the average time to prioritize "Go Wish" cards (22 minutes)

---

[41] Menkin ES. Go Wish: a tool for end-of-life care conversations. *J Palliat Med. 2007. Apr;10(2):297-303.*
[42] Lankarani-Fard A et al. Feasibility of discussing end-of-life care goals with inpatients using a structured, conversational approach: the Go Wish card game. *J Pain Symptom Manage. 2010 Apr;39(4):637-43.*

would still need to complete the **Consent Form to Relieve Unbearable Suffering by Palliative Sedation** (in about half this time) to provide specific guidance.

Another example of a conflict between two items in the top five "Go Wish" cards is relevant for religious patients: "To be at peace with God" and "Not being a burden to my family." Some patients do wish to stop *Manual Assistance with Oral Feeding and Drinking* once they meet their criteria of Advanced Dementia; but some religious leaders consider such stopping to be "euthanasia by omission." In contrast, the **Plan Now, Die Later—Ironclad Strategy** asks Advance Care Planners to explicitly indicate their preferences.

The swinging pendulum for Proxy Directives is between two styles: **covenant** and **contract**. The "covenant" style expects proxies to fulfill their faithful promise based on knowing (and perhaps loving) the patient well; these may include "shared memories" about the patient's lifelong values. This is how Dr. Joseph Fins romantically described the **covenant** type of relationship in 1999. He also wrote: "an informed and loving proxy [can] confront [] a difficult moral choice."[43] Physicians prefer the **covenant** style. Why? It is easier to ask one person—the designated proxy—to consent or refuse to treatment than to try to interpret the patient's previously written instructions. Also, laws provide immunity for making mistakes *in good faith*. In 1999, Dr. Fins assumed either the first named proxy would serve or the alternate proxies would know the patient as well. He did not anticipate numerous subsequent studies showing **proxies are wrong** about patients' treatment preferences **one-third** of the **time**.[44]

Dr. Fins did admit the **contractual** "view is most appropriate when the patient's preferences are clear... [since it] *appropriately* protects the vulnerable patient from outright violations of his preferences." {Original emphasis.} Dr. Fins did not otherwise note that the contractual style enhances the power of proxies to fulfill patients' *Known Wishes*, if challenged. This is the main reason the **Plan Now, Die Later—Ironclad Strategy** uses the **contract** style. Even so, the Advance Care Planner can choose the **covenant** for one major decision: s/he can select **My Choice Card "B"** that states: "Permit others to decide if help with feeding and drinking should, or should not, stop." Otherwise, the "ironclad strategy" uses the **contract** style of Proxy Directive. *In eight simple, clear words, this is your proxy's job description:*

"Make sure others will honor my *Known Wishes*."

Instead of selecting a proxy who has loved you a lifetime, s/he **must** advocate your *Known Wishes*—as expressed in your **Natural Dying—Living Will** and your other signed consent forms. To the extent that your *Known Wishes* are comprehensive, specific, and clear and

---

[43] Fins JJ. From Contract to Covenant in Advance Care Planning. *Law, Medicine & Ethics 27* (1999): 46-51

[44] Shalowitz DI, Garrett-Mayer E, Wendler D. The accuracy of surrogate decision makers: a systematic review. *Archives of Internal Medicine* 166 (2006): 493-497. Another study showed of those who "inaccurately predicted patients' extending life versus relieving pain preferences," almost nine out of ten replaced their own wishes for those of the patient: Marks MA, Arkes HR. Patient and surrogate disagreement in end-of-life decisions: can surrogates accurately predict patients' preferences? *Med Decis Making. 2008 Jul-Aug;28(4):524-31.*

convincing and do apply to your future specific mental/medical condition, physicians will understand them and courts of law will accept them. There is one additional benefit of relying on your *Known Wishes*. Serving as a proxy carries a high risk of emotional burden; however a recent literature review revealed eighteen studies that showed these burdens can be reduced if proxies have confidence their decisions are consistent with patients' treatment preferences.[45]

Proxies who sign the recommended **Natural Dying Agreement** will be signing a *contract* that is *bilateral* and therefore legally stronger than a *unilateral* contract, which are typically found in Proxy Directives where the form is merely a patient's REQUEST for the proxy to perform certain functions, and may not even have notified the proxy of this request.[46] A *bilateral contract* is an important component of the **Plan Now, Die Later—Ironclad Strategy**. Suppose an unrelated person challenged your proxy's actions by claiming that stopping *Manual Assistance with Oral Feeding and Drinking* is not in your "best interest" and threatened to take your proxy to court to disqualify him/her as your proxy. A *bilateral contract* would let your proxy argue: "How can you challenge my actions and claim they are not in the patient's 'best interest'? Performing this service is precisely why the patient entered into a (bilateral) contract with me to be his proxy, and paid me *a professional fee* to perform this exact service. In fact before he would agree to designate me as his proxy, the patient insisted that I assert in writing that I had no moral or religious conflict of conscience to perform this precise service." (Note: If no professional fee is involved, the argument would change to: "The patient chose me because he trusted me based on our long-standing relationship and his knowledge that I am devoted to try hard to make sure his suffering would not be prolonged.")

Knowing the proxy's job description, let's divide the qualities to look for into three areas:

The areas are: **1.** General personal characteristics; **2.** Relationship with you; and, **3.** Ability to function in this area. (Your State's requirements still must be met; for example, your proxy usually cannot be your physician or an employee of a community care facility or a residential care facility where you are receiving care. Check your State's forms for specific details.)

1. **General personal characteristics**: Your proxy must be **willing**, **able**, and **available**. Almost all other Proxy Directives are unilateral requests that *assume* your proxy is "**willing**"; few provide a formal way to notify your selected proxy. (The **Plan Now, Die Later—Ironclad Strategy** *requires* your proxy to sign a *bilateral contract*, the **Natural**

---

[45] Wendler D, Rid A. Systematic review: the effect on surrogates of making treatment decisions for others. *Ann Intern Med.* 2011 Mar 1;154(5):336-46.

[46] To illustrate the difference between *unilateral* and *bilateral contracts*, consider this story: Suppose my dog ran away and I asked Sally to let me know *if* she found it. As an incentive, there would be a $50 reward. Sally would have NO obligation to look, let alone look hard, to find my dog. She might not even try since a *unilateral contract* is only a request. Sally's service is thus NOT obligatory. However if my dog walked into her home and she returned it to me, I would still give her the "award." In contrast, suppose I dropped off my dog at Sally's Salon and *I paid her $50* because *she promised* to groom my dog. We would then have a *bilateral contract*. If Sally promised but then failed to perform the service of grooming my dog, she would be legally guilty of breaching our contact.

Dying Agreement, which signature should be witnessed.) "**Able**" includes staying cognitively intact, energetic and healthy, and likely to live longer than you. (Recommended: designate alternates, just in case.) "**Available**" means your proxy can respond quickly to make decisions and "be there" at your bedside long enough to... (and these words should become your proxy's *mantra*): "**Make sure others will honor your *Known Wishes*.**"

No quality is more important than being **trustworthy**, specifically **to advocate your end-of-life *Known Wishes***. Your proxy should be **decisive** even when asked to make difficult, life-determining decisions. S/he should NOT be subject to paralytic fear. Proxies should not be personally hindered by their **moral** qualms or **religious** tenets. They should not be so **emotionally involved** in you that they cannot agree to medical orders "to let you go," if your suffering became unbearable. In other words, you proxy should NOT be swayed by the **selfish** goal to keep you alive to be a **companion**. Similarly, s/he should NOT consent for you to receive life-sustaining treatment mainly because they need to retain the "important" role of serving as your **caregiver**. They should NOT have a financial **conflict of interest** that influences their deciding when it is time for your **Natural Dying**. In situations where your *Known Wishes* do not apply, they must understand and follow the concept of "Substituted Judgment": This requires proxies to make the same decisions that *YOU* would have made—NOT the decisions they would make for *themselves*. It is easier if your proxy and you have similar values and beliefs, but what is critically important is that your proxy promises to make decisions based on **your** *Known Wishes*.

Other desirable personal characteristics are to be a good **listener, responsive**, and have enough **courage, energy, conviction, persistence**, and **diplomacy** to get the job done in the face of subtle or direct threats, if conflicts arise (because they often do). Examples: As life-determining decisions need to be made, family members may get into their familiar power struggles. In such situations, your proxy needs to remain firm and decisive. Physicians may resist complying with your *Known Wishes*. Here, your proxy must demonstrate **diplomacy**, and if that does not work **courage** to follow through. S/he may for instance use the specific authority you granted by signing the form, **Designation of Proxies/Agents; Specifying Their Authorities** and insist you be discharged "Against Medical Advice" (AMA)—if necessary to fulfill your *Known Wishes*. Your proxy should be able to relate to medical and other professionals with mutual respect. S/he should be able to balance being firm but respectful with authority figures and as s/he tries to resolve conflicts.

2. **Relationship with you**: Your proxy should **care** about you and be **devoted** to your attaining the goal of a *timely, peaceful transition*. While it may be helpful if s/he knows your general values and treatment preferences, what is critically important is that s/he really understands your *Known Wishes*. Ideally, you memorialized your *Known Wishes* in an audio or video recording as you sorted the **My Way Cards** or as you explained your choices on the resulting written form, the **Natural Dying—Living Will**. It would be nice if your proxy has known you a long time, but sometimes people find the number of available

candidates for proxies dwindle over time. They sometimes ask a professional person who works in the field to serve as their proxy or alternate proxy. With adequate documentation of your *Known Wishes,* these professionals can get "up to speed" quite quickly.

3. **Ability to function in this area**. *Ideally*, your proxy will have a working **knowledge** of medicine, of the law, and of ethics—as these disciplines relate to end-of-life issues. (Actually few professionals are this well-rounded.) Realistically, your proxy should be **resourceful** to learn what s/he needs to know on an "as-needed basis," and be willing to ask for input from others who do know. Good things to know/learn: How to request another physician's second opinion, a consultation from the institution's ethics committee, and advice from an attorney who specializes in health care law or elder law; how to tap into pastoral and spiritual resources, social resources, and patient advocates and Ombudsmen. Your proxy should also know what hospices are local, and perhaps physicians who specialize in Palliative Care. Your proxy should know how to tap into such resources as the National Hospice and Palliative Care organization (www.nhpco.org) and the American Bar Association's tool kit (which has sections specifically designed to help proxies)[47], books, and websites including the list of Internet resources on www.CaringAdvocates.org. Your proxy may join organizations that help their members to function in this challenging area. This field is constantly changing. New challenges, new forms, and new court rulings continue to have impact on the way physicians practice medicine in the environment of health care law.

Even the most devoted proxy/agent cannot be by your side 100% of the time, always available to present all your legally valid Advance Care Planning forms to anyone who must learn your *Known Wishes.* The next TOPIC describes two vehicles that work together towards this goal.

18: So All Concerned Know Your End-of-Life Wishes: the "Natural Dying Medallion" and National Registries

Your completed set of well-designed forms will not help you attain your goal unless your future decision-maker places them in front your future physicians when critical decisions must be made. The **Plan Now, Die Later—Ironclad Strategy** incorporates two ways to make these forms available: One is a **medallion** (a metal dog tag) that has sufficient space to alert first responders to several urgent wishes. The other is a **national registry** from which authorized people can request an immediate FAX or Internet download of all your Advance Care Planning forms. Medallions have the national registry's toll-free number and Internet address engraved.

Most States[48] now offer what Dr. Bruce Haynes recommended in 1993 for California's Emergency Medical Services: "In regard to resuscitation... the patient is seen under emergency

_____

[47] http://apps.americanbar.org/aging/publications/docs/consumer_tool_kit_bk.pdf
[48] Florida requires instead a reduced size copy of the signed DNR form on yellow paper.

conditions and accurate identification may be difficult... The most accurate form of identification for patients outside of licensed facilities is a medallion or bracelet attached to the patient... [which] should be standard in each county and have controlled availability **so that it may, by itself, be immediately honored**... Medallions should only be issued after receiving a copy of the completed...approved DNR Request Form from an individual."[49]

Typical **DNR** medallions may not ensure *timely, peaceful transitions*. The **Natural Dying Medallion** informs first (9-1-1) responders about several urgent instructions that can be engraved, if you wish. When emergency medical personnel see these instructions, they will be more likely to facilitate rather than inadvertently sabotage your goal.[50] Here are some examples:

- What medical treatment DO you want or NOT want? Do you want *CPR attempted,* or not? Do you want your *intra-cardiac device restarted,* or not? Do you want *an IV drip or oral fluids* to rehydrate you, or not?
- Do you want to be transported to a hospital—*ONLY* if needed for Comfort Care?
- Did you want all to know you *gave consent for Palliative Sedation*—to avoid pain and suffering?
- Do you want authorized people to obtain immediate FAX or Internet download copies of all your Advance Care Planning forms if they so request by a toll-free call or by Internet?
- Do you want your medallion to have the name and phone number of your proxy?

To explain: The most urgent order is "No IV hydration" because first responders are trained to start intravenous drips that run at full speed so physicians can administer life-prolonging medications. But if your goal is a *timely, peaceful transition* via medical dehydration, then *automatically* starting an IV could inadvertently postpone/sabotage your goal. What you engrave on your **Natural Dying Medallion** can prevent this from happening. Second, some hospices have expertise in providing *Palliative Sedation* at home, but you may agree to be hospitalized ONLY if needed for Comfort Care just in case, so you do not suffer. If resistance is encountered about not restarting an intra-cardiac device, your proxy may need to prove your *Known Wishes* by showing first responders your **Natural Dying Physician's Orders**.

Requirements about alert jewelry differ among States—for safety, security, and appearance:

Safety: Before a medallion can be issued, almost all States[51] require an approved DNR form signed by both a physician and the patient or proxy.[52] Caring Advocates also offers a **DNR-**

---

[49] Suggested in 1993; retrieved on May 21, 2009. http://www.emsa.ca.gov/pubs/emsa-111.asp. {Emphasis added.}
[50] First responders who were not trained to respond to these specific orders can refer to the patient's **Natural Dying Physician's Orders** and if necessary, call their "base station physician" for further guidance. Later, under non-emergency situations, your (possibly new) physician can read your FAXed or downloaded Advance Care Planning forms, to learn about your specific *Known Wishes*.
[51] Oklahoma does not require a physician's signature; instead the State requires two qualified witnesses to sign.

Registry Medallion with these words typically engraved: "For cardiac arrest: DNR. DO treat me otherwise." These medallions may include information to maximize the chance that treatment will keep you alive, such as certain diagnoses and drug allergies. **DNR-Registry Medallions** can be used if you DO want a DNR order, but do NOT want **Natural Dying**. The words "Do treat me otherwise" instruct health care providers not to mistakenly consider a "Do Not Resuscitate" order as a "Do Not Treat" order. That could cause *premature dying*, as Dr. Fred Mirarchi's research has so convincingly demonstrated. (See "Stories," Chapter 2.)

Security: Some States require no identifying information. Others require only one or two of the following: patient's name, date of birth, and Unique Identifying Number. Caring Advocates uses all three. This makes it much less likely that someone will place one person's DNR medallion on another when that person still wanted CPR or other life-sustaining interventions.

Appearance: All States require the inscription, "Do Not Resuscitate" or "DNR" on medallions. Most States accept the medical emergency logo. Here is a small sampling of other requirements: Oklahoma: the State name; Missouri: an outline of the State's geographic shape; Texas: the letters "OOH" ("out of hospital"); California: "EMS" ("Emergency Medical Services"); Florida: physician's name, signature, and phone number. Some States also accept the letters **POLST, MOLST,** or **POST**; however these letters do not actually instruct emergency medical personnel what to do; they just indicate that a form *exists*. First responders who see these letters must A) *locate* the form, B) *read* the form, and C) *interpret* the form. The last task may not be straightforward if the physician ordered more than one level of treatment and/or Limited Treatment. In such cases, **no longer**—in the words of Dr. Haynes—will "the bracelet or medallion" be **sufficient** "**by itself** [to] be immediately honored."

Consider ordering a **Natural Dying Medallion** your proxy keeps safe, since you never know when it might be needed, such as after a sudden car accident that leaves you in a coma.[53]

The templates for engraving some representative medallions are on the next page. Below is a photo of one:

---

[52] Some States allow nurse practitioners and physician assistants. Some States have options other than requiring patients' signatures, such as a witness to an informed oral consent, as in the State of New York.

[53] The medallions of most other companies are too small to engrave all these instructions and identifying information. Order online or by phone from Caring Advocates, or use the form included in My Way Cards decks.

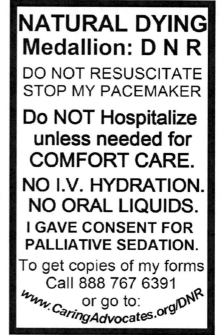

Left: Using Texas as an example, this Medallion could be the front of either the **Natural Dying Medallion** or the **DNR-Registry Medallion**. It has both the Caring Advocates logo and the widely accepted "medical emergency" logo. *Middle*: This back of a California medallion has the words required by the Emergency Medical Services Authority plus the Date of Birth. It also has the required toll-free number and URL to request the patient's DNR and Advance Care Planning forms. *Right*: This back of a **Natural Dying Medallion** illustrates additional orders so Emergency Medical Personnel can facilitate the goal to attain a *timely, peaceful transition*. States vary in terms of required physical requirements. Florida must be yellow. California must be stainless steel. Photos of actual medallions and engravings: www.CaringAdvocates.org/DNR.

National (or regional) registries: Some professionals do not think Electronic Medical Records can completely solve the problem of obtaining Advance Care Planning forms quickly. Even in an electronic format, it may take a while to find Advance Care Planning forms in a several hundred-page medical chart. The trend continues for specialized services as States and regions announce new programs for electronically available Advance Directives and POLSTs. The oldest national registry specializing in Advance Care Planning forms is the U S Living Will Registry; among the newest is Paratus.

Having forms available assumes you have completed them. An effective strategy begins with the *details* of how you fill out the forms. A prime example is the TOPIC discussed next: A new potential battle front is emerging with the introduction of a hybrid type of Advance Care Planning form—a doctor's order form that is filled out in advance.

19: POLST (Physician Orders for Life-Sustaining Treatment) forms threaten to override your Advance Directives

The Need for POLST forms: More than four out of ten deceased people required medical decision-making as their lives came to an end. Of these, seven out of ten had previously lost the capacity to make those decisions. Yet only 2% of those who had Living Wills wanted "all care possible."[54] Over the years, polls have revealed that only three to four out of ten people complete Advance Care Planning.[55] Taken together these figures leave a huge gap: millions of patients who did not create clear instructions still need medical decisions as they near death. In the past, it was sometimes difficult to avoid the default choice of aggressive, burdensome, unwanted, expensive medical treatment. Another "solution" now seems available: in the U S, a new form is gaining acceptance. Their names vary slightly, as they may contain the term "Medical" or "Physician," and either "life-sustaining" or "scope" of treatment. Their general term is Physician Orders for Life-Sustaining Treatment or **POLST**. Other forms have the acronyms **MOLST** and **POST**.

Advantages of POLST forms: First, they are *immediately actionable physician's orders*. In contrast, Living Wills contain treatment requests that physicians must first interpret (and then agree to comply with). Second, by law or by common practice, these *orders are valid across treatment settings*. In practice however, these orders are often changed after a patient is *admitted* to a new setting. Consider the Washington State POLST that clearly states: "This POLST is effective across all settings including hospitals **until replaced by new physician's orders**..." {Emphasis added.} Furthermore, physicians are not obligated to continue to use another POLST form if they void one; they can instead (and often do) substitute a hospital's order form, which rarely if ever requires the signature of a surrogate decision-maker.

Third, this more practical "advantage" of POLST forms is rarely mentioned: these forms can be used to order "Limited Intervention" or "Comfort Measures Only" for patients who have lost their decisional capacity and could not otherwise give informed consent or engage in Advance Care Planning. This is one way to fill in the huge gap mentioned above. Important benefits: some patients may suffer less; their care may be less expensive. But the key question is: Will they receive the care that they really wanted? (See "A Tale of Two Mothers" in "Stories.")

Granting physician's power: POLST forms give physicians much power. In California, for example, physicians can consider family members as potential surrogates but they also may

---

54 Silveira MJ, Kim SY, Langa KM. Advance directives and outcomes of surrogate decision making before death. *N Engl J Med. 2010 Apr 1;362(13):1211-8.*

55 In the UK, only 8% have Living Wills, although 47% say they would make one **if it were easy**. http://pdfs.island.lk/2010/02/22/p11.pdf. In the UK, physicians determine the "best" treatment for patients; patients can request but not demand treatment. Physicians must honor patients' Advance Treatment Refusals, however, if presented in the form of legally valid Advance Decisions (Living Wills).

determine which person is "best able to speak for the patient." Note: this physician-selected surrogate, who signs a POLST form as a "legally **recognized** surrogate," must be distinguished from the "legally **designated** surrogate" whom a patient might have diligently chosen when their minds were still "sound," that is, possessed decisional capacity.

POLST forms can override Advance Directives: It is most worrisome aspect that POLST forms can override diligently created Advance Directives, which patients expected others to honor in the future. This *should not* happen; this *may not* happen, but this **can** happen. If this **does** happen, the difference could be a matter of life and death for patients who completed a "Will to Live" Directive (www.nrlc.org/medethics/WilltoLiveProject.html), whose presumption is to preserve life based on human dignity rather than to make end-of-life treatment decisions based on the "quality of life ethic." For most readers of this book, the difference could be sabotage of your plan for a *timely, peaceful transition*. The risk is that 9-1-1 Emergency Medical Personnel will start an IV Drip (as they are trained to do automatically). An April, 2011, report when twelve states had POLST forms, "to the extent that there is a risk of conflict, the states differed in how to respond. The POLST form controls in three states (ID, NC, UT). The most recently completed controls in two states (CA, WA), and the advance directive controls in one state (TN). Two states (NY, WV) mandate that the substituted judgment/best interest standard be followed. Four states (HI, MN, OR, VT) do not address the conflict issue at all." [www.assets.aarp.org/rgcenter/ppi/cons-prot/POLST-Report-04-11.pdf. Retrieved 7-11-11.] The **Plan Now, Die Later—Ironclad Strategy** now considers this challenge in two states:

A **"semi-transparent" example**: The State of Idaho's **POST** form is NOT transparent. It provides check boxes to indicate that the patient's Living Will, DPA or DPAHC are known to "also exist," but it does NOT indicate which form would prevail in case of a conflict. In contrast, the State's sample Advance Directive form in the statute *is transparent:* it offers Advance Care Planners with *only these two choices: Either* **incorporate the POST** as "compatible with this [Advance] Directive," *or* **agree in advance to modify** the Advance Directive: "If a POST form is later signed by my physician, then this **living will shall be deemed modified to be compatible** with the terms of the POST form." {Emphasis added.} What's missing? To clearly disclose how the conflict will be resolved on *both* the **POST** form *and* the Advance Directive form; and most importantly, to offer Advance Care Planners a THIRD choice [in my words]: "I want my *Known Wishes*-as expressed in my Advance Directive—to be **durable**; therefore I want my Advance Directive to override a later-dated POST, if the two forms conflict."

A **"more subtle" example**: California's POLST form includes this informational statement: "POLST does not replace the Advance Directive. When available, **review** the Advance Directive and POLST form to ensure consistency, and **update forms appropriately to resolve any conflicts**." Note: the POLST form does not specify WHO shall do the updating. More importantly, the POLST form does not mention California Probate Code Section **4781.4**, This section states: "If the orders in an individual's request regarding resuscitative measures

[POLST] directly conflict with his or her individual health care instruction, as defined in Section 4623, then, to the extent of the conflict, **the most recent order or instruction is effective.**" {Emphasis added.} [Section 4623 refers to a "patient's written or oral direction concerning a health care decision for the patient."] *Interestingly*, a new check box **with a date** was added to the 2011 POLST, which was not on the 2009 version:

|___| **Advance Directive dated** _____ **available and reviewed**

POLST forms are often completed and revised after patients have lost decisional capacity, when it is impossible to update patients' Advance Directives. Thus *only* POLST forms *can be updated.* The obvious question is: how likely are POLST forms to be the "most recent"? Here, California's form is quite clear. A POLST must be signed and dated every time it is revised, and:

Directions on the back page of POLST forms say **review POLSTs "periodically,"** *and* when:

- **The person is transferred from one care setting or care level to another, or**
- **There is a substantial change in the person's health status, or**
- **The person's treatment preferences change.**

The risk of changing orders: A new, conflicting POLST form will take precedence over **your prior**, longstanding *Known* Wishes—and this may lead to your *prolonged dying* or your *premature dying* that you do not want. There is only one "safeguard": POLSTs are intended only for patients *whose physicians do not expect* them to live longer than a year. Bottom line: POLSTs forms give physicians much power over your autonomy. Physicians can **A)** determine that you have less than a year to live; **B)** decide which person is best able to speak for you; and **C)** change orders about potentially life-sustaining treatments. The only constraint is that they must, *in good faith* **judge their own orders** as "consistent with the person's medical condition and preferences."

Question: If you knew that after you lose decisional capacity, your diligent efforts to complete all your Advance Care Planning forms including your Living Will *could be changed* by your future treating physician (whom you may not currently know)... would you still put in all that Advance Care Planning effort? Perhaps not... but wait! Here's the good news: The next TOPIC shows how the **Plan Now, Die Later—Ironclad Strategy** can overcome these challenges.

20: So POLSTs do NOT override your Advance Care Planning

To preserve your Advance Care Plan's **durability** given the threat of POLST, take these steps:

1. Answer "Yes" to this question on your **Natural Dying Advance Directive**: "In the event of a conflict with other Advance Care forms, including a POLST/MOLST/POST, do you want this **NDAD/NDPO** to prevail—regardless of when other forms are dated?"

In theory, this *should* suffice: Every future physician A) *should* consult with your legally **designated** proxy/agent and B) *should* take into consideration your written *Known Wishes* as expressed in your **Natural Dying Advance Directive** (which incorporates your **Natural Dying—Living Will**). In practice, it is best to provide additional ways to make your future physician aware of your preference and to provide your proxy/agent with the means to motivate your physician and others so they *WILL* comply with your *Known Wishes*.

2. When you visit your physician to discuss and to sign consent on your **Natural Dying Physician's Orders**, sign your name near the first sentence in Order #2 that reads, "NATURAL DYING PHYSICIAN'S ORDERS **overrides** Physician Orders for Life-Sustaining Treatment for Limited/Full Treatment *if in effect*." Underline or circle the word, "**overrides**." Physicians are legally obligated to review the most recent physicians' orders before writing new orders. When they do, this highlighted order with your signature **should** make them realize this order reflects your **durable** *Known Wish*—which their "new" orders then **should** reflect.

3. Ask your physician to add this order to your POLST: "In the event of a *conflict* with other forms including this **POLST**, the patient's **Natural Dying Physician's Orders** will prevail—regardless of when other forms are dated." In the event you do not have decisional capacity, instruct your authorized proxy/agent to ask your physician to write a similar order. Where on the form can such an order be added? Two examples are: In New York, in the space after words, "**Other Instructions** about starting or stopping treatments discussed with the doctor..." In California, in Section B, under "**Additional Orders**."

There may be an additional hurdle to overcome in California, however. A statement on their POLST reads: "Depending on local EMS protocol, 'Additional Orders' written in Section B **may not be implemented by EMS personnel**." {Emphasis added.} This flies in the face of the almost universally accepted clinical practice that health care providers are *obligated* either to follow physician's orders or to state and discuss the reasons why they object. The statute that created California's POLST gave its EMS Authority to approve the POLST form. To date, no one has challenged this regulatory body for **also** carving out one category of health care providers as not being *obligated* to honor physician's orders. This is one reason why it is a good idea to provide your proxy/agent with the additional "ammunition" described next.

4. Provide your proxy/agent with legal information to help motivate your future physician to make sure that your *Known Wishes* are honored. To continue to use California as an example, Probate Code Section **4782** states: "A health care provider who honors a request regarding resuscitative measures is **not subject** to criminal prosecution, civil liability, discipline for unprofessional conduct, administrative sanction, or any other sanction... **if** the health care provider (b) has **no knowledge** that the **action or decision** would be **inconsistent** with a **health care decision** that the **individual signing the request would have made on his or her own behalf under like circumstances.**"[56] Some attorneys believe this section simply means that physicians will preserve their immunity for writing orders ONLY if these orders are consistent with *Known Wishes* in the individual's Living Will and proxy's request.

Your proxy/agent may have to explain these legal nuances to your future physician. Below is a sample script. A good way to use this script is to read it or refer to it—as you **discuss** the issue of a conflict between Advance Directives and POLST with the attending physician. Generally, it is *not wise to send letters* unless they have first been reviewed by your attorney.

> Dr. _____, thanks for agreeing to discuss the conflict between the **POLST** for Mr. _____ and his **Natural Dying Advance Directive/Natural Dying Physician's Orders**.
>
> From what I have read, you might lose your immunity for being sued if you A) had **knowledge** of your patient's *Known Wishes*, but B) wrote orders inconsistent with the decisions your patient would have made, or inconsistent with what his/her proxy/agent (that is, **me**)—now requests. Based on Probate Code Section **4782**, the safest legal course you can take is to comply in good faith with these consistent requests.
>
> Of course there is ambiguity in the new POLST law. One section of California Probate Codes states POLST is NOT an Advance Directive; another section states the two forms are to some extent equivalent since the most recently signed form takes precedence. Consult an attorney, if you wish, but also consider the statements in the next paragraph.
>
> Both common law regarding informed consent, and statutes regarding the honoring of *Known Wishes* ("known desires") have longer case law histories than conflicts about the new POLST form. As I understand the POLST law, it did not change the part that physicians can expect to retain their immunity ONLY if they follow *in good faith*, the patient's written health care instructions and the proxy/agent's oral requests (provided these two are consistent). Bottom line: although certain sections of the Code are ambiguous, following the traditional path has a lower legal risk.

Finally, instruct your proxy/agent to inform your future physician that his job is not only to write orders that reflect your *Known Wishes*, but also to help make sure others will honor them. In California, your proxy should ask the medical director of your local EMS to inform the staff base station physicians (whom 9-1-1 personnel call for advice when in the field).

---

[56] The older Section 4733 has a similar statement: physicians shall comply with *Known Wishes* in an individual health care instruction or made by an authorized person.

This TOPIC presented details on how to overcome challenges from POLST forms for two reasons: POLSTs are becoming more widely used, and to exemplify how the **Plan Now, Die Later—Ironclad Strategy** works. Let's now consider this strategy more broadly.

21: The Four Pillars of Your Plan Now, Die Later—Ironclad Strategy

As indicated previously (TOPIC 4), some Living Wills are quite **short**. Completing them seems **simple**. You can express your wishes merely by checking (selecting) a few boxes from the choices they offer. However consider this quote by a famous attorney/ethicist/philosopher:

> *The greatest insult to the sanctity of life is indifference or laziness in the fact of its complexity.*
> **—Ronald Dworkin**

The following question reflects the perspective of this book and its author:

Suppose you seek a successful, compassionate strategy for life's final chapter...
Considering what is at stake—*How much and how long you will suffer before you die...*
Do you select a plan because it is "SHORT and SIMPLE"? Or because it is "EFFECTIVE"?

The goal of the **Plan Now, Die Later—Ironclad Strategy** is a *timely, peaceful transition.* To attain this goal, you must prevent *premature dying* and prolonged, unnecessary, end-of-life suffering, and this includes avoiding *To Delay is To Deny.* This happens if your wishes are fulfilled... but only after a long, drawn-out conflict. The *ideal* strategy effectively deters would-be challengers, thereby discouraging conflicts *before* they begin. Once started, litigation can last months to years. In this context, the "ironclad strategy" is like a *few ounces of prevention.* (But it is still less than a pound!) Considering what is at stake—***How much and how long you will suffer before you die***—it is worth the effort.

The **Plan Now, Die Later—Ironclad Strategy** strives to succeed by being ethical in two areas: the clinical and the legal. The strategy requires a discussion with your physician who is asked to sign two forms. The entire process also strives for diligence. It even includes such details as: **A)** It is a stronger legal statement to write and to cross out than never to have written at all; and **B)** Reasons you explain in your own words and own handwriting are legally more compelling than checking a box and signing your name at the end of a long document.

Where do you start? Sorting **My Way Cards/*Natural Dying Living Will Cards*** lets you learn and make decisions about each *symptom, loss of function, unwanted behavior,* and *conflict with lifelong value.* Write down your preferences—on the enclosed *wallet card* or on a *My Decisions Table* (available as a download or FAX from www.MyWayCards.org).[57]

Although you, the Advance Care Planner (legally known as the "principal"), is responsible to set up the entire strategy, the plan will "spring into action" in the future. Then, its success will depend on four "PILLARS." Success is defined by attaining a *timely, peaceful transition.*

What a return on investment!

Spending **one to three hours** in Advance Care Planning NOW
has the potential, if you reach the stage of Advanced Dementia, to prevent
one to three years (or more) of prolonged dying and its associated suffering.

It should be obvious by now that success depends not only on the important task of your deciding what you want and expressing it specifically in a clear and convincing way, but also on adding a strategy that will effectively overcome a variety of potentially sabotaging challengers in the future. The two illustrations in Chapter 2 in "Stories" show **A)** Living Wills are NOT self-enforcing and **B)** physicians may NOT comply with your proxy's requests. Thus **you need** *four* **PILLARS, not** *one*. The next page summarizes these PILLARS by describing HOW your PREVIOUS effort (PAST, when you engaged in Advance Care Planning) can help attain your goal WHEN that "time comes" (NOW, when you reach the stage of Advanced Dementia).

The Four Pillars:
You, your physician, your proxy, and your notary

I. **You previously expressed** your **specific** end-of-life treatment preferences or *Known Wishes* **well**—that is, in a **clear and convincing** way—and NOW they clearly apply to your current **specific** mental/physical condition.

II. **Your prior physician** *verified* that you gave your *informed consent* after you discussed these *wishes*, using a physician's order form that *can* be implemented NOW and *must* be considered by other, current physicians. For strategic purposes, your physician's **authority** is physically combined with your Advance Directive's **durability**.

---

[57] For readers who want these details now: You can send, FAX, or upload the results of your decisions to Caring Advocates. The cards and www.MyWayCards.org include instructions on how to FAX or upload or send your results to Caring Advocates—the organization that transforms your sorting decisions into your two-page **Natural Dying—Living Will**. Along with your Living Will, a letter advises you to give Caring Advocates permission to send your physician a **Natural Dying Physician's Orders**: for your physician and you to discuss and to sign.

III. **Your proxy/agent** uses the *power* you previously granted him/her **to override** current conflicting desires expressed by your "future demented self"—to fulfill your prior, ***irrevocable*** *Known Wishes*. Your proxy/agent's power can also motivate other, "would-be challengers" to comply NOW with your *Known Wishes*.

IV. **Your notary** certified you swore *under penalty of perjury* that your *Known Wishes* and other specific instructions to your proxy/agent are *true and correct*—so that courts of law will admit your declaration as evidence—which can motivate others' compliance.

Overview of "Plan Now, Die Later—Ironclad Strategy" Forms

PILLAR I: These **forms** comprise an Advance Directive: a Living Will and Proxy Directive.[58]

1. **Natural Dying—Living Will** that can be attached to a:

2. **Natural Dying Advance Directive** that refers to an attached:

3. **Designation of Proxies/Agents; Specifying Their Authorities** that refers to a:

4. **Natural Dying Organ Donation Consent Form** (which is optional).

These four forms allow clinicians and others to **understand** your *Known Wishes*. The recommended *way* to express them can provide future proof that you had *decisional capacity, diligence, emotional stability*, and made your decisions with *solemnity*, which decisions were *consistent* over time. These are the same criteria that certain judges used to deny requests to forgo life-sustaining treatment, such as tube feeding an Advanced Dementia patient. Proof can take the form of an audio (or video) recording as you sorted the **My Way Cards** or as you discussed your choices on your **Natural Dying—Living Will**. Note: Even if you satisfy all these criteria, your *Known Wishes* will still only be REQUESTS to your future physician. (See the two illustrations in Chapter 2 in "Stories.") For an "ironclad strategy," you need three more PILLARS. The first is **Form 5**, the **Natural Dying Physician's Orders**, which is physically **inseparable** from **Form 2**, as shown below and on the back cover of this book.

---

[58] Why does the Advance Directive part of the "Plan Now, Die Later—Ironclad Strategy" use four separate forms? In part so the **Natural Dying Advance Directive** and the **Natural Dying Physician's Orders** can each be *one page*, which permits them to be printed back-to-back on the same sheet of yellow heavy card stock so they *cannot be physically separated*. The **Natural Dying Advance Directive** and the attached **Natural Dying— Living Will** express your LEGALLY DURABLE *Known Wishes*; the **Natural Dying Physician's Orders** form has **CLINICAL AUTHORITY**. *Inseparable*, these forms are the cornerstone of the "ironclad strategy."

NATURAL DYING ADVANCE DIRECTIVE 2	5 NATURAL DYING PHYSICIAN'S ORDERS

NATURAL DYING ADVANCE DIRECTIVE [2]

To my proxy and to my future physician:

If I meet ANY of these conditions:

1. My pain and suffering are unbearable,

2. Further medical treatment would not provide me any benefit (is *futile*), or

3. I meet the criteria I previously selected for Advanced Dementia that I may express by completing a **Natural Dying—Living Will,** [1] then the time has come for my Natural Dying.

Patient's signature:
Notary/signature of witnesses:

[5] **NATURAL DYING PHYSICIAN'S ORDERS**

PND: Permit Natural Dying.
DNAR: Do Not Attempt Resuscitation.
DNH$_2$O: Do Not Rehydrate by I.V. Drip or by giving fluids by mouth.
DNI: Do Not Intubate (to assist breathing).
DNHOSP: Do Not Hospitalize unless needed to provide Comfort Care.*
DNAA: Do Not Administer Antibiotics.*
DNAED: Do NOT ASSIST Eating or Drinking by hand. Do OFFER food and fluid by placing nearby—if patient desires.

***Provide anything needed for Comfort Care.**
Patient's signature to **consent**:
Physician's signature for **consent**:
Physician's signature to **implement** orders:

Combining FULL versions of these two forms
on one sheet provides both the
AUTHORITY of a physician's orders, and the
DURABILITY of a patient's Advance Directive.
[7] Add the **Natural Dying Agreement** and **Affidavit** [8]
to strengthen your "*ironclad strategy.*"

PILLAR II:

5. **Natural Dying Physician's Orders** is the form you and your physician sign to give your informed consent and the form on which your physician writes relevant orders. **Form 5** can refer to another attached form:

6. **Consent Form to Obtain Relief from Unbearable Suffering by *Palliative Sedation*** for you to state detailed preferences and get your physician to sign.

PILLAR III:

   7. **Natural Dying Agreement** (a contract to enhance your designated proxy's power).

PILLAR IV:

   8. **Natural Dying Affidavit** (a form you swear before a notary that your proxy can use to motivate physicians and institutions to comply with your *Known Wishes*).

22: A Description of Each Strategic Form

Form 1: Create your **Natural Dying—Living Will** by making decisions as you sort **My Way Cards/*Natural Dying Living Will Cards*** (unless you used the *Criteria* in Chapter 4 in "Stories" to indicate your *Known Wishes*). The two-page **Natural Dying—Living Will** memorializes the results of your choices. For each of the 48 items/cards—the *symptom, loss of function, unwanted behavior,* and *conflict with lifelong values* of Advanced Dementia and other terminal illnesses—you decide "**Treat & Feed**" *versus* "**Natural Dying.**"[59] In the future, your proxy/agent compares your choices with your medical and mental condition. If overall, your proxy/agent thinks you meet your criteria, s/he then consults with your future physician to determine if the time has come for **Natural Dying**, using the process of "shared decision-making." The **Natural Dying—Living Will** form also allows you to state *how strictly* you want your proxy/agent to honor your current instructions—from always trying to feed you to overriding your request for assistance to be fed and to drink EVEN IF you request.

Natural Dying—Living Wills can be used in several ways: **A)** as a stand-alone set of end-of-life *Known Wishes*; **B)** with another Advance Directive such as free ones from Internet sources (who typically copy the form illustrated in your State's statute), or **C)** along with other popular forms (such as "Five Wishes")—provided that you indicate, "I want ***this* NDAD/NDPO** to prevail, even if the dates on the other forms are more recent"—a question that you are asked as you complete the next form:

Form 2: The one-page **Natural Dying Advance Directive** is the *pivotal* form in the **Plan Now, Die Later—Ironclad Strategy**. It is on the back of the **Natural Dying Physician's Orders** and refers to the **Natural Dying—Living Will** and four other forms. The **Natural Dying Advance Directive** asks for your proxy's name and contact information, the names of "Other important professionals and organizations involved in your care," and any individuals whom you do NOT want to make medical decisions for you in the future.

---

[59] Each sorting is done twice; the second time refines "**Natural Dying**" into two categories: **ND** = to consider the card/item either "Along with other items/cards" and **E** = "Enough suffering—by itself—for Natural Dying."

Form 3: The **Designation of Proxies/Agents; Specifying Their Authorities** is a four-page form. Another page provides reasons to consider as you decide if you want your proxy's authority to begin as soon as you sign the form. An optional page is included for the signatures of two qualified witnesses. This form provides space to add your second and third choice proxies. Importantly, this **form grants broad authority to your proxies** not typically included in other Proxy Directives. (Cross out any authority you do not want to grant.)

Form 4: The **Natural Dying Organ Donation Consent Form** is a two-page, optional form that gives you a choice between **A)** allowing your future physicians, institutions or State to define "after I die" or "Upon my death," for purposes of "procuring" your vital organs (thereby satisfying the "Dead Donor Rule"); and **B)** the alternative of using the criteria you previously specified for **Natural Dying**. Note: the criteria for "Death by neurological criteria" (brain death) and especially for "Donation after Circulatory Death" (DCD) are still evolving and are debated among bioethicists. (See Chapter 1, in "Stories.") To my knowledge, **Form 4** is the first to offer these stable criteria: First, *your consent must be voluntary*. Second, your clinical condition must clearly dictate that it is *time to stop all life-sustaining treatment*.[60] You may need some time to choose between these alternatives. This Consent Form is not part of the "ironclad strategy"; you can delay including it (or not include it).

Form 5: The completed one-page **Natural Dying Physician's Order** form confirms that you and your physician discussed and then you gave your informed consent to its four orders. This means you decided these physician's orders *did* reflect your end-of-life wishes. There are two important reasons your physician signs: **A)** to verify your informed consent; and **B)** to confirm his/her willingness to sign the orders you need to fulfill your end-of-life wishes. This form allows you to state your wishes to refuse *Manual Assistance with Oral Feeding and Drinking*, which you can choose to make **irrevocable**. (Detailed instructions are in the **Appendix**.) The form lets you write the names of institutions to which you do NOT want to be transferred, if you doubt they will comply with your specific end-of-life wishes. The form importantly allows you to give your consent to *Palliative Sedation* if **Form 6** is attached.

The completed **Natural Dying Physician's Orders** form adds **clinical authority** to your *Known Wishes*. Physicians who subsequently treat you can use their "authority" to change the orders, but your signed **Natural Dying Physician's Orders** is physically combined with your **Natural Dying Advance Directive** and some State laws say if your future physician is aware of your **durable** *Known Wishes*, s/he **must** honor them—or otherwise risk losing immunity. Some legal suits may require the physician to bear financial liability for damages.

How IMPLEMENTATION works: When your proxy/agent believes you have met your criteria

---

[60] Among the articles on which this point of view is based is: Miller FG, Truog RD. Rethinking the Ethics of Vital Organ Donations. *Hastings Center Report* (2008) *38(6):* 38-46.

for **Natural Dying**, s/he will contact your (currently treating) physician and engage in the process of "shared decision-making." Then your physician should consult clinicians involved in your care and others such as your family members. Only then will your last physician sign in the box, **To IMPLEMENT Orders for Natural Dying**, at the bottom of the page.

Form 6: For relief from endless, unbearable, end-of-life pain, attach the two-page **Consent Form to Obtain Relief from Unbearable Suffering by *Palliative Sedation*** to your **Natural Dying Physician's Orders** form. This form lets you specify your wishes in detail. Read and complete it *before* you visit your physician, or come prepared to ask specific questions. Discuss and sign this form in front of your physician. You have TWO IMPORTANT CHOICES: **A)** If you chose ***Respite Sedation***, point out that it is NOT likely others will confuse "sedation" with "euthanasia" (which potential criticism is why some physicians are hesitant to provide this method of Comfort Care). **B)** If you want relief from **mental anguish** and from "**existential suffering**" as well as from **physical discomfort**, ask your physician if s/he will treat all three. (Unfortunately, the AMA considers treating "existential suffering" as "beyond the scope of clinical care.") If your physician objects by refusing to sign this consent form, seek another physician who will *NOW*—while you still have mental capacity and physical energy. Otherwise, you may suffer from endless, unbearable pain at the end of your life. Even if another physician will be your last, s/he must have a good reason not to honor your *Known Wishes* as reflected by your previous informed consent.

Form 7: The seven-page **Natural Dying Agreement** form is an *irrevocable, bilateral contract* that grants additional power to your proxy/agent. Completing this form helps to clarify your wishes and to demonstrate your conviction about *WHAT you want* and can be documented in your own handwriting and your own words, in the space provided.[61] The form derives its power by being designed to overcome an *asymmetry* in the law. Without this form your "future demented self" has the power to sabotage your plan for a *timely, peaceful transition*. This "Agreement" overcomes this potential future challenge; it empowers your proxy/agent to override incompetent requests by your "future demented self" for assistance to be feed or drink. Your proxy can also use this power in another important way. It can serve as the basis for a compelling counter-argument to overcome challenges by others; for example, challenges by objecting physicians and attorneys who represent institutions' risk management departments. (Read three pages of "Fred's" story—at age 90. Also read a sample counter-argument offered in TOPIC 13.)

Note: the legal arguments in "Paragraph 4" of the **Natural Dying Agreement** are not designed for general readers; they are not easy to understand. (Frankly, it took a long series of discussions with three healthcare attorneys to refine this part of the Agreement.) They can be

---

[61] You should explain your reasons to those you ask to sign this form: your ***physician*** and each ***proxy/agent***. The form provides common reasons. Some States require an Ombudsman to explain this Agreement to residents of skilled nursing facilities, but a ***person*** who has no conflict of interest is recommended for all.

shown to others, however. Also, general readers may find this **interesting**: many physicians are also NOT aware of these nuances of law. To motivate compliance with your *Known Wishes*, your proxy/agent can show this part of the form to your future physician and explain that they may be protected by immunity ONLY IF they act *in good faith* to comply with your written and your proxy's oral requests. (See also the script and cautions in TOPIC 20.) Sharing this information may suffice for your physician to honor your *Known Wishes*. If not, your proxy can also present the next form, which an institution's risk management department may evaluate.

Form 8: The one-page **Natural Dying Affidavit** form has enhanced legal force based on your swearing an oath before a ***notary*** (under penalty of perjury) that its contents are *true and correct*. The form's content summarizes your *Known Wishes* and then directs your proxy "to seek declaratory or injunctive relief to effectuate [your] originally expressed, competent wishes..." and to sue any entity who fails to honor your *Known Wishes*, or who accedes to requests by your "future incompetent self" to delay your **Natural Dying**. Instruct your proxies to consider your **Natural Dying Affidavit** as a "trump card" they can hold, to use ONLY if necessary to motivate objecting physicians and institutions—*either* to honor your wishes *or* to refer you promptly to other providers/institutions who will honor your wishes. Your proxy may also show the possible legal causes of action and Advance Directive lawsuits listed in TOPIC 14.

Different levels of help are available

Many people complete these forms without any help although some view the videos on the website, www.MyWayCards.org. One level of Caring Advocates' membership includes some time to call a non-clinical staff person to ask logistic questions. Patients who are ill and people who want extra security or convenience can enlist the services of a Caring Advocates Planning Professional for part or all of the Advance Care Planning process. This can be done locally, in-person, or online using Caring Advocates' web application, www.InterviewByInternet.com.

The **Appendix** provides detailed instructions on how to complete the forms and a Table that summarizes WHO signs WHAT forms and that suggests what forms to read *before* you visit your physician.

While it is strategic and perhaps legally prudent to discuss your *Known Wishes* with your proxy/agent, it is kind, considerate and loving to also discuss them with your loved ones.

23: How can you tell if you have "just a little" Dementia?

There are new criteria to diagnose dementia: An April 19, 2011 press release announced, "For the first time in 27 years, new criteria and guidelines for the diagnosis of Alzheimer's disease have been published... [They] include two new phases of the disease: **presymptomatic** and **mildly symptomatic** but pre-dementia. [This] reflects current thinking that Alzheimer's begins... years, perhaps decades before memory and thinking symptoms are noticeable." William Thies, PhD, Chief Medical/Scientific Officer of Alzheimer's Association, wrote, "It is our hope... [this will] ultimately lead to effective disease-modifying therapies."[62] Much of recent excitement is about the use of biomarkers (brain imaging and spinal fluid chemistry) which can detect people at risk in the phase *before they have any symptoms*; or predict which patients with mild cognitive impairment are likely to progress to dementia.

It is not easy to know what symptoms are worrisome: Larry King, like many people, got the "memory thing" wrong. In his first CNN special, "Unthinkable: the Alzheimer's Epidemic,"[63] he said it's not Alzheimer's if you misplace your keys but it might be, if you forget "what keys are for." While moderate and late-stage dementia patients do not know the function of keys, if you are concerned with early diagnosis, a better criterion is not being able to remember (that is, *to integrate*) NEW information. For example, a person who has early dementia will repeatedly ask if she gave her son the keys that she did not want to lose. If asked, she can explain why it is important not to lose keys—which is why she asks again and again: she is worried. What is her problem? She cannot remember that her son has repeatedly answered by saying, "Yes, you gave me the keys a little while ago" (which is NEW information).

Symptoms other than memory: The press release stated: "The diagnosis of Alzheimer's dementia may not always have memory impairment as its most central characteristic; a decline in other aspects of cognition (such as word-finding, vision/spatial issues, and impaired reasoning, judgment, and problem solving) may be the presenting or most prominent symptoms at first."[62] Also, the early phases of the various kinds of dementia are different.

Psychological tests are powerful: Some professionals feel a combination of psychological tests has nearly as much power to make an **early clinical diagnosis** as do new biomarkers.

Do you want to know? You may wish to know if you or a loved one has dementia, but are reluctant to ask a physician to run the tests to make the diagnosis... and there are some good reasons. Even if the cost is covered by insurance, once one receives an *official* diagnosis of dementia, s/he no longer can buy long-term care insurance (and may have a problem getting health insurance). Depending on the State, s/he may be required to prove s/he can still drive a car. Employment opportunities may become limited. Worry and self-image can lead to anxiety and depression. Social status may change. Residential opportunities become more limited.

---

[62] www.alz.org/documents_custom/Alz_Assoc_diag_criteria_guidelines_press_release_041911.pdf
[63] www.cnn.com/SPECIALS/2011/larryking/. It first aired on May 1, 2011.

The benefits and risks of knowing you have dementia: A few dementias can be treated effectively, which your neurologist should rule out. For most dementias, there is almost no effective treatment (YET). Other benefits of knowing include: a good subsequent work-up can guide your physician NOT to give you treatment that is inappropriate; for example, Aricept makes Fronto-Temporal Dementia worse. Neurologist Dr. Douglas Scharre wrote, "Earlier diagnosed patients may be better able to express their wishes and participate more fully in their future care plans. Families could be educated and encouraged to start planning ahead for needed social and legal services and might increase patient supervision to promote safety and avoid financial predators. Overall this may lead to an improvement in the quality of life for cognitively impaired patients and a reduction in burden for their caregivers." Dr. Scharre developed a useful test called **SAGE** (described below). First we consider another *downside* associated with making the diagnosis of dementia, for patients who are depressed...

...for a while, their risk of suicide is increased,[64] so: Provide supervision after disclosing the diagnosis. Also consider waiting until the time is right to disclose the diagnosis of this most dreaded disease. Until then, apply the principle, "Therapeutic Privilege," which is exemplified by this classic example: A man regains consciousness after a heart attack and asks, "What happened?" His physician knows his diagnosis but WITHHOLDS the information. Instead s/he says, "We are still doing tests." If the physician said, "You had a heart attack," the patient might get anxious, mobilize stress hormones, and have another heart attack. Similarly, one may tell a patient s/he has a problem with memory, but further tests or further time will determine more.

No test is perfectly accurate, but the **SAGE** is very good; full statistical data were reported.[65] In contrast, a recent article about a new biomarker scan to detect amyloid in brain to diagnose Alzheimer's was criticized for NOT including data about how frequently false positives and false negatives were experienced.[66] The **SAGE** test is free and usually takes less than 15 minutes (although patients with dementia may not be able to complete it). Scoring is not hard. A plus for busy physicians and their staff is that it requires NO time to administer. The test can be downloaded[67] and completed with confidentiality, in the privacy of your own home. If the score is low, however, it is highly recommended that you take another version of the test in your physician's office so your physician can be sure that you (or the patient) received NO help from others. (Four versions reduce "learning effects.") Note Dr. Scharre's caveat: "**SAGE**

---

[64] Draper D, Peisah C, Snowdon J, Brodaty H. Early dementia diagnosis and the risk of suicide and euthanasia. *Alzheimer's & Dementia. 6(1) 2010:* 75-82.

[65] Scharre, DW et al. Self-Administered Gerocognitive Examination (SAGE): a brief cognitive assessment instrument for mild cognitive impairment (MCI) and early dementia. *Alzheimer Dis Assoc Disord. 2010 Jan-Mar;24(1):*64-71. Inter-rater reliability was 0.96 (ICC coefficient). Test-retest reliability was 0.86 and might be higher if repeated in the same environment and controlled for learning effect. Screening using this instrument correlated about 85% with a neuropsychologic battery, and showed 95% specificity and 79% sensitivity in detecting cognitive impairment.

[66] http://www.citizen.org/pressroom/pressroomredirect.cfm?ID=3337 Retrieved May 11, 2011.

[67] The test can be downloaded from either www.CaringAdvocates.org or from www.sagetest.osu.edu.

screening is not a diagnostic test of any condition." Yet it is the simplest test I know of that can help distinguish mild cognitive impairment patients from normal persons.

→ A great benefit: **SAGE** results could motivate patients to complete Advance Care Planning.

For patients who have mild cognitive impairment or have recently been given the diagnosis of early dementia of *any type* that is progressive, there is a time urgency to complete Advance Care Planning before their finite window of mental capacity closes forever. Sorting **My Way Cards** informs patients and their families what it may be like to live with Advanced Dementia. This news can be softened by saying that the course is quite variable and not every patient reaches that stage (leaving out the reason why: they may die of something else, before). Also note the Alzheimer's Association has wonderful resources for support as do other community organizations. Moreover there is considerable potential to enjoy life in new (but simpler) ways.

What if it is already too late, for patients who have more than "a little" dementia?
For patients who do not possess sufficient decisional capacity to express their end-of-life treatment preferences, "the substituted judgment standard is regarded as the primary standard to guide surrogate decision-makers" yet there are several reasons why family members of "persons with advanced dementia do not use this standard." (Instead, they use the "Best Interest" standard that is usually relegated to situations where the person's preferences are NOT known.) The most common reason to change the priority of standard was "over half of the surrogates discussed the **need for family consensus** on decisions."[68] A recent U K study had this consistent finding: "Family disagreements compounded decision-making difficulties. This was particularly evident in end-of-life decision-making, when the **need for decisions to be unanimous** was, perhaps, particularly strong." Interestingly: "Those who opted for the more life-prolonging treatment seemed to be more likely to express regret."[69]

Rather than waiting until an end-of-life decision **must** be made, when the pressure of time may add to other feelings of crisis, here is another option: Each person who knows the patient well can sort a deck of **My Way Cards** as they apply the "Substituted Judgment" standard to each item. They do this by imagining what the patient would have chosen—WHEN WELL—before s/he received the diagnosis of dementia. The results from the sorting/decisions of several family members and significant others are then compared. If there are significant discrepancies, a facilitator can mediate to try to resolve the differences. If a consensus can be reached, all involved can feel more certain the decision they must someday make will be what the patient would have wanted. (For an example of a contentious situation where this option might have worked, see "Stories," Chapter 5, which refers to the case of Joan Zornow.)

---

[68] Hirschman K, Kapo J, Karlawish J. Why doesn't a family member of a person with advanced dementia use substituted judgment when making a decision for that person? *Am J Geriatr Psychiatry 2006;14*:659-67.
[69] Livingston G, et al. Making decisions for people with dementia who lack capacity: qualitative study of family carers in UK. *BMJ 2010;341*:c4184 doi:10.1136/bmj.c4184

CONCLUSION: Revisiting "Ironclad" —a Strategy to Avoid Conflict

"I'm sorry I did not have time to write you a short letter."

—Mark Twain

*I would have preferred to have written a **short** and **simple** book. Given the alternative, I hope I have written an **effective** one.*

—Stanley Terman

The goal of this book is to help readers attain *timely, peaceful transitions*. Importantly, this includes **A)** avoiding days to weeks of unending, unbearable pain and suffering; and **B)** preventing months to years of lingering in the stage of Advanced Dementia.[70]

The cornerstone of the "ironclad strategy" is one double-sided piece of paper that contains two physically inseparable forms. To express your **legally durable** *Known Wishes*: one side has the **Natural Dying Advance Directive** to which the **Natural Dying—Living Will** is attached. To provide **clinical authority**: the other side has the **Natural Dying Physician's Orders** to which the *Consent Form to Obtain Relief from Unbearable Suffering by Palliative Sedation* is attached; your physician's signature verifies your discussion and informed consent to these specific orders. The **Natural Dying Physician's Orders** include refusal of *Manual Assistance with Oral Feeding and Drinking*—if consistent with your selecting **My Way Cards** items 8.2, 8.3, 8.4 and 8.5 to generate your **Natural Dying—Living Will**. To determine WHEN it is time for **Natural Dying**, your proxy/agent and your physician will engage in the process of "shared decision-making" by comparing your mental and mental conditions with the other **My Way Cards** items you selected that express your *Known Wishes*.

Two additional forms strengthen the strategy. The **Natural Dying Agreement** is an *irrevocable bilateral contract* between you and your proxy/agent that grants your proxy/agent considerable additional power. The **Natural Dying Affidavit** is your *sworn declaration*. It is designed to convince a court to expedite fulfilling your wishes. This **Affidavit** also is a "trump card" to alert would-be challengers they can be sued if their actions delay your Natural Dying.[71]

The Specific Disclaimer regarding the term "ironclad strategy" prior to Chapter 1 ended with this caveat: "Placing a sheet of iron around a wood ship made it virtually impenetrable to being

---

[70] Of **non**-demented patients, 5% to 35% have unbearable end-of-life pain and suffering. The percent of demented patients in pain is unknown and may be underestimated since they cannot complain and may not manifest typical behaviors for pain. Mistreatment of demented patients by caregivers was nearly 50%, according to Wiglesworth A. et al. Screening for Abuse and Neglect of People with Dementia. *J Am Geriatr Soc. 2010;58(3):493-500*

[71] Two other forms are not strategic. The "Designation of Proxies/Agents; Specifying Their Authorities" (or your State's Proxy Directive form) is logistic, and the "Natural Dying Organ Donation Consent Form" is optional.

sunk by cannons, but it was still vulnerable to, for instance, fire. This book shows you how to avoid 'fires'; but nothing in life comes with a 100% guarantee." This "Conclusion" will explain why the "fires" seem to be getting hotter; that is, why the opposition seems to be growing. But first, the "Conclusion" describes a positive trend that can help make sure others *will* honor your *Known Wishes*. Note that there are two "American ways" to motivate physicians and others. One is to make them aware that failure to comply risks a lawsuit that might hold them financially responsible for large damages and/or have a negative impact on their professional reputation. The other way is to deny physicians payment for services and to threaten sanctions.

In their 2008 case law review, Attorney Holly Lynch and colleagues[72] argued against the theory that there can be no damages for prolonging a life. They also concluded there were few lawsuits that provide a strong incentive for physicians to adhere to Advance Directives. But then they outlined a legal theory and proposed a framework in which to proceed. To summarize briefly: Civil action for damages can be based on the **intentional tort** [legal wrong] **of medical battery** and the **negligent tort of medical malpractice**. "The patient's recognized right to refuse care has been violated, leading to an injury"; hence "Wrongful Living" is a compensable harm that includes any subsequent harm that would not have occurred *but for the unwanted provision of life-sustaining treatment.* For example, Lynch and colleagues point out the flaw in the reasoning in the complicated case of Edward Winter. This man clearly indicated he did not want his heart resuscitated. But it was. He would not have experienced a subsequent stroke that increased the cost of his continued care *but for his receiving unwanted resuscitation.*[73]

Lynch and colleagues propose the following steps: "First, the court should ask whether the health care providers have behaved **recklessly** in providing life-saving or life-sustaining care or have **intentionally disregarded** a patient's clear refusal." Second, **the "patient should be permitted to recover for all of the pecuniary** [monetary] **expenses resulting from the violation of the right to refuse**... [which] includes recovery of **living expenses** in addition to **medical expenses**... [and] **"damages for pain and suffering.**"[74] {Emphasis added.} Third, a positive expected impact of such lawsuits is: "With the possibility of significant damages for saving people against their will rather than allowing them to die, hospital counsel will no longer be able to assert that they prefer a wrongful living suit to a wrongful death suit." Finally, another positive: if physicians are incentivized to comply with Advance Directives, then patients will in turn be more motivated to complete these forms.

The American Bar Association Commission on Law and Aging proposes another way to motivate physicians to comply with patients' advance treatment refusals. Chairman Attorney

---

[72] Lynch HF, Mathes M, Sawicki NN. Compliance with advance directives. Wrongful living and tort law incentives. J Leg Med. 2008 Apr-Jun;29(2):133-178.

[73] *Anderson v. St. Francis-St. George Hospital, Inc.* No. 95-869 (Ohio, Oct. 10, 1996); 671 N.E.2d at 226.

[74] Lynch et al also offered elegant reasons to dismiss likely arguments from various sources but space prevents even a summary of them here. Here is the conclusion of one: "A patient's refusal of care can be enforced without having a detrimental impact on any other party who might have made a different choice for himself or herself, and without weakening the traditional default rule in favor of life."

Jeffery J. Snell may soon present a Resolution[75] that "urges the Centers for Medicare and Medicaid Services (CMS) to take **preventive and corrective action** in response to evidence that some institutional and individual health care providers are violating their obligations under the Medicare and Medicaid Conditions of Participation [by] **thwarting the treatment wishes expressed by terminally ill patients, and seeking reimbursement for these practices**." {Emphasis added.}

The ABA Resolution uses strong language to explain three reasons why **unwanted treatments** are not reimbursable. **A)** "It is unlawful to submit [such] claims." Any submission implicitly certifies compliance and thus "constitutes a '**false or fraudulent claim**' under the False Claims Act." **B)** "When a competent and informed patient or surrogate expressly declines treatment, such treatment **cannot be considered 'medically necessary'** or in the 'best interest' of the patient under any conception of medical care that recognizes patient autonomy… Unwanted medical treatment provides no benefit to the patient, only the provider, and… violates longstanding principles of informed consent." **C)** "Unwanted medical treatment is arguably a 'worthless service' because the patient or surrogate has already determined that it is 'of no medical value' [and] unwanted medical treatment is **worse than 'worthless'** because it may cause emotional and psychological harm, and possibly physical harm in the form of additional suffering that the patient sought to avoid."

The ABA Resolution cited the Patient Self-Determination Act of 1990, which specifically stated that "providers must give written information to patients regarding their 'rights under State law . . . to make decisions concerning such medical care, including the right to accept or refuse medical or surgical treatment and the right to formulate advance directives.'" State laws usually provide legal immunity to health care providers—but ONLY if they honor the patient's *Known Wishes* (provided those wishes are available). Health care providers who provide unwanted treatment, which by definition conflict with *Known Wishes,* are vulnerable to being sued.

The ABA Resolution recommends the Centers for Medicare and Medicaid Services take three steps: **1)** Send a "**clarifying notice**… to elucidate the legal obligations and limitations upon providers in delivering medical treatment to seriously or terminally ill patients, specifically with respect to reimbursement"; **2)** "Establish a requirement that hospitals have **procedures in place** to ensure that the expressed wishes of terminally ill patients regarding care be respected"; and **3)** "Investigate alleged violations of this rule and **enforce corrective actions and sanctions as warranted**."

The ABA Resolution offers a specific example for implementing the second step that would require physicians to consider Advance Directives. "Include a requirement that providers certify on the relevant claim form that the **care provided was not in contravention of the expressed wishes** of a competent adult, the instructions in that person's advance directive, or the directive of his or her lawfully appointed surrogate decision-maker."

---

[75] Perhaps at their meeting in August, 2011.

The ABA Resolution states, "Protocols such a Physician Orders for Life-Sustaining Treatment (POLST) *can also help* to ensure that the goals and wishes of seriously ill patients are known and respected across care settings." If CMS does implement these steps, physicians' incentive to be paid may lead to an increase in their use of **POLST**s. Why? Physicians can control **POLST** forms. So let's consider how **POLST**s compare to the **Natural Dying Physician's Orders**—the form this book recommends as a last/final "Comfort Measures Only" form.

Advantages of POLST forms over the NDPO form

As of May, 2011, **POLST**s have an advantage over **NDPO**s: the forms are already "endorsed" in about a dozen regions, including some entire States. Such recognition evolved in three ways: by statute, by regulation, or by grassroots professional adoption that gradually led to consider the form as standard care. Interestingly, the State from where the initial leadership of **POLST** sprang—Oregon— was a place where "grassroots" led to its being adopted.

Where **POLST** forms are accepted, emergency medical personnel have been trained to honor the brightly colored forms across treatment settings. This means that 9-1-1 first responders who see a pink, green, or yellow form should know how to respond.

In contrast, **NDPO**s are "just" physician orders, albeit on a brightly (but differently) colored piece of paper that happens to have a valid Advance Directive on the back. Emergency medical personnel who have not received specific training about this form may need guidance on how to respond to its orders. They can phone either **A)** the physician who signed it, or **B)** their local base station "on call" EMS physician. This may sound a bit cumbersome but this is common practice and the same hurdle may also apply—at least in California—to *any additional order* written on the statute-recognized and EMS-Authority-approved "standard" **POLST**. That is because California's form states: "Depending on local EMS protocol, 'Additional Orders' written in Section B **may not be implemented by EMS personnel**." {Emphasis added.}

A way to overcome this disadvantage: To facilitate compliance, **NDPO** forms can be combined with a **DNR Medallion** on which the FAX number and web address are engraved for retrieving Advance Directives that can help motivate the compliance of health care providers.

Consider the above legal arguments of Holly Lynch (HL) and the ABA Resolution (ABA) if a **Natural Dying Medallion** had the words "*NO I.V. Hydration*" engraved: Emergency medical personnel who still inserted an I.V. would risk being sued for "**recklessly** providing life-saving or life-sustaining care" and/or "**intentionally disregarding** a patient's clear refusal" (HL)—for which "**corrective actions and sanctions**" might be imposed (ABA).

Advantages of the NDPO form over POLST forms

A) Durability: Orders on **POLST** forms are NOT durable. Even though providers are expected to honor these orders across treatment settings, once a patient is admitted to a new institution, physicians can—and often do—write new orders. For example, Washington's **POLST** says, "This

POLST is effective across all settings including hospitals **until replaced by new physician's orders...** {Bold emphasis added.}." New orders may not honor *Known Wishes.* In contrast, the **Natural Dying Physician's Orders** are physically inseparable from the patient's **durable** *Known Wishes* since the patient's **Natural Dying Advance Directive** is attached.

B) Compliance: Health care providers are expected to follow physician's orders, but emergency medical personnel are not required to follow physician orders on California's **POLST**s since this form says: "Depending on local EMS protocol, 'Additional Orders' written in Section B **may not be implemented by EMS personnel.**" In contrast, **Natural Dying Physician's Orders** are like all other physician orders: patients can expect other health care providers either to comply or to promptly state their objections. The **NDPO** has NO statement that emergency medical personnel are not required to follow any of its signed, written orders.

C) Particularized Known Wishes: Judges may not consider **POLST**s (**MOLST**s) as *specific* or as *clear and convincing* expressions of a patient's *Known Wishes* unless accompanied by a "particularized" Living Will the patient previously completed when s/he had decisional capacity. Example: *in Zornow,* Judge Polito wrote, "Any blanket MOLSTs or directives were **impermissible unless particularized.**" (See "Stories," Chapter 5.) In contrast, the **Natural Dying Advance Directive** and the **Natural Dying—Living Will** to which it refers, strive to be a *specific,* and a *clear and convincing* expression of the patient's *Known Wishes* as well as being consistent with the specific **Natural Dying Physician's Orders**.

D) Authority: POLSTs do not grant legal standing to surrogate decision-makers. The California **POLST** refers to these persons as *"legally recognized* decision-makers." Yet it would be more appropriate to refer to these surrogate decision-makers as *"clinically recognized* decision-makers." California Probate Code does not define the term, "legally recognized decision-maker." In contrast, the Code, in Section 4607(a), does define "Agent" as "an individual **designated** in a power of attorney for health care to make a health care decision for the principal." Only persons who have decisional capacity can **legally designate** a proxy/agent to have authority to make the same decisions as the patient can make. Two examples of decisions are: Proxies can fire one physician and hire another if the first physician refuses to comply with the patient's *Known Wishes* for reasons of moral conscience or religious beliefs. For similar reasons, proxies can demand patients be discharged from hospitals or skilled nursing facilities Against Medical Advice ("AMA"). For patients who have only a **POLST**, their *clinically recognized* decision-maker's lack of legal standing may render this individual impotent to make such demands. (See the semi-fictional story Sara, "Stories," Chapter 5.)

E) Safety/protection from undue influence: Patients who have **POLST** forms are more vulnerable to having orders written that reflect the bias of the treating physician or the interests of next-of-kin (who may have a financial conflict of interest) since **POLST** forms do NOT require witnesses or an Ombudsman to make sure the patient has signed "willfully and voluntarily"—as per California Probate Code 4675. (See "Martha's tale" in "Stories," Chapter 5.) In contrast, like all Advance Directives, the **Natural Dying Advance Directive** requires two qualified witnesses or a notary, and in some States also an Ombudsman for patients who reside in skilled nursing facilities. The **Natural Dying Agreement** highly recommends an Ombudsman or other person who has no conflict of interest. Another safeguard that **POLST** forms lack that **NDPO** forms include: **POLST**s do NOT prompt physicians to contact other treating clinicians and other people the patient had listed as significant—before implementing the orders.

F) Effectiveness: Regarding dealing effectively with people's **two greatest end-of-life fears**, **POLST**s (**MOLST**s) do NOT prompt patients and physicians to discuss two important treatment decisions that are included as standard orders on the **NDPO** form: **A)** To relieve unending, unbearable pain and suffering: *Palliative Sedation* or *Respite Sedation*; and, **B)** To avoid lingering in Advanced Dementia with an increased risk of unrecognized and untreated pain and suffering: advance refusal of *Manual Assistance with Oral Feeding and Drinking*. The characteristic of **effectiveness** may be the most important reason why people will choose a **NDPO** as their last **POLST**-type of form, when the time comes for Comfort Measures Only. It may also be the driving force for the grassroots adoption of the **Natural Dying Physician's Orders**. Consumer activists are more likely to strive for this cause than health care professionals.

Thoughts about the future: POLST forms were introduced in the early 1990s so they are older than **NDPO** forms (introduced in 2007). Regulatory agencies typically revise their forms every two years. After a few years of experience with **POLST**s, regulatory agencies may feel comfortable with adding another form, the **Natural Dying Physician's Orders**. This will more likely happen if the grassroots experience leads to repeated requests by consumer activists that they need **NDPO**s because these forms can do what **POLST**s cannot: reduce their two greatest end-of-life fears. This will in turn depend upon educating people to realize that they need to learn about all their end-of-life treatment options, rather than just those that slide easily through the political machinery because they do not *seem* (perhaps, incorrectly) to step on the toes of organizations that feel threatened by them. In the meantime, your proxy has a "trump card"—the **Natural Dying Affidavit**—to make the **Plan Now, Die Later Strategy** effective.

Evidence that the opposition to Natural Dying is growing

Now let's consider the evidence that opposition to **Natural Dying** seems to be growing.

1. Positive evidence: In the U S, the most recently designed Advance Care Planning forms are **POLST** forms. More often than not, these forms use the word "*always*" or "*must*" to modify a **statement** that *oral food be offered patients*. "Statement" is emphasized because NO form includes a checkbox to indicate patient have a *legal choice*. A checkbox would *encourage physician-patient discussion* about this choice. These forms implicitly *mandate* "offering food orally." As the reader is now well-aware, an argument can be made to require advanced informed consent to cease *Manual Assistance with Oral Feeding and Drinking* under certain circumstances—to avoid violating the First Principle of Medical Ethics, DO NO HARM.

2. Negative evidence: The most knowledgeable leaders in the field recently recommended "Comfort Feeding Only," but were *silent* about advance refusal of *Manual Assistance with Oral Feeding and Drinking*. Dr. Palecek and others wrote: A *"Comfort Feeding Only order* eliminates [] ambiguity by instituting an individualized care plan linked to specific patient *behaviors* that directs the cessation of oral feeding at the point of patient distress."[76] But Boly and colleagues demonstrated clinicians *cannot rely on the behaviors* of Minimally Conscious State patients to indicate if they are experiencing pain.[77] Thus we must consider the distinct possibility that forced-fed Advanced Dementia patients do suffer as they slowly starve to death.

3. Evidence from recent court cases, in chronological order (*with my questions added*):

A) California Supreme Court, 2001: "Certainly it is possible, as the conservator here urges, that an incompetent and uncommunicative but conscious conservatee [Robert Wendland, in the Minimally Conscious State] might perceive the efforts to keep him alive as **unwanted intrusion** and the **withdrawal of those efforts as welcome release**. But the decision to treat is reversible. The decision to withdraw treatment is not."[78] {Emphasis added.} (*Did the court ignore this fact: enduring longer, more intense suffering longer is also irreversible?*)

B) New York, 2002, after hearing the patient's niece state that the patient is a devout Catholic, the judge ruled: "Other than the execution of the Health Care Proxy and Living Will/Power of Attorney, there was absolutely no evidence offered by Petitioner that the patient vocalized or represented a desire to be removed from life-sustaining measures or to have medical treatment discontinued if she was presented with such a circumstance."[79] (*If valid, legally accepted forms do not count as evidence for this judge, is there **any** evidence the judge would accept?*)

C) New York, 2005, since the patient's sister claimed the Jewish patient had become more orthodox before she got dementia, the judge quoted from the *Halacha* (Jewish law) instead of asking the three physicians who testified for their opinions regarding: Is Advanced Dementia a terminal illness?[80] (It is.) (*State law requires respecting religious preferences, but does it also require the ancient* Halacha *to trump the opinions of modern physicians about prognosis?*)

D) New York, 2010: to arrive at his ruling *in the Matter of Carole Zornow,* Judge Polito referred to the teachings of four Catholic Popes and the U S Conference of Catholic Bishops'

---

[76] Palecek EJ, Teno JM et al. Comfort Feeding Only: A proposal to bring clarity to decision-making regarding difficulty with eating for persons with Advanced Dementia. 2010. *J Am Geriatr Soc.* 58:580–584.

[77] Boly M. et al. 2008. Perception of pain in the minimally conscious state with PET activation: an observational study. 2008. *Lancet Neurol. Nov;7(11):*1013-20. Minimally Conscious State patients are in many ways, clinically similar to Advanced Dementia patients.

[78] Conservatorship of Wendland (2001). 26 C4th 519; 28 P3d 151

[79] In the Matter of University Hospital of The State University of New York Upstate Medical University, Petitioner, for an Order Determining the Validity of a Health Care Proxy Executed by Yvette Casimiro, 754 N.Y.S.2d 153 (2002).

[80] Borenstein et al v. Joan Simonson et al, 8 M3d 481, 797 N.Y.S.2d 818 ((2005).

revision of the *Ethical and Religious Directives for Catholic Health Care Services*, # 58.[81] The ruling also provides more complete versions of religious citations in its Appendices. This is interesting: If the judge had merely wanted to make sure that *the one patient before him* who suffered from Advanced Dementia would someday receive a feeding tube, he could have stopped after writing he accepted "the undisputed documented hospital **or** nursing home record. Accordingly, the prior directives and MOLSTs, except for the DNR, are permanently revoked."[82] Instead, Judge Polito went on at length to explain why several Catholic doctrines mandate tube feeding. In reaching his decision, it is noteworthy that the judge accepted a nurse's eight-year-old chart note as meeting his clear and convincing standard for evidence. In contrast, the judge decided that the six of Joan's seven adult children—all of whom agreed their mother indicated she would NOT want to receive tube feeding under these circumstances—could not meet this standard of evidence. Finally, the judge made this strong recommendation: "The Court would suggest legislative action by reviving [revising] [New York State's] Family Health Care Decision Act design to set forth the '*sanctity of life*' as the main ethic, and allow the limited '*quality of life*' ethic to be specifically limited to those who so personally indicate under the [clear and convincing] level of proof required..." (*Does* **A)** *such repetitive deference to Catholic teachings* and **B)** *the recommendation to revise the law to be consistent with Catholic teaching indicate this secular judge may have had a religious agenda?*)

In honoring one's end-of-life wishes, these are the two most salient ethical/moral lessons:

- Force-feeding patients in Advanced Dementia violates the First Principle of Medical Ethics, DO NO HARM.

- Not attempting to obtain informed consent for *Manual Assistance with Oral Feeding and Drinking*—as people engage in Advance Care Planning—especially those at risk for reaching the stage of Advanced Dementia (which is to say *millions* of us... and *most of us* —if we live long enough) is a gross abdication of a critically important professional duty.

Can you attain the goal of a *timely, peaceful transition*? Yes. Conflicts are less likely to escalate to court if you express specific *Known Wishes* in a clear and convincing way, which applies to a *specific* medical/mental condition. (This sentence is an operational way to state what Judge Polito probably meant by the word "particularized"). Important: Judge Polito would honor such *Known Wishes*—even if the law were changed as he recommended. That is because the law is clear: everyone must honor "particularized" Advance Directives—even

---

[81] In the Matter of Carole ZORNOW, as, Petitioner pursuant to Article 81 of the Mental Hygiene Law for the Appointment of a Guardian of Joan M. Zornow, an Alleged Incapacitated Person. Supreme Court, Monroe County, New York. http://law.justia.com/cases/new–york/other–courts/2010/2010–20549.html and 2010 WL 5860446 (N.Y.Sup.).
[82] About this evidence, I would ask: **i)** Did the judge know if the patient, nurse, and chart were in hospital **or** in a nursing home in 2002? **ii)** Did the nurse inform Joan of her treatment alternatives and their consequences, such as prolonged dying with possible increased pain and suffering? **iii)** Granted the patient was referred to as "alert," but did patient also have decisional capacity to make this critically important decision?

conservative attorneys (including Wesley J. Smith) admit this. This is why many Advance Care Planning professionals say that a clear and convincing, specific Living Will form will suffice. *I disagree.* Even the best "PILLAR I" still requires "PILLARS II, III, and IV." (See TOPIC 21.)

Change is slow: Two definitive publications published more than a decade ago showed that tube feeding in Advanced Dementia is useless or worse.[83] Yet clinicians continue to insert tubes at the rate of over 6 per 100 hospital admissions from nursing homes, about one-third of U S nursing home residents currently have feeding tubes, and judges continue to rule tubes must be inserted or remain in place to provide artificial nutrition and hydration—for both religious and non-religious reasons. The "**movement**" to reduce using feeding tubes has limited success in twelve years. The ***proposal*** to refuse in advance, *Manual Assistance with Oral Feeding and Drinking* has greater obstacles. There is a strong cultural bias that feeding is nurturance to the needy, and that eating and drinking are critically important for social interaction. (Not for dying patients.) In 2011, this ***proposal*** is less advanced than the tube feeding movement was *before* 1999. Thus change in medical practice or policy may take too long to benefit the huge number of baby boomers who are destined to suffer from dementia. Also unfortunate: even if there were a promising treatment for dementia today, it too would not likely benefit baby boomers, whose disease has been "incubating" for decades. So: baby boomer cannot expect new cures, treatments, clinical standards of practice, or social policies to save them from multiple burdens of Advanced Dementia. This leaves one option: take independent action *now*.

➔ To meet the standards judges have set as they ruled to feed severely brain-damaged patients:

1) Express your specific *Known Wishes* in a *clear and convincing* way. This is a *content issue*.

2) For the *process issues*: Demonstrate you made your end-of-life decisions *diligently* and with *solemnity*, when your *emotions were stable* and when you possessed *decisional capacity*.[84] Record yourself on audio or video, either in an **interview** as you sort the **My Way Cards/ *Natural Dying Living Will Cards*** or in a **discussion** with your proxy/agent (and/or loved ones) about your *Known Wishes* as you refer to your **Natural Dying—Living Will.**

3) Repeat the sorting/deciding process to provide proof your choices are *consistent over time*.

➔ To make sure others will honor your *Known Wishes*, you should also:

---

[83] Finucane TE et al. Tube Feeding in Patients With Advanced Dementia: A Review of the Evidence. (1999). *JAMA. 282(14):*1365-1370; and, Gillick MR. Rethinking the Role of Tube Feeding in Patients with Advanced Dementia. (2000). *N Engl J Med.* 342:206-210.

[84] For patients who want to be sure they can overcome future challenges that they did NOT possess decisional capacity when they made these decisions, we recommend: Have a Planning Professional interview as you sort the cards using the **"Show & Ask" technique**; take a health literacy test before sorting; and take the questionnaire, "What do you know about Pain Control, Advanced Dementia, and Natural Dying?" after you complete sorting.

4) Complete all the **Plan Now, Die Later—Ironclad Strategy** forms (PILLARS II, III, & IV).

5) Designate a proxy/agent (and alternates) whom you can trust to be an effective advocate.

6) Store all your forms in a national registry from where they can be quickly retrieved.

7) In case your proxy/agent is not by your side when Emergency Medical Personnel or others "need to know," authorize your proxy/agent to have you wear the **Natural Dying Medallion** you previously ordered—*after* your physician has signed Orders to Implement Natural Dying.

➔Yes, these seven steps are more effort than others recommend for Advance Care Planning...

Yet considering what is at stake—*how much and how long you will suffer before you die*—and the strength of the opposition who may challenge your *Known Wishes*, it is worth the effort.

Will the "ironclad strategy" actually work? The answer is rather complicated. Legal proof can come only if this sequence of events happens: **A)** a conflict escalates to the courts; **B)** a judge in a lower court rules against the "ironclad strategy"; and **C)** an appeals court reverses this decision and decides to publish its ruling. Then the ruling will set legal precedence in its jurisdiction. To avoid lawsuits, risk management departments and malpractice insurance companies may educate physicians. Eventually, new standards of practice may be adopted.

Note however: the goal of the **Plan Now, Die Later—Ironclad Strategy** is to avoid conflict by deterring "would-be" challengers; and this includes *never going to court*. Like the sign that says, *"Don't even **think** about parking here,"* the ironclad strategy's forms, accompanying arguments, and legal citations that an informed proxy/agent can present to physicians and institutions are designed to appear *so effective on their face* that they will have this result: **"Don't even *think* about not honoring these *Known Wishes*."**

If this kind of success is achieved, then the victory will be silent; there will be no applause. Families will retain their privacy as they navigate through one of life's most awesome paths... with a minimum of *internal* and *external conflicts*. Without conflict there will be no court trial, no newspaper articles, and no TV coverage. Just a *peaceful transition*... one that is quiet and private... as a treasured loved one goes *gently into that night*. This is, after all, how it used to be (prior to the era of modern medicine). It is still the way it should be. And now, it can be.

Edward R. Murrow ended his weekly TV programs by saying, "Good night... and good luck."

Since this book is for those who choose to rely not on *luck* but on *effort*, let me end with... "Good night... with good planning."

Stanley A. Terman, PhD, MD

APPENDIX: Details on How to Complete Each Strategic Form

Form 1: The **My Way Cards**/*Natural Dying Living Will Cards*:

Instructions are included in the deck (and the e-book version) of **My Way Cards**.

Form 2: How to complete the *pivotal* Natural Dying Advance Directive (NDAD):

This form asks several questions to which "Yes" is usually the better answer. These are the questions:

It is best to have previously considered and discussed alternatives to **Natural Dying**.

You can sort **My Way Cards** to create **Form 1, Natural Dying—Living Will**, or use *Criteria* in "Stories."

Empower your Proxy and Physician to stop *Manual Assistance with Oral Feeding and Drinking*. Explicitly refuse tube feeding. (Some States, like New York, require explicit authorization.)

Conflict may arise by the use of other forms such as "Five Wishes," which has different criteria for the maximum amount of pain medication. Important: To prevent a more recently signed **POLST/MOLST/POST** from overriding all your diligent Advance Care Planning efforts, answer "Yes" to: "In the event of a *conflict* with other forms—including a **POLST/MOLST/POST**—do you want *this* **NDAD/NDPO** to prevail, even if the dates on the other forms are more recent?" (See TOPICS 19 and 20.)

Use the **Designation of Proxies/Agents; Specifying Their Authorities** form if you want to grant your proxy expanded authority. To decide when you want your proxy's authority to begin, read the included short essay, **Should your proxy/agent's authority begin immediately?** Indicate your decision on page 4. You may answer "No" and not use this form if you wish to use only your State's forms. If you do use this form, check to make sure your proxies and witnesses qualify per your State's requirements.

If you attach a **Consent Form to Obtain Relief from Unbearable Suffering by *Palliative Sedation*** to your **Natural Dying Physician's Orders** answer "Yes."

Regarding the **Natural Dying Agreement** and **Affidavit**, if you have not yet signed and notarized these important strategic forms but intend to do so, you can answer "Yes," but make sure you complete them; otherwise, someday those concerned about you may look for forms that do not exist.

→ Form 2 is reproduced in full, on next page. It asks you to sign in EITHER ONE of TWO boxes:

Sign **one** of these **two** *DURABLE authorizations:* So my Proxy/Agent can serve as my strategic advocate, **to decide** *WHEN* it is time for **Natural Dying, I select my Proxy**. I realize my Proxy still **must consult** with my Physician: [⬚⬚⬚⬚⬚⬚⬚⬚⬚⬚⬚⬚⬚⬚⬚⬚⬚⬚⬚⬚]. *(OR)* **To decide** *WHEN* it is time for **Natural Dying, I select my Physician:** [⬚⬚⬚⬚⬚⬚⬚⬚⬚⬚⬚⬚⬚⬚⬚]. Date: ____ / ____ / ____ .

Signing in the lower box for "my <u>Physician</u>" is recommended only if you have a *special relationship* with a *known* and *trusted* physician who is devoted to treat the disease from which you are likely to die.

Natural Dying Advance Directive (NDAD): to refuse <u>all</u> life-sustaining treatment

The **Natural Dying Advance Directive** is the *pivotal* form of the "Plan Now, Die Later—Ironclad Strategy." The **NDAD** is *only* for those who wish to refuse *all* life-sustaining treatment if their future mental or physical condition meets their *previously selected CRITERIA*. **NDAD** is the basis for *actionable* **Natural Dying Physician's Orders**.

Signatures to "PLAN NOW":

A competent adult **patient** can sign in "**A**" after being informed about the *process* of **Natural Dying** by his/her physician. The patient may have read about Natural Dying by sorting **My Way Cards** or had a discussion with a **Planning Professional**—a *trained* Nurse, Social Worker, Marriage Therapist, Nurse Practitioner, Physician Assistant, Pastoral Counselor, Psychologist, or Attorney who conducted an *initial* informed consent discussion and assessment of decisional capacity, formed an opinion, and then signed in "**B**." After answering some questions the **patient** can: authorize a person to be his/her Proxy/Agent (which is recommended) *or* ask his/her Physician to decide *WHEN* it is time for **Natural Dying**. Either way, the decision will be based on the *CRITERIA*, below.

A) To **patient**: Have you considered and discussed alternatives to **Natural Dying** at the end of life? <u>Yes</u>/<u>No</u>. Did you express your specific wishes for Advanced Dementia by creating a **Natural Dying—Living Will**? <u>Yes</u>/<u>No</u>. Do you empower your Proxy and Physician to stop manual assistance of your **oral** feeding and drinking? <u>Yes</u>/<u>No</u>. Do you refuse **tube** feeding? <u>Yes</u>/<u>No</u>. In the event of a **conflict** with other forms—including a **POLST/MOLST/POST**—do you want *this* **NDAD/NDPO** to prevail, even if the dates on the other forms are more recent? <u>Yes</u>/<u>No</u>. Do you authorize your decision-makers to use the *CRITERIA* below* to time your **Natural Dying**? <u>Yes</u>/<u>No</u>. Did you sign/attach your **Designation of Proxies/Agents; Specifying Their Authorities**? <u>Yes</u>/<u>No</u>. Did you sign/attach a **Consent Form to Relieve Unbearable Suffering by Palliative Sedation**? <u>Yes</u>/<u>No</u>. Did you sign (or do you intend to sign) a **Natural Dying Agreement and Affidavit**? <u>Yes</u>/<u>No</u>. Should your Physician/Proxy **wait** to distribute copies of this **NDPO/NDAD** *until it is time* to implement its orders? <u>Yes</u>/<u>No</u>. Do you agree to *disclose* your **NDPO/NDAD** to all healthcare providers in all settings at *that* time? <u>Yes</u>/<u>No</u>.

Sign **one** of these **two** *DURABLE* authorizations: So my Proxy/Agent can serve as my strategic advocate, **to decide** *WHEN* it is time for **Natural Dying, I select my Proxy.** I realize my Proxy still **must consult** with my Physician: _____ *(OR)* To decide *WHEN* it is time for **Natural Dying, I select my Physician**: _____ . Date: ____ / ____ / ____ . My first choice Proxy's name is: _____ ; phone: _____ , e-mail: _____ .
Physician providing comfort care: _____ ; Psychiatrist/psychologist/counselor: _____ .
Others (religious/spiritual leader, attorney, hospice worker, advocates, caregivers, end-of-life organization): _____
_____
I do **NOT** want these people to make **medical decisions** on my behalf: _____

➔ **Notary public** or **qualified witnesses** *must sign* using a separate "Acknowledgment/Witness Page."

B) To the **Planning Professional**: If you informed patient about **Natural Dying** on ____/____/____ , and formed the opinion that the patient had the mental capacity to make end-of-life decisions, **print** YOUR name & degree: _____ ; **sign**: _____ ; phone: _____ ; e-mail: _____ .

Signatures to "DIE LATER":

* *CRITERIA* the patient wants future decision-makers to consider, to decide if it is time for **Natural Dying**, are:
- Is terminally ill and has unbearable and untreatable pain or suffering; or
- Meets the *criteria selected in* **Natural Dying—Living Will** for *Advanced Dementia* or *terminal illness*; or
- Has an exceedingly low chance of returning to a level of health that would permit survival independent of continuing intensive medical treatment as a hospital or skilled nursing facility would provide; or
- Has reached the clinical point discussed with _____ on (date) ___/___/___ , or previously wrote in other Advance Directive forms and/or recorded on audio or video dated ___/___/___ .

C) To the **Proxy**: If the patient previously authorized you to decide *WHEN* it is time for **Natural Dying**, and you believe that time has come *NOW*—based on the above *criteria* and your **current consultations with treating physicians**, and you have agreed to try to find a *Physician willing to implement the attached NDPO*, then **sign**: _____ ; **print**: _____ . Date: ___/___/___ .

D) To the **Implementing Physician**: If you agree it is *NOW* time for **Natural Dying**, then sign and date the **NDPO** (on the *other side of this sheet*) in the *box* at the bottom, after the words, "**TO IMPLEMENT Orders.**"

© 2011 Stanley A Terman, PhD, MD. *Unique Identifying Number*: _____

Even physicians who promise "to be there" when "that time comes" may be temporarily unavailable. Signing in the "my <u>Physician</u>" box transforms this form into a pure Living Will. If you sign in this (lower) box, you will have NO human advocate to help fulfill your *Known Wishes* other than this one physician. This choice is NOT recommended if you want the **Plan Now, Die Later—Ironclad Strategy.**

Signing in the upper, "my <u>Proxy</u>", box creates a combination Living Will/Proxy Directive form. You can authorize your proxy/agent to seek the services of another physician, if necessary. The **Plan Now, Die Later—Ironclad Strategy** *REQUIRES* you to sign in this box and to name a proxy/agent.

Write in your proxy's name and contact information and the names of "Other important professionals/ organizations involved in your care," including your Comfort Care physician, counselors, attorney, relatives, friends, and organizations.

To prevent your future physician from asking people whom you do NOT trust to make future medical decisions on your behalf, write their names (or if there are none, write the word, "None") on the line after this sentence, "I do NOT want these people to make **medical decisions** on my behalf: _____ ."

A Caring Advocates Planning Professional will use **Section B** if you have a discussion with him/her; your physician may review his/her report or stated opinion before signing to verify your consent.

Note that **Sections C and D** are for *later use*, when it is time for **Natural Dying.**

Form 3: Designation of Proxies/Agents; Specifying Their Authorities.

If you only want *some* of the expanded authority in this Proxy Directive, cross out the phrases that correspond to what you do NOT want on its pages 2 and 3. (Other instructions are given with **Form 2.**)

Form 4: Natural Dying Organ Donation Consent Form:

This optional form is described in TOPIC 22. Chapter 1 in "Stories" provides background information.

Form 5: How to complete the Natural Dying Physician's Orders (NDPO):

This form has four orders for you to consider, for which you may then give your informed consent:

Order 1: If someday, you have an intra-cardiac device, its continued functioning may prolong your dying. Point out to your physician, the detailed order under the DNR order that says:

Discontinue and do not restart cardiac pacemakers, defibrillators, or Left Ventricular Assist Devices.

This is important. Some physicians are reluctant to deactivate a pacemaker if the functioning of your heart currently depends on it—even if you are suffering from unbearable pain from terminal cancer.

Order 2: If you want these **NDPO** orders to prevail over other, possibly conflicting orders (that a future physician may someday sign), underline or circle the word "**overrides**" and sign in the margin.

Note: Order 2 includes the attached *Consent Form to Relieve Unbearable Suffering by PALLIATIVE SEDATION*. This form has one page of background information. During your office visit, ask your physician to discuss your selected choices and then to sign the consent form. (Note: If you do not want relief from unbearable suffering, cross out all the words from "Attached:" to "SEDATION.")

Find out if there are any nearby facilities to which you would NOT want to be transported; for example, a faith-based hospital or skilled nursing facility whose policy or staff physicians may not honor your end-of-life wishes. Write the names of these facilities on the last line of Order 2, after the words, "List **facilities NOT to transport**: _____ ." (You can also write in the names of facilities you prefer.)

Order 3: allows for antibiotic treatment for pneumonia and other infections—if needed for Comfort Care—even as you are dying. Administration of fluids should be minimized so your dying is not prolonged. Recent clinical evidence shows it is more comfortable to die by medical dehydration than from untreated pneumonia, so antibiotics can be given, if required for Comfort Care.

Order 4: can be made *irrevocable*. Think about this alternative to erring on the side of life before you visit your physician; if you wish, cross out certain words—*before* your office visit, as indicated, below:

DO NOT ASSIST FEEDING & DRINKING (DNAFD) BUT OFFER FOOD & FLUID.

<u>Always</u> place food and fluid near the patient, if awake. Respect patient's decision if repeatedly refused. Never force oral ingestion if patient turns head away, bites down on the straw or spoon, or spits out food. Respect patient's prior wish for Natural Dying and if Proxies are empowered to refuse help with feeding & drinking over patient's current objection. **Unless** patient explicitly indicated otherwise when competent, **fulfill patient's request for help feeding/drinking even if mentally unable to make medical decisions.**

If you cross out all the words in bold font—the first sentence, "~~Always place food and fluid near the patient, if awake~~," and these words in the last sentence: "~~Unless~~" and "~~fulfill patient's request for help feeding/drinking even if mentally unable to make medical decisions~~."—then the remaining words will be: "patient (that is, you) explicitly indicated otherwise when competent." The "otherwise" refers to the words you crossed out (preferably with a thin line so that others can still read them).

Crossing out these words reflects your **irrevocable decision** NOT to let your "future demented self" receive help feeding and drinking since that would sabotage your goal of a *timely, peaceful transition*. Here is an example of what you can write under this key paragraph, where it asks: "*If PATIENT crossed out any words above or has other instructions, patient should write them here, sign & date:*"

"*I forbid anyone—including my proxy (agent)—to change this irrevocable Order.*"

OR, to respect certain **religious beliefs**, cross out NO (or different) words and write something like:

"*I always want help with oral feeding and drinking for as long as possible.*"

Natural Dying Physician's Orders (NDPO): For Emergency First Responders (EMTs); healthcare providers in hospitals, nursing homes & hospices; family members; & others.

First follow my orders to withhold the interventions below; <u>then</u> contact me. <u>Safeguard</u>: Competent patients can revoke any order to accept treatment that is potentially life-sustaining. To verify this order, call me at number below.* My "**NATURAL DYING** Physician's Orders" (NDPO) are based on the patient's <u>attached</u> "**NATURAL DYING** Advance Directive" (NDAD) and on discussions that led to my understanding his/her end-of-life preferences.	Patient's full name: ———————————— Patient's date of birth &/or patient number: ———————————— Patient's address and phone:

D N R _{MD initial}	**1**	**DO NOT (ATTEMPT) RESUSCITATION. Do NOT call "911" for CPR.** Patient considered and discussed alternatives, and now refuses **all** potentially life-sustaining treatments. Discontinue and do not restart cardiac pacemakers, defibrillators, or Left Ventricular Assist Devices.
No IVs **D N I** **D N H** _{MD initial}	**2**	**NATURAL DYING PHYSICIAN'S ORDERS (NDPO)** overrides Physician's Orders for Life-Sustaining Treatment for Full/Limited Treatment *if in effect*. My orders are **COMFORT MEASURES** *ONLY*. **DO NOT REHYDRATE (DNH$_2$O), No IVs**: Patient has clearly chosen Medical Dehydration. Re-hydration may prolong duration of suffering while dying. Eliminate pain & suffering with opioids and sedatives using routes that minimize fluid. Consider transdermal patches, sublingual drops, IM injections. **DO NOT INTUBATE (DNI).** Remove obstruction. Use suction, + pressure devices, oxygen, opioids. **DO NOT HOSPITALIZE (DNH)** *unless* needed to provide *Comfort Care.* <u>Attached</u>: *Consent Form to Relieve Unbearable Suffering by PALLIATIVE SEDATION*. List risks in transferring patient: eg, bone fragility; psychological factors (delusions, delirium, combativeness). List **facilities NOT to transport**: ➔
D N A A _{MD initial}	**3**	**DO NOT ADMINISTER ANTIBIOTICS – UNLESS NEEDED FOR COMFORT CARE.** ALWAYS CONTINUE ALL COMFORT CARE MEDICATIONS but minimize administration of fluids.
D N A F D _{MD initial}	**4**	**DO NOT ASSIST FEEDING & DRINKING (DNAFD) BUT OFFER FOOD & FLUID.** **Always** place food and fluid near the patient, if awake. Respect patient's decision if repeatedly refused. Never force oral ingestion if patient turns head away, bites down on the straw or spoon, or spits out food. Respect patient's prior wish for Natural Dying and if Proxies are empowered to refuse help with feeding & drinking over patient's current objection. **Unless patient explicitly indicated otherwise when competent, fulfill patient's request for help feeding/drinking even if mentally unable to make medical decisions.** *If PATIENT crossed out any words above or has other instructions, patient should write them here, sign & date:* ———————————————

SAFEGUARDS BEFORE IMPLEMENTING: My *initials* represent my best attempts to inform <u>family members</u> ____ and <u>other important people</u> ____ (*patient's list <u>attached</u>*), and to contact <u>psychiatrist</u> or <u>psychologist</u> who assessed patient's ability to make medical decisions & emotional & cognitive barriers (anorexia nervosa, treatable depression, dementia, etc) to exercise sound judgment ____, and <u>physician</u> who may state patient has already received the maximum benefit from pain management/palliative care ____.

<u>PATIENT'S CONSENT</u>: I, _____, discussed the above **Orders**, which reflect my wishes so I signed here: **EVALUATION COPY**. **PHYSICIAN'S** signature to verify <u>Patient's Consent</u>: We discussed these orders on (date) ___/___/___ when patient had capacity. I reviewed the **NDAD** and the Planning Professional's opinion (if available): **EVALUATION COPY**. Print: _____.

* **Phone**: _____ ; Cell: _____ ; email: _____ ; City: _____ .

- -

<u>**TO IMPLEMENT Orders**</u>, Physician signs here: [_____] . Date: ___/___/___
 ➔ *NOT A VALID ORDER UNLESS SIGNED HERE* ➔

HIPAA permits disclosure of Natural Dying Physician's Orders to healthcare professionals as needed.

When you visit your physician, explain why you crossed out these words. It may help to read the commonly given reasons listed in the **Natural Dying Agreement** form as you compose your own words.

Required signatures: After you discuss your choices with your physician, **you** sign to give your informed consent. It is IMPORTANT to make sure **your physician** signs his/her name below yours. That way, both signatures will confirm that your physician and you discussed these Physician Orders and that you then gave your signed informed consent.

NOTE: If your physician has limited experience with the **Natural Dying Physician's Orders**, you might explain: At the time informed consent for future treatment decisions is obtained, physicians **do NOT sign in the box** after the words, "**TO IMPLEMENT Orders**" (unless an alert patient wants Natural Dying immediately). Physicians usually sign in this box ONLY in the future—AFTER both proxy and physician agree (by the process of "shared decision-making")—that you have met the criteria for **Natural Dying** you previously specified by sorting **My Way Cards**, as memorialized in your **Natural Dying—Living Will**.

Although your physician's signature that verifies your consent could legally suffice, we recommend you also ask your notary (or qualified witnesses) to acknowledge your signature on this physician order form because they can then also write something like: "[Your printed name] *added some words* and *crossed out other words* in Order 4." (They do NOT need to indicate *which* words.)

Form 6: How to complete the Consent Form to Obtain Relief from Unbearable Suffering by *Palliative Sedation*:

This form has one page of background information for you to consider. Your physician and you sign.

Form 7: How to complete the Natural Dying Agreement:

This form lets you state your end-of-life treatment preferences in detail. Read points **2.A**, **2.B**, and **2.C**. Cross out any phrases that do NOT reflect your end-of-life wishes. Sign on its page 3. There are also spaces for you to write your own words in your own handwriting, reasons you made these choices. The form gives examples of some common reasons for you to consider. This additional documentation will strengthen your strategy by demonstrating your strong conviction that others should honor your *Known Wishes*. As explained previously, this Agreement is designed to overcome the *asymmetry* that exists in the law and can sabotage your plan for a *timely, peaceful transition*: Patients who lack capacity **can receive** life-sustaining treatment if they request, but people **cannot refuse** life-sustaining treatment unless they possess capacity. The law gives your "future demented self" power to sabotage your plan. The **Natural Dying Agreement** overcomes this potential future challenge by empowering your proxy to override requests by your "future demented self." —But this is only one application of this strategy. Importantly, it also provides the basis for a compelling counter-argument to others who may object to your wishes. (See TOPIC 13.)

Minor details: The reason there are two lines to sign on its page 4: you may need to sign once in front of your physician and a second time before your witnesses or notary. Each proxy/agent must sign Page 6, so you may need extra copies of this page. Be sure to ask your physician to sign this form on page 7.

Who is a "person asked to explain this Agreement" with no conflict of interest, who may sign on Page 7? In some States s/he must be an Ombudsman, whose signature is required on all Advance Directive forms for vulnerable residents, such as those who reside in skilled nursing facilities. For other patients in other states, such a person is optional but still recommended.

Form 8: How to complete the Natural Dying Affidavit:

This is the only form that requires a notary (in many States). It is important that you read, understand, and discuss this declaration BEFORE a notary takes your oath, since the notary will ask you if you have read this declaration and then ask you to swear that it is true and correct. (Allow 5 to 15 minutes.)

Once completed, your proxy/agent has two choices: **A)** S/he can present this Affidavit to an institution or physician when you are admitted—to demonstrate how serious you are about wanting them to honor your end-of-life treatment preferences (*Known Wishes*). The downside of this choice of timing is that it might threaten them unnecessarily and change their attitude as they provide you care. **B)** Your proxy can keep the Affidavit safe but ready to present as a "trump card"—to use only if the physician or institution needs extra motivation to comply with your end-of-life wishes.

This Affidavit may help motivate an institution or physician who would otherwise be reluctant to comply with your *Known Wishes*. If this sworn declaration by itself does not suffice, your proxy/agent can then cite the lawsuits listed in TOPIC 14.

BEFORE you visit your physician:

- *Sign your* **Natural Dying—Living Will**;
- *Complete and sign the* **Natural Dying Advance Directive***;*
- *Complete and sign the* **Natural Dying Consent Form to Obtain Relief from Unbearable Suffering by** *Palliative Sedation*—or think about questions you wish to ask your physician;
- *Read the* **Natural Dying Physician's Orders** *and the* **Natural Dying Agreement** *so you can sign them in front of your physician, as s/he signs.*

Any time (before or after you visit your physician): Ask all your proxies/agents to sign the **Natural Dying Agreement**; ask a notary to take your oath for the **Natural Dying Affidavit**; and, if you do not ask "qualified" witnesses to verify your signatures on the other documents, ask a notary to acknowledge them. It is also best to have the signatures of your proxies/agents notarized.

To Create Your "Ironclad Strategy": Who Signs What?

FORMS	Principal/ Patient	Proxy/ Agent	Physician	Notary or Qualified Witnesses	Other person with no conflict of interest OR Ombudsman
(Read or complete forms in shaded boxes BEFORE you visit your physician.)					
1. Natural Dying—Living Will	✓			✓	(Some States require for patients residing in skilled nursing facility.)
2. Natural Dying Advance Directive	✓	✓ *(LATER)*		✓	(Some States require for patients residing in skilled nursing facility.)
3. Designation of Proxies/Agents (and/or your State's form)*	✓			✓	(Some States require for patients residing in skilled nursing facility.)
4. Natural Dying Organ Donation Consent Form	✓			✓	(Some States require for patients residing in skilled nursing facility.)
5. Natural Dying Physician's Orders	✓		✓ *NOW & LATER***	✓ *(Recom-mended.)*	
6. Consent Form to Obtain Relief from Unbearable Suffering by Palliative Sedation	✓		✓		(Some States require for patients residing in skilled nursing facility.)
7. Natural Dying Agreement	✓	✓ *NOW*	✓	✓	Highly recommended for ALL patients (even those who do not reside in a skilled nursing facility).
8. Natural Dying Affidavit	✓			✓ NOTARY	

*Check your State's specific requirements for the specific qualifications of proxies and of witnesses.

** *NOW*, to verify your INFORMED CONSENT; *LATER*, to IMPLEMENT the Natural Dying orders.

About the Author

Stanley A. Terman is a board-certified psychiatrist. He received an AB from Brown University, a PhD (Biophysics) from MIT, and an MD from the University of Iowa. During his first five years in California, he was on the teaching faculty of the University of California, Irvine. He has since been the Chief of Staff of a psychiatric hospital and contributed to several bioethics committees. His psychiatric specialties were helping families and couples. For the last fifteen years, he has devoted his career to reducing the suffering of terminally ill patients and their families. In 2000, he founded a non-profit 501(c)(3) organization whose name changed to Caring Advocates in 2005. He is the current CEO and Medical Director of this organization. The **goal** of Caring Advocates is to help people attain *timely, peaceful transitions*; its **means** is to educate people about their end-of-life choices, to help them create an "ironclad strategy," and then to help make sure others will honor their *Known Wishes*.

Dr. Terman is the author of **The *BEST WAY* to Say Goodbye: A Legal Peaceful Choice at the End of Life** (2007), **Lethal Choice** (2008) (a medical legal thriller about Physician-Assisted Dying), and **Peaceful Transitions** (whose first edition was published in 2009).

Dr. Terman created a new tool for Advance Care Planning, **My Way Cards** (*Natural Dying Living Will Cards* for religious observers) to create a **Natural Dying—Living Will**. The two goals of sorting cards are: **1)** To inform people what it is like to live with Advanced Dementia (and other terminal illnesses). The cards use plain, straightforward descriptions that have almost no medical jargon or medical diagnoses, and are supplemented with illustrative line drawings to enhance understanding; and **2)** To create a legal document that will be an effective Advance Directive, especially when combined with other forms, such as the **Natural Dying Agreement** and **Affidavit**. Dr. Terman is the co-developer of the combined document, the **Natural Dying Advance Directive/Natural Dying Physician's Orders**. The latter can be considered a "final" or "last" **POLST** (Physician Orders for Life-Sustaining Treatment) that was especially designed for Advanced Dementia and for patients who want to be sure they will receive aggressive control of end-of-life pain and suffering (using *Palliative Sedation*, if needed).

Dr. Terman has lectured and given workshops around the world. In 2010, he went to Australia twice to present the **My Way Cards**, once in an invited keynote address.

Dr. Terman lives with his wife, Beth, and their three Pomeranian dogs in Carlsbad by the Sea, where they walk while listening to music, almost every day. He is blessed with three wonderful children and three grandchildren.